preface

Our intention has been to produce a text which covers completely all the GCSE specifications in ICT which came into force in September 2001. We have therefore not followed the specifications of a particular board, but have sought to present the subject in a way which is accessible to all students, whether they are engaged in full or short courses, and in the Foundation or Higher Tier. While we have tailored the text to classroom use, every effort has been made to make it readable and accessible to those who would like to use it for revision or for self-study.

In a world where ICT permeates so much of our lives, it would be strange to produce a printed book in isolation from the technology. Therefore, throughout this book are references to a special website (**www.oup.com/uk/ictforgcse**) that has been created to support the text with downloadable files and activities. The website will also support the updating of materials for students and teachers alike, as well as providing a place where materials and experiences of teaching and learning ICT at this level can be shared and discussed.

ICT for GCSE provides:

◆ Easy-to-understand pathways through the information.
◆ Double-page spreads for each topic, most of them with questions at the end to test knowledge and understanding.
◆ 'Things to do' spreads, each of which offers a range of practical tasks to develop and test skills, knowledge and understanding of different types of application. Some of these may be used as GCSE coursework tasks where applicable.

◆ Specific guidance for the completion of coursework, with clear advice as to what should be included to ensure the best grades in the subject.
◆ Up-to-date information regarding the use of communications technology as required by the new GCSE specifications.
◆ Clear links to relevant websites and to the *ICT for GCSE* website.
◆ Examination questions, representing all the GCSE examination boards.
◆ A glossary of key terms
◆ An index.

We are grateful to Assessment and Qualification Alliance, EDEXCEL, NICCEA, OCR and WJEC for permission to use their past examination questions.

Thanks go to John Day, and to Diana Forster, Tony Lees and Don Manley at Oxford University Press, for all their help, tolerance and encouragement. Without them this book would never have been produced.

We would also like to thank our respective partners, Anne and Liz, for their unstinting support whilst we were writing this book, as well as our children for tolerating our passion for ICT in schools! Particular thanks go to Dominic Rushbrook for his help and invaluable advice on all things technical, and to Steve Rymarz and colleagues at the City of Norwich School for their creative ideas resulting from teaching ICT over many years.

Tim Roderick and Geoff Rushbrook
October 2001

contents

The term **information system** is given to any record-keeping system. We come across information systems all the time. Common examples of information systems are address books, dictionaries, telephone directories and train timetables. What these examples have in common is that data has been collected (**input**), processed and displayed (**output**) in order to provide useful information.

Computers have two important advantages over manual information systems – they can work automatically and extremely quickly, to calculate or to sort data into some useful form. This calculation or sorting of data is known as **data processing**.

Throughout your GCSE ICT course you will come across the terms **data** and **information**. It is very important that you understand what these mean. Data is the term used to describe any numbers, text or raw facts. Data on its own has no meaning. Data only becomes information after being processed and taking on some meaning.

Let's take the following example of data:

> **NCFCP12W7D3L2P24**

This data only becomes information when it is understood and its meaning becomes clear:

> **Norwich City Football Club.**
> **Played 12 games. Won 7. Drawn 3. Lost 2. Points 24.**

Another example: 8.75 is data; '£8.75 is the hourly rate for the job' is information.

Examples of computerised information systems

Police National Computer

The Police National Computer (Fig 1.1) helps police forces in their fight against crime. Over half a million criminal records are held on the system. Each year the computer gets 65 million requests for information from police officers who want to find information about suspects, or cars. This information is given to officers in seconds.

A National Automated Fingerprint Identification System (NAFIS) is also linked to the Police National Computer. This fingerprint system gives the police fast access to databases of convicted criminals' fingerprints as well as marks collected from scenes of crime. This allows the police to search the records to find matches for

Fig 1.1 The Police National Computer is an example of an information system.

crime-scene marks and to confirm the identity of anyone arrested.

Driver Vehicle Licensing Authority (DVLA)

By law, all drivers of vehicles on public roads have to have a driving licence. The Driver Vehicle Licensing Authority (DVLA) issues driving licenses and vehicle registration documents. Details on every driver, and every vehicle, are kept on a massive computerised database involving millions of records. Apart from licensing drivers and vehicles, the DVLA database can be accessed by the police in their fight against crime.

If these millions of driver and vehicle records were paper-based, it could take minutes or hours to find the information required. By using a computer, the information can be found in seconds. Compared with paper-based systems, computer information systems are particularly impressive when carrying out searches across a number of different categories: for example, finding all blue Vauxhall Astras with an X registration.

London Ambulance Service

The London Ambulance Service has to deal with over 1500 emergency calls a day. When a person dials 999 and asks for an ambulance, the computer automatically finds the address of the caller. This takes less than a second. Once other details have been taken, the call is automatically routed by the Command and Control system's computer to the officer controlling ambulances for that part of London.

The computer tells the controller which is the nearest available ambulance, and which is the nearest hospital to the incident. This information can then be passed on to that ambulance crew. By using a computerised information system such as this, valuable minutes and seconds can be saved – vital in life-and-death situations.

Medical information systems

Most doctors today use a medical information system to keep details about their patients and their illnesses. Patient information can be brought up on computer screen whilst you are seeing the doctor. The medical information system, apart from having your name, age and address, will also have a record of your illnesses and of any drugs given to you.

Once the doctor has found out the cause of your illness, all she or he has to do is to enter any drugs prescribed, and the computer will print off a prescription that can be taken to a chemist.

Advantages and disadvantages of computerised information systems

Advantages	Disadvantages
◆ Save enormous amounts of paper and filing space	◆ Some systems can be complicated and/or require a lot of time to be spent on staff training
◆ Rapidly find, calculate and sort data	
◆ Work automatically	◆ The computer(s) running the information system may not work due to an electrical failure or a hardware/software fault. If everything is computerised, no work can be done at these times
◆ Data can easily be **imported** (brought in) from another system or program	
◆ Data can easily be entered (by keyboard or scanner) or updated	
◆ Data can easily be **exported** (moved) from one system or program to another	◆ Data held about people may be incorrect
◆ When computers are linked together in a computer network, more than one person can access the information at the same time	◆ Some people may attempt to access confidential information. Therefore, security is extremely important

QUESTIONS

1 Explain what is meant by the following terms: information system, data processing, data and information.

2 Give four common examples of information systems.

3 Give two examples of computerised information systems.

4 What are the advantages and disadvantages of using a computerised information system?

A computer system is made up of two important parts: **hardware** and **software**.

Hardware

Hardware is the name given to the physical parts of a computer. In other words, the parts of the computer that you can *touch*. Hardware also includes equipment, known as **peripherals**, which can be added to a computer system. Common peripherals include **printers**, **scanners** and **modems**.

The different items of hardware are normally grouped into five categories (Fig 1.2):

1 Central processing unit (**CPU**)   The CPU is the brain of a computer and controls how the rest of the computer works (see pages 12–13).

2 Memory   Memory enables a computer temporarily to store instructions and data (see pages 12–13 and 22).

3 Storage devices   These include floppy drives, hard-disk drives, CD-ROM drives, DVD drives and tape drives. Some of these devices can read data whilst others, such as a floppy drive, allow data to be saved as well as read (see pages 22–5).

4 Input devices   An input device is anything that can get data into a computer. A mouse, a keyboard and a scanner are all examples of input devices (see pages 14–17).

5 Output devices   To get processed information out of a computer, an output device, such as a printer or computer screen, is needed (see pages 18–21).

Software

Software is the name given to computer programs that tell (instruct) the hardware how to work. Without software the computer hardware would do absolutely nothing, as there would be no instructions. Anything that can be stored is also called software. Saving a word-processed letter, or a spreadsheet, as a computer file is an example of software.

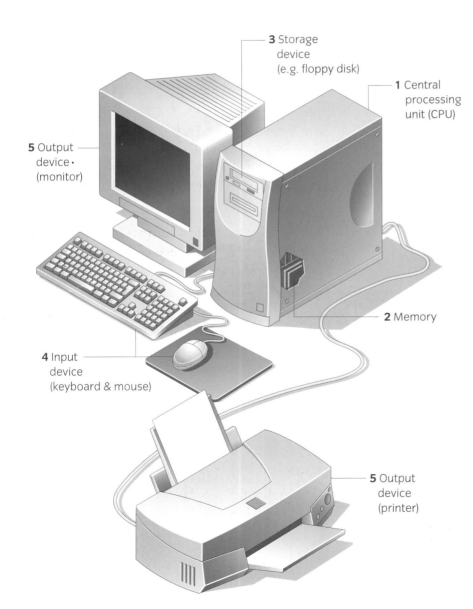

3 Storage device (e.g. floppy disk)

1 Central processing unit (CPU)

5 Output device (monitor)

2 Memory

4 Input device (keyboard & mouse)

5 Output device (printer)

Fig 1.2 The five categories of hardware.

The two main types of software are:

System software

System software, usually called an **operating system**, is the name given to the software that controls the hardware and how all other software works (see pages 30–1). The most commonly used operating system is Windows, made by the Microsoft Corporation.

Included under the heading of system software is **utility software**. This software aims to protect and maintain the system software, just like a mechanic maintains the smooth working of a car's engine when it is serviced. Examples of the tasks undertaken by utility software include protecting software against damage caused by computer viruses, making copies of files (backing up) and recovering files after software has stopped working (crashed).

Application software

Application software (Fig 1.3) is the name given to software that instructs a computer to carry out a specific task. It is application software that people choose to help them with a task when they use a computer.

For example, to write a letter on a computer, a word-processing application such as Microsoft Word would normally be chosen. Other examples of application software include database, desktop publishing, drawing, painting, and spreadsheet programs (see pages 36–7).

Another type of software, which contains parts of both system software and application software, is **language software**. Language software is the name given to the instructions (programs) produced by programmers to create system and application software. There are four main levels (generations) of language software.

Level 1 – Machine language   This involves programming the computer using the digits 0 and 1 that make up the binary code (see pages 12–13).

Level 2 – Assembly language   Assembly language has the same structure and commands as machine language but allows programmers to use names instead of numbers. Both assembly and machine languages are specific to one type of central processing unit (CPU) and therefore will not run on other computers.

Level 3 – High-level languages   Most of the programs we use today are written in a high-level language such as C++, PASCAL, Visual Basic and JAVA. High-level languages are different from low-level languages such as machine and assembly languages. High-level languages are so called because they use keywords similar to English and are easier to write than machine and assembly languages. Importantly, high-level languages enable programs to run on most types of computer.

Level 4 – Fourth-generation languages   Fourth-generation languages (4GL) are even closer to human languages and are often used to access databases.

Fig 1.3 Microsoft Word is an example of application software.

QUESTIONS

1 What is the difference between software and hardware?
2 List the five categories of hardware.
3 What are the two main types of software? What is the difference between them?
4 Explain the function of utility software.
5 Give three reasons why high-level languages, rather than low-level languages, might be used to write computer programs.

All computers, regardless of how big or small they are, have three things in common.

- Raw data has to be **input**.
- Data has to be **processed** using instructions from computer programs.
- Processed data has to be **output**.

There are three main types of computer: **microcomputers** (often referred to as personal computers or PCs), **minicomputers** and **mainframe computers**.

A microcomputer is one that is built around a microprocessor. Although less powerful than minicomputers and mainframe computers, microcomputers have evolved into very powerful machines. So much so, that today's latest desktop PCs are as powerful as, and much cheaper than, mainframe computers of only a few years ago.

Microcomputers come in different shapes and sizes. Desktop, mini-tower, tower, notebook, palm top and personal digital assistants (PDAs) are all examples of microcomputers. **Notebook** computers are designed to be portable (moved around). They are much smaller, and weigh less, than desktop computers. Notebooks can be powered by either battery or mains electricity.

In recent years, as chips (see page 12) have become smaller and more powerful, so have microcomputers. **Palm top** computers are smaller and lighter than notebooks (Fig 2.4). Palm tops are designed to fit into bags, briefcases and pockets. They are increasingly popular for workers 'on the move', particularly as they can be attached to mobile phones for e-mail. **Personal digital assistants (PDAs)** are even smaller, often the size of a diary or a large pocket calculator (Fig 2.5). PDAs do not pretend to offer all the functionality of desktop computers but are excellent organisers – keeping track of appointments, telephone numbers and names and addresses. PDAs can easily be set up to exchange data with other PDAs or a desktop computer.

Fig 2.4 Palm top computers, powerful and small, are for people continually on the move.

Fig 2.5 A personal digital assistant (PDA) is an excellent organiser for the busy person.

Minicomputers are used on computer networks. They are larger and more powerful than desktop computers. A **mainframe computer**, however, is the largest and most powerful type of computer (Fig 2.6). Mainframe computers are used to link hundreds of computer users via a network. This network can link users in the same building, or users thousands of miles away in different countries.

Fig 2.6 This powerful mainframe computer is at the CERN research centre, Geneva. In the foreground are the tape drives that store programs and record data from the various instruments in the laboratories. In the background are the processor stacks that manipulate the data.

QUESTIONS

1 List three things that all computers have in common.
2 What are the three main types of computer? What is the difference between them?
3 Give six examples of different types of microcomputer.
4 The following people require a computer for their jobs. Which computer(s) would you recommend? Give reasons for each of your answers.
   a) A small shop with two workers.
   b) A worker in a multinational bank with branches in many different countries.
   c) A company director who has frequent meetings.
   d) A sales representative who travels a lot between shops and has to give computer presentations to clients.
   e) An office worker in a large company based on one site.

Every time you start a computer, it follows instructions on what to do (see pages 8–9).

Just as we have a brain, so does a computer. The brain of a computer is the **central processing unit** (**CPU**), also known as the **processor**. This processes all of the information and instructions (code) used by a computer. Just as we depend on our brain to control all parts of our body, so a computer depends on its central processing unit to control its other parts.

The CPU enables the computer

◆ to carry out the instructions within the software
◆ to handle the control signals
◆ to carry out arithmetic operations
◆ to store data.

A popular range of processors is the Pentium series produced by Intel (Fig 2.7). The chip shown here is made up of over 27 million tiny switches, called transistors, mounted on a slice of silicon (Fig 2.8).

Everything that the chip, and therefore the computer, does results from the turning off and on of different combinations of these transistor switches. The off and on states of the transistors are used to represent the noughts (0) and ones (1) that make up the binary number system (see table below). These noughts and ones are known as **bits** (**bi**nary digi**ts**). A bit is the smallest chunk of information that a computer can work with – either the binary 0 or the binary 1. The more bits a processor can use, the faster it can compute (works things out) and the more memory it can access easily. When you use a computer, millions of transistor switches are continually being switched on or off by an electric current.

Speed

The speed with which a CPU processes data and instructions is measured in either **megahertz** (**MHz**) or **gigahertz (GHz)**. Each year, faster and faster chips (also known as intergrated circuits) are being produced. Speeds of over 1 GHz are now common. To give you an idea of how fast chips work, one gigahertz equals 1 000 000 000 cycles per second!

Fig 2.7
A Pentium III processor.
◀

Fig 2.8 A close-up of a Pentium III processor showing the connectors on the chip.

Binary Number System

Decimal Number	Binary Number
0	0000
1	0001
2	0010
3	0011
4	0100
5	0101
6	0110
7	0111
8	1000
9	1001
10	1010

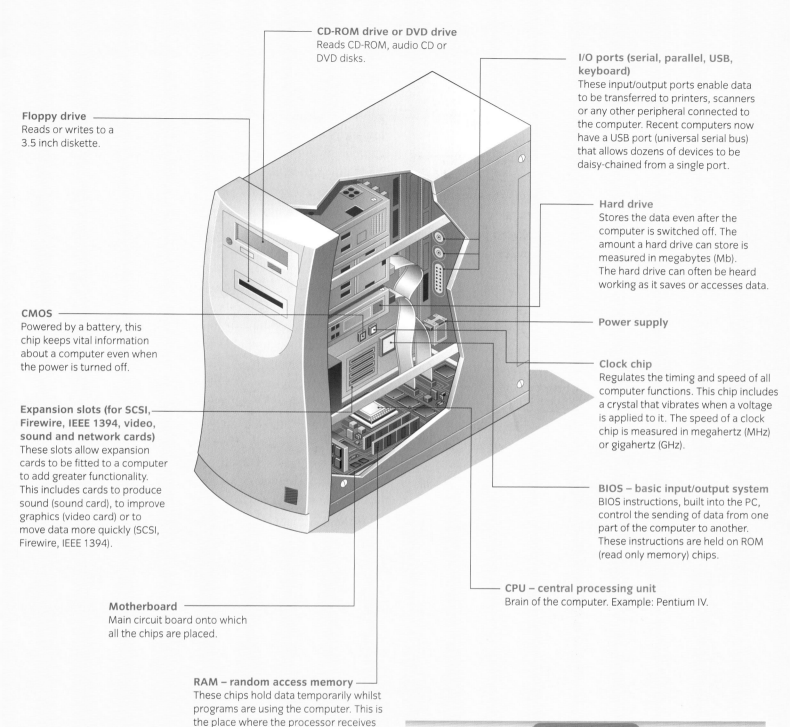

CD-ROM drive or DVD drive
Reads CD-ROM, audio CD or DVD disks.

Floppy drive
Reads or writes to a 3.5 inch diskette.

I/O ports (serial, parallel, USB, keyboard)
These input/output ports enable data to be transferred to printers, scanners or any other peripheral connected to the computer. Recent computers now have a USB port (universal serial bus) that allows dozens of devices to be daisy-chained from a single port.

Hard drive
Stores the data even after the computer is switched off. The amount a hard drive can store is measured in megabytes (Mb). The hard drive can often be heard working as it saves or accesses data.

CMOS
Powered by a battery, this chip keeps vital information about a computer even when the power is turned off.

Power supply

Clock chip
Regulates the timing and speed of all computer functions. This chip includes a crystal that vibrates when a voltage is applied to it. The speed of a clock chip is measured in megahertz (MHz) or gigahertz (GHz).

Expansion slots (for SCSI, Firewire, IEEE 1394, video, sound and network cards)
These slots allow expansion cards to be fitted to a computer to add greater functionality. This includes cards to produce sound (sound card), to improve graphics (video card) or to move data more quickly (SCSI, Firewire, IEEE 1394).

BIOS – basic input/output system
BIOS instructions, built into the PC, control the sending of data from one part of the computer to another. These instructions are held on ROM (read only memory) chips.

CPU – central processing unit
Brain of the computer. Example: Pentium IV.

Motherboard
Main circuit board onto which all the chips are placed.

RAM – random access memory
These chips hold data temporarily whilst programs are using the computer. This is the place where the processor receives the instructions and data it needs to do its job. Data held in RAM is lost when the computer is turned off, which is why hard or floppy disks are needed to store data.

Fig 2.9 Inside a personal computer.

QUESTIONS

1 What is the main purpose of **a)** an operating system and **b)** application software?
2 Why is the central processing unit so important to a computer?
3 Explain what is meant by the following terms: bits, megahertz, BIOS, hard drive, motherboard, RAM.
4 If data is held in RAM, why is it important to save your work?

Getting data into a desktop system

Data must be provided in a suitable form for any computer system to be able to process it. So, it is always important to think of the different ways of entering data into a computer, particularly as all data needs to be as accurate as possible. **Input** means to enter data into a computer for processing. An **input device** is any device that can get data into a computer.

The most easily recognised information system is a desktop computer, also known as a personal computer (PC). The most common way of putting data into a PC is through a **keyboard**. This has a set of alphabet keys, a set of digit keys, and various function keys. So the data entered by the person operating the keyboard is in the form of individual letters, words or numbers. The keyboard has the disadvantage that it is easy to make mistakes by hitting the wrong keys.

There are ways of inputting letters, words and numbers automatically into a system. For example, when a person buys a National Lottery ticket, he or she fills in the play slip by putting lines through sets of numbers on a grid. This slip is then fed into a machine that reads the marks. The computer system turns each set of marks into a set of six numbers and enters them into the draw. This method of entering data is called **optical mark recognition** (**OMR**) and relies on precisely positioned marks on a form being read by a special **scanner** (Fig 2.10). This data is then processed by the system. If you have multiple-choice tests as part of your examinations, you will probably have to answer them on an OMR form. These answer sheets will be passed through a scanning system to mark your answers. This way of inputting data is very fast and accurate.

Fig 2.10 Data can be entered into a computer in different ways. Lottery slips are an example of optical mark recognition (OMR).

Another way of entering handwritten or printed text into a computer system is to scan the text using an **optical character recognition** (**OCR**) program. The scanned text is turned into a file that can be edited, reformatted and reprinted by a word processor. The accuracy of OCR is variable and can be poor, particularly if the original pages to be scanned are of a poor quality.

Data can also be entered into a PC through a **microphone**. The computer responds to this data by carrying out instructions, such as printing a document or turning the spoken words into text in a word processor. These are **voice-activated** or **voice-input** recognition systems. A **touch screen** is another way to input data (Fig 2.11). The touch screen is a specially mounted screen that is sensitive to touch, and bypasses the need to use a mouse or keyboard. Some special-needs students use touch screens, as do banks and other organisations which provide information to the public. Another touch-sensitive device is the **track pad** found on notebook computers, which replaces the mouse or the tracker ball.

Pictures can also be input into systems. When the picture has already been printed, you need a **scanner**. It is also possible to use a **digital camera** that stores pictures not on film but in an electronic format. Pictures from the camera are transferred to a computer via a cable and a computer program.

You can draw pictures directly into a computer using a range of input devices. The most common input device is a **mouse**. The mouse (which all modern computer systems have) can be used to good effect with simple painting programs and with computer-aided design systems. Other more sophisticated input devices can be used in paint programs to help an artist to control precisely where the paint is applied and how much is used. Many graphic designers involved in computer-aided design (CAD) use a **pressure-sensitive digitiser** (a special pad connected to the computer) with an electronic pen or wand. The harder you press, the more paint you get!

An alternative to a mouse could be a **tracker ball** or, if you want to play games, a **joystick** or **games controller**.

Moving pictures can be captured by a computer using a **video digitiser**. This method is often used by the television industry to edit TV programmes. With digital video cameras now available in shops, the editing of videos through computers will become commonplace.

Fig 2.11 Touch screens, such as the one shown here, are popular in public places as there is no need to use a mouse or a keyboard.

QUESTIONS

1 What is an input device?
2 List eight different input devices that can be connected to desktop computers. Write a sentence explaining **a)** how they work and **b)** who might use each device. (For example, a special-needs student would use ... .)
3 Explain what is meant by the terms OMR and OCR.

How do you get data into other information systems?

So far, all the input devices mentioned can be connected to desktop computers. However, you regularly come across others and probably don't realise it! Fast-food outlets, for example, have tills with special keyboards. Each key on the till represents one item of food. When the key is pressed to order the item, it gives to the computer system the name of the item and how much it costs. These are then printed on the customer's receipt. Other special keyboards designed to do just one job can be found on children's toys, games consoles and programmable robots used in primary schools. Every time you use a remote control for a television, video recorder, or stereo hi-fi system, you are inputting data on a special keyboard, which then gets processed by an information system. When you use teletext on a TV, you are accessing an information system through a type of keyboard.

Barcodes are a way of putting information into a system. Libraries use barcodes on all of their books, videos and CDs. Your library ticket will have a barcode on it as well. When you borrow anything from a library, the data from the barcodes is scanned into a large computer database. This allows the library to know who has which books, videos and CDs.

High-street shops and all supermarkets use scanners to read the barcodes on goods. The data collected from the barcodes is used to produce customer's bills and to tell a store what has been sold. Goods are then automatically re-ordered. These systems, known as **EPOS** (**electronic point of sale**), enable large amounts of data to be input very quickly and accurately.

Fig 2.12 Input devices: getting data into a computer.

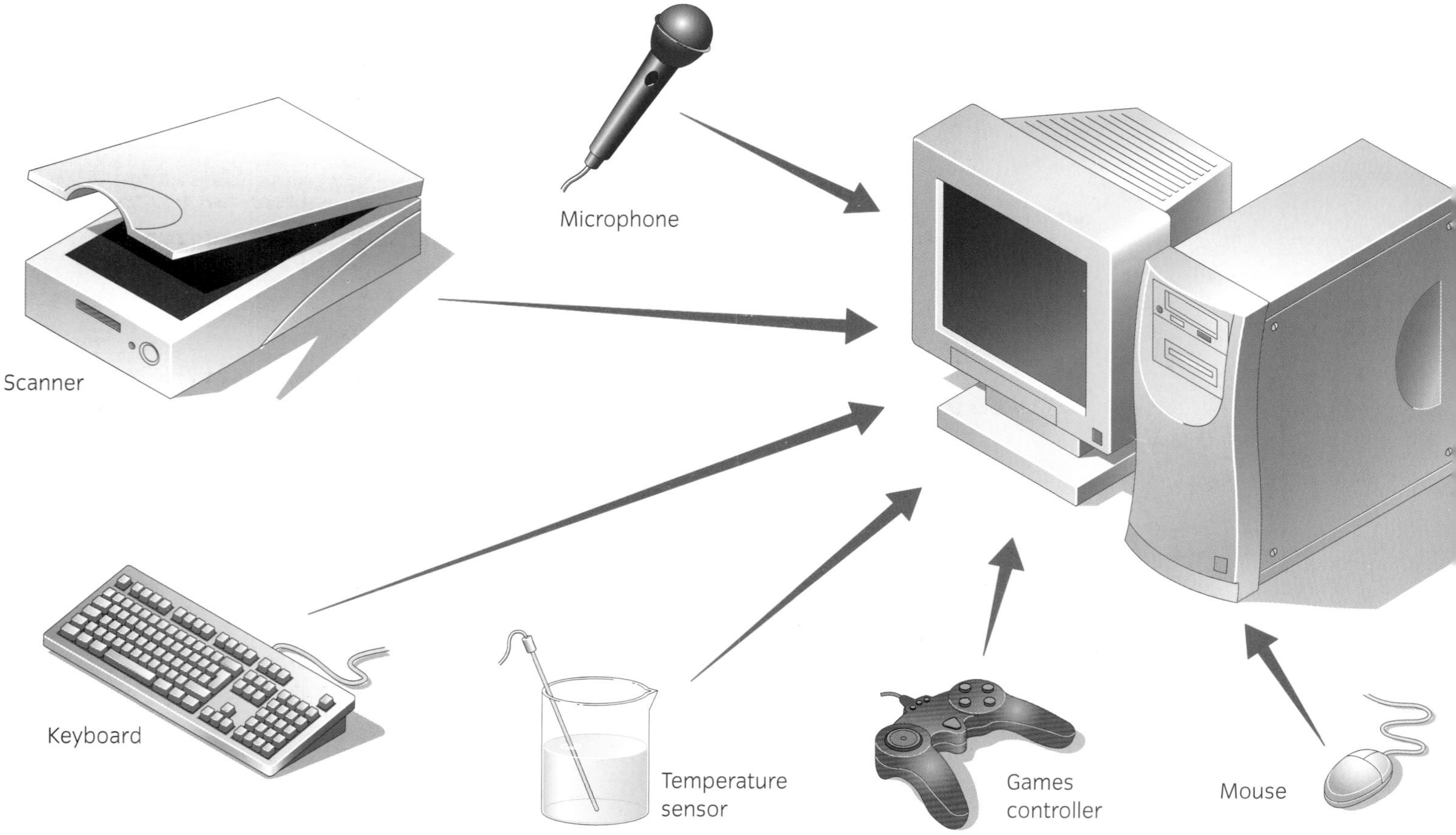

Scanner

Microphone

Keyboard

Temperature sensor

Games controller

Mouse

Millions of people now pay for their shopping using credit, debit or store cards. The **magnetic strip** on the back of such a card is 'read' as it is being swiped by a salesperson. This swiping transfers account information, and the cost of the goods, into the banking system. This type of system is referred to as **EFTPOS (electronic funds transfer at point of sale)**. A card that does not have a magnetic strip is also now appearing. This has a built-in electronic circuit and a set of gold-coloured contacts. Putting the card in a special reader inputs the information held in the circuit. Such cards are called **smart cards**. They are more sophisticated than magnetic swipe cards.

Banks each day process millions of cheques. Every cheque has the cheque number, account number and branch code printed in magnetic ink. A **magnetic ink character reader** (**MICR**) reads this information, along with the amount of the cheque, into the banks' information systems. This process is similar to OMR input on desktop computers.

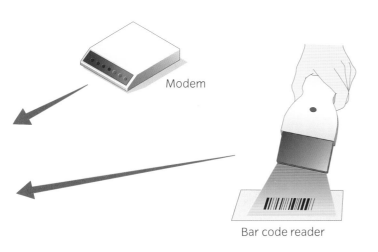
Modem

Bar code reader

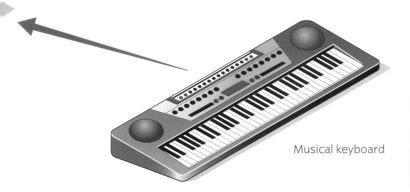
Musical keyboard

The music industry uses **MIDI** systems. Here, data is input through a piano-type keyboard or by sensors that respond to being struck. A wide variety of sounds can be generated from one keyboard or set of pads. This can involve the use of 'real' sounds recorded into the system through a microphone and then sequenced by the information system to produce the desired musical effects.

Sensors are available which respond to a wide variety of stimuli. They can be used to collect data automatically into a system. For example, the Meteorological Office has weather forecasting systems that collect data from sensors around the world and in space. These sensors collect data on temperature, wind speeds and direction, hours of sunshine and humidity. This data is processed to help meteorologists to predict the weather. As we know, the forecast is not always accurate, but large amounts of precise data are collected.

Information systems that control such things as doors use sensors to input data so that the systems can decide what to do. When you approach an automatic door, a sensor tells the system you are there and makes the door open. Burglar alarms use sensors to inform the system when doors or windows have been opened or broken. This causes an alarm to sound or the police to be telephoned automatically.

Remember An information system can process any form of data, but to do so it needs an appropriate input device.

QUESTIONS

1 Write a paragraph explaining how libraries use input devices to keep track of all their books, videos and CDs.
2 What are the advantages to supermarkets of using barcodes and an electronic point of sale system?
3 What advantages are there for the Meteorological Office in using sensors as input devices?
4 Explain what is meant by the following: EFTPOS, MICR and MIDI
5 What sort of information could be held on a smart card?

To get processed information out of a computer, you need an **output device**, such as a printer or computer screen. **Output** means the results of processing data. The most common output devices are **computer monitors** and **printers**. Computer monitors, also known as **visual display units** (**VDUs**), come in many different sizes and resolutions. However, output can also be to a modem, a plotter, speakers, a computer disk, another computer or even a robot.

Monitors

A PC monitor or screen contains a matrix of luminescent dots of **R**ed, **G**reen and **B**lue (known as **RGB**). These can be blended to display millions of colours (Fig 2.13). Mapping the location and colour information of each bit of data creates a computer image. This is known as a **bitmap** (**bmp**). The bitmapped image seen on a monitor is made up of thousands of **pixels**. Pixel stands for picture (**pix**) **el**ement.

The two most common ways of displaying output from a computer are by a **cathode-ray tube (CRT)** monitor and a **liquid crystal display** (**LCD**). A monitor can sit easily on a desktop computer but would be far too big and heavy for a portable notebook computer. Therefore, notebooks use either a liquid crystal display or a gas-plasma display, in which the gas is neon. Like a LCD screen, a plasma screen is only a few centimetres thick, and so can be hung on a wall. It can be larger than a LCD, as well as being brighter and visible from a wider angle.

Printers

There are two main types of printer in common use – the **ink-jet printer** and the **laser printer**. The slow and noisy **dot-matrix printer** has almost died out. The only advantage of a dot-matrix printer over other printers is that, like a typewriter, it is an impact printer. This means that, if you use carbon paper, you can print on more than one sheet of paper at a time. Laser printers produce attractive documents at a high resolution and are much faster. Ink-jet printers can produce wonderful colour pictures.

Laser printers are used in many workplaces because they are quiet, print quickly, can be stocked with a large number of sheets of paper, and produce very high-quality documents. Print quality is measured in the number of **dots printed per inch** (**dpi**). The printout from most laser printers tends to be 300 to 1200 dpi.

Black and white laser printers work by transferring black powder from a toner cartridge to a sheet of paper. A drawback of most laser printers is that only A4 paper can be used.

With the introduction of colour laser printers, this type of printer will continue to be preferred for offices and businesses.

Fig 2.13 Colour on a computer monitor is produced by red, green and blue (RGB) luminescent dots, known as pixels.

Although a colour laser printer is far more costly to buy than a colour ink-jet printer, it produces higher quality images and is cheaper to run.

It is now possible to buy a low-priced, good quality, black-and-white or colour ink-jet printer. The quality of printout can be nearly as good as that of a laser printer, but ink-jet printers are slower, their ink-filled print heads have to be cleaned and their cartridges need to be replaced more frequently than the toner cartridges of laser printers. Colour ink-jet printers are ideal for use at home, where small-quantity output is required for cards, photographs and schoolwork. Ordinary paper can be used but for the best results, particularly in colour, special glossy paper needs to be used. This can be quite costly.

Fig 2.14 Most colour printing is done using only four colours: cyan (blue-green), yellow, magenta (purple-red) and black. Usually, each colour is printed separately from its own plate.

In offices, another type of colour printer is also used. This is the **colour thermal printer**. All three types of colour printer use the four-colour process, which is the most widely used method in colour printing (Fig 2.14). The four colours are **C**yan (blue-green), **Y**ellow, **M**agenta (purple-red) and blac**k**. This system is known as **CYMK**, with K standing for black. In both the colour laser printer and the colour thermal printer, each of the four colours is printed separately, one on top of the other. But in the ink-jet printer, all four colours are printed at the same time. As with all printers, the choice of colour printer for an office is dependent on the speed and quality required, and the cost.

In magazines, where-high quality printouts are required, an **image setter** is used. An image setter transfers text and artwork from computer files directly onto paper or film. Image setters print at a very high resolution of over 1000 dpi.

QUESTIONS

1 Explain what is meant by an output device.
2 What are the two most common types of output device?
3 Explain what is meant by the following terms: VDU, RGB, pixel, LCD, CMYK.
4 What sort of monitor could be used with **a**) a desktop and **b**) a notebook computer? Give reasons for your answer.
5 Write three short paragraphs explaining the *advantages* and *disadvantages* of each of these printers: dot-matrix, ink-jet and laser.
6 If you had to produce a quality magazine that would sell in newsagents throughout the UK, which output device would you use? Give reasons for your answer.

Plotters

Car designers, architects and engineers, for example, who wish to print accurate charts, diagrams and 3D drawings, output not to a laser printer but to a **plotter**. A plotter uses coloured pens or toner to draw an image on paper. The paper is handled in different ways depending on the type of plotter. **Flatbed plotters** hold the paper still while the pens move. **Drum plotters** roll the paper over a cylinder, while **pinch-roller plotters** are a mixture of the two. The advantage of a drum plotter is that it can produce very large drawings.

Sound

Most computers sold to homes and schools have a sound card fitted. This allows both the recording of sound (input) and the playback of sound (output) via speakers. The sound output may be from a WAV, MP3, MIDI file or music from a CD. Some software will allow word-processed text to be read back to the user. This can be very important to young children or the visually impaired. Voice output has now become so widely used that the computer voice of the scientist Stephen Hawking is known all over the world.

Connecting to the Internet

A **modem** is both an input and an output device. A modem enables a computer to send data to, and receive data from, another computer, over a telephone line. This allows computers to send and receive e-mail, and to access the Internet. We have already seen that a PC is a **digital** device using binary code to switch on and off millions of transistor switches. The telephone system is an **analogue** device designed to transmit the human voice. Imagine an uneven wavy line. This is how the human voice would appear in an analogue system as it varies in frequency and strength.

When sending data, a modem converts digital data into analogue signals by varying (**mod**ulating) the frequency of a carrier wave. The modem receiving these signals performs the opposite operation. That is, it changes (**dem**odulates) the analogue signals back into digital code. The speed at which a modem transfers data is measured in **kilobits per second**.

Other digital devices are now replacing the modems described above. One such device is **ISDN** (**integrated services digital network**) which provides much faster transfer of data. This has advantages for those businesses and organisations that frequently send and receive large amounts of data and want fast access to the Internet. Another advantage is that ISDN enables users to talk to and to see each other using videoconferencing.

Cable television companies are now offering fast Internet access via their cabling system, and **ADSL** (**asymmetric digital subscriber line**) is a new technology that transforms a telephone wire into a high-speed digital data line. With ADSL, data can be sent and received much faster than through traditional modems or ISDN. ADSL also has the advantage of being connected 24 hours a day to an Internet service provider (ISP). This means that it is no longer necessary for a computer to 'dial-up' an ISP every time it wants to access the Internet or to send/receive e-mails. Another advantage of ADSL (and ISDN) is that, despite its being permanently connected to the Internet, you can still make and receive calls on the telephone.

Control

Computers can also output control signals. These **electronic signals** are used to control a range of external devices. For example, a computer could control the lights, heating and alarm system in a house. In industry, computers are used to control **robots** and machine tools that help in the manufacture of, for example, cars and computers.

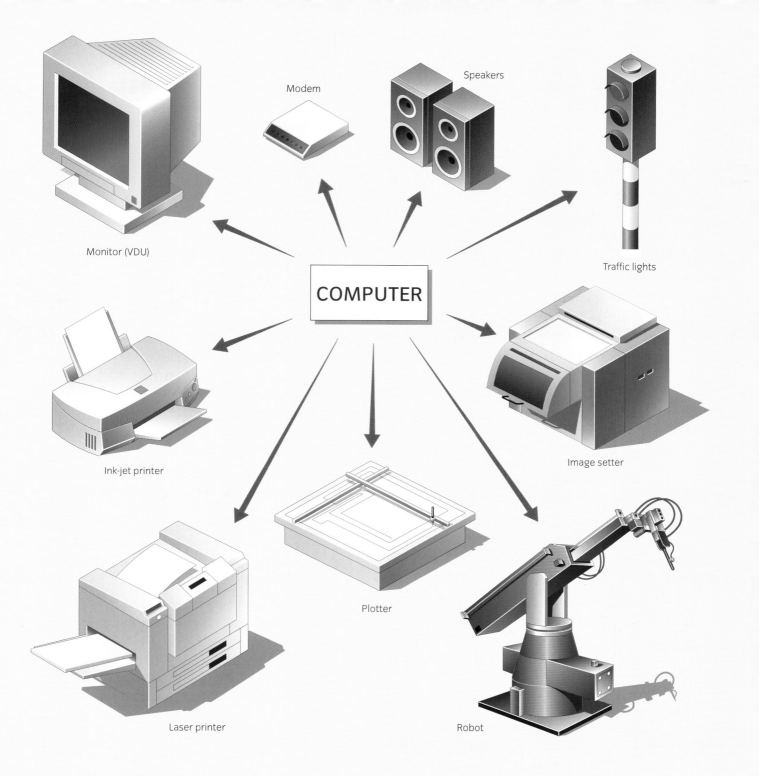

Fig 2.15 Output devices: getting data out of a computer.

1 What output device would you use if you were a car designer or an architect? Give reasons for your answer.
2 List six main types of output devices (printers, monitors, …).
3 What is a modem? Why is a modem both an input *and* an output device?
4 Give two applications of ISDN.
5 What are the advantages of using ADSL to send and receive data?

There are two main ways in which a computer stores data: in **memory** and in **media** (such as floppy disks, hard drives and CD-ROMs).

Storage space

You have already seen, on pages 12–13, that a bit (**bi**nary digi**t**) is the smallest chunk of information a computer can work with. A group of 8 bits make up a **byte** (**bi**nary **te**rm). Bytes are used as a measure of the amount of computer storage space in both memory and media. A single byte (binary term) equals a letter, number or symbol on a keyboard. Thus a brief letter typed in a word processor is made up of hundreds of bytes. If you think of all of the programs on a computer, plus all the files that are saved, you can see that on each computer disk there are millions of bytes. To deal with this, computer memory and storage size is given in **kilobytes (kb)**, **megabytes (Mb)** or **gigabytes (Gb)**.

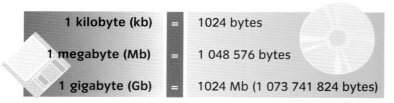

1 kilobyte (kb)	=	1024 bytes
1 megabyte (Mb)	=	1 048 576 bytes
1 gigabyte (Gb)	=	1024 Mb (1 073 741 824 bytes)

Memory

Inside a computer is a **RAM** (**random access memory**) chip (or chips) that holds the operating instructions for the computer, its programs and the data. The advantage of RAM is that the computer can access data held in RAM almost immediately. The major disadvantage is that data held in RAM is lost when a computer is turned off or goes wrong. This is why we need to use hard or floppy disks, or other media, to store data.

As computer programs and operating systems have become more complex, the size of RAM has increased. Today, most PCs come with 64 Mb or 128 Mb of RAM as standard.

When a computer is made, basic input/output instructions are put on **ROM** (**read-only memory**) chips. These instructions can be read, but not changed, and are available every time the computer is switched on.

Data storage

It is very important to have a device on which to store data and programs when a computer is turned off. These devices can be grouped into two main types: **magnetic media** (such as floppy disks, hard drives and tape drives) and **optical drives** (which use lasers to store and read data). Examples are CD-ROM, CD-R and DVD.

Magnetic media

The most common, and cheapest, way to store data is on magnetic media, such as floppy disks, hard drives and tape drives. Some computers, such as the iMac, do not have a built-in floppy disk drive but the vast majority

*Fig 2.16
Extra RAM (random access memory) chips can be fitted to increase the memory of a computer. Graphic designers often use computers with large amounts of RAM as this allows them to work on large pictures more quickly.*

Fig 2.17 Inside the plastic case of a floppy disk is a flexible magnetic disk which stores data.

Fig 2.18 Structure of a hard drive

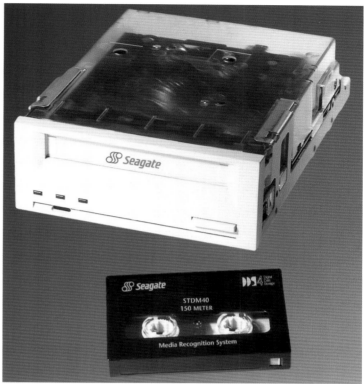

Fig 2.19 Back-up tapes such as this are used to make copies of large amounts of data on computer networks.

do, as a 3.5–inch floppy disk is an easy way to transfer information from one computer to another. Early floppy disks were indeed 'floppy', but now the flexible magnetic disks are protected by a plastic case (Fig 2.17). Most floppy disks can store up to 1.44 Mb of data. Given the file sizes now in use, this is not large.

In recent years, disk drives that can store more data, and work more quickly, have been produced. The most common is called a **Zip drive**. Special 3.5-inch removable disks can store 100 Mb or 250 Mb of data. Zip disks are particularly useful for backing up (copying) important data or for moving data easily from one computer to another.

As floppy and removable disks are magnetic, it is important to keep them away from all sources of magnetism, otherwise all of the data could be lost.

Another common device in which to store data is a rigid magnetic disk known as a **hard drive** (Fig 2.18). Although it is possible to add external hard drives to computers, most hard drives are inside computers, protected by rigid cases. Hard drives can access data

much more quickly than floppy drives and, most importantly, can store much more data. Hard drives of 20 Gb are now common.

When you need to back up large amounts of data, you can use **tape** cartridges, known as DAT tapes (Fig 2.19). These cartridges look like audiocassette tapes, although they are often smaller. Backing up to tape is vital for computer networks and organisations or businesses which need to copy important data that is held on hard disks. This is a slow process and is often done at night, at the end of a working day.

QUESTIONS

1 What are the two main ways in which a computer stores data?
2 Explain what is meant by the following terms: bit, byte, kilobyte, megabyte and gigabyte.
3 What is the difference between RAM and ROM chips?
4 List one major advantage of having a large amount of RAM in a computer.
5 Give three examples of magnetic media.

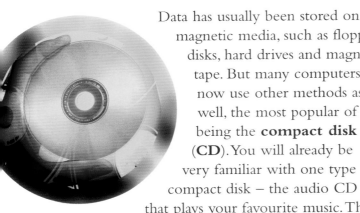

Fig 2.20
A CD-ROM disk can store large amounts of data. CD-ROMs are read-only media, which means that only the data on the disks can be used. It cannot be deleted or changed.

Data has usually been stored on magnetic media, such as floppy disks, hard drives and magnetic tape. But many computers now use other methods as well, the most popular of being the **compact disk** (**CD**). You will already be very familiar with one type of compact disk – the audio CD that plays your favourite music. There is, though, another type of CD that is used only with computers. This is known as the **CD-ROM** (**C**ompact **D**isk **R**ead-**O**nly **M**emory). The CD-ROM (Fig 2.20) allows a user to access up to 650 Mb of stored data. (This amount of data would need over 460 floppy disks.)

Compact-disk drives are also known as optical-disk drives because they use lasers to store and read data. Many computers with CD-ROM drives can play audio CDs, but the term CD-ROM is always taken to mean any CD format which stores data, rather than audio tracks. CD-ROMs are **read-only** media, which means that you can use only the data on the disks. You cannot delete it or change it. The major advantage of optical drives such as CD-ROMs is that they can store large amounts of data. Because of this large storage capacity, most types of software are distributed on CD-ROMs, as they would be too large to fit on floppy disks.

Because CD-ROMs are read-only media, **CD-R** and **CD-RW** have been developed. **C**ompact **D**isk **R**ecordable and **C**ompact **D**isk **R**ewritable are types of CD that allow data to be written to (stored on) disks. Many home computers are now being sold with CD-R drives to enable users to regularly back up data saved on hard disk.

Digital (computer) photographs can also be put directly onto compact disks known as **picture** or **photo CDs**.

Films from any 35 mm camera can be cheaply scanned onto a photo CD, allowing up to 100 pictures per disk to be used on a computer. A major advantage of the photo CD is that the pictures are scanned onto the disk in different resolutions, thereby allowing professional, high-quality photographs to be printed.

The latest optical technology is the **DVD** drive. **D**igital **V**ersatile **D**isks are becoming increasingly popular, as they can store much more data than CD-ROMs. In fact, a DVD can store up to 17 Gb of data. This is the equivalent of 26 CD-ROMs. This massive storage capacity means that full-length feature films can be put on DVD. As a result, DVDs are often referred to as digital video disks.

DVD-Video holds video programs and is played in a DVD player linked to a TV. DVD-ROM, like CD-ROM, holds computer data and is read by a DVD-ROM drive linked to a computer. The massive storage capacity of DVD, coupled with the fact that digital technology produces better pictures, means that videotapes, audio CDs and CD-ROMs are likely to be replaced by DVDs over the coming years.

QUESTIONS

1 What do the following terms stand for: CD-ROM, CD-R, CD-RW and DVD?
2 CD-ROMs are read-only media. What does this mean?
3 Why are DVDs becoming increasingly popular?
4 Look carefully at the table opposite. What storage device would you use to do each of the following tasks? Give reasons for your answers.
   a) Transfer a word-processed document from one computer to another.
   b) Regularly back up data on a computer network.
   c) Distribute a full-length feature film with accompanying data.
   d) Regularly back up data saved on a computer's hard disk.
   e) Distribute 500 Mb of application software.

Storage	Advantages	Disadvantages
Magnetic media		
Floppy disk Storage capacity: 1.4 Mb	◆ Cheap ◆ Used everywhere ◆ Light, fits in a pocket, and so highly portable	◆ Smallest storage capacity (1.4 Mb) ◆ Reads/writes data slowly
Hard drive Storage capacity: several gigabytes and getting larger	For now, the best all round storage medium: ◆ Stores/retrieves data quickly – much faster than floppy disks ◆ Stores much more data than floppy disks ◆ Cheap on a cost per megabyte basis	◆ Not portable
Tape Storage capacity: typically 2, 4 and 8 Gb	◆ Used on many networks to back up data on hard disks ◆ Low-cost storage	◆ Not generally used with desktop computers ◆ Slow – so only used for network back-ups
Removable drives Storage capacity: 100 Mb to 2 Gb	Removable drives such as Zip and Jaz drives: ◆ Store much more data than floppy disks (Zip 100 and 250Mb, Jaz 2Gb) ◆ Very good for backing up files ◆ Removable and portable ◆ Relatively cheap	◆ Other computers must have a Zip or Jaz drive fitted to read these disks ◆ Do not hold as much data as hard drives ◆ Generally not as fast as hard drives
Optical storage		
CD-ROM (Compact disk read-only memory) Storage capacity: 650 Mb	◆ Stores large amounts of data – up to 650Mb per CD-ROM ◆ Very cheap to produce, particularly on a large scale ◆ Good way of distributing software	◆ As CD is read-only, data cannot be changed or deleted ◆ Slower access times than hard drives, so video images generally not full screen ◆ Cannot read DVD
CD-R (Compact disk recordable) Storage capacity: 650 Mb	◆ As with CD-ROM, a CD-R stores large amounts of data ◆ Possible to add data (write) to the CD-R in more than one session ◆ Good for backing up files	◆ Must have a CD-R recorder to write to a disk ◆ CD-R software has varying capabilities
CD-RW (Compact disk rewritable) Storage capacity: 650 Mb	◆ As with CD-ROM, CD-RW stores large amounts of data ◆ CD-RW can be erased and reused as many times as required ◆ Good for backing up files	◆ Must have a CD-RW recorder to write to a disk ◆ CD-RW does not work in all CD players
DVD (Digital versatile disk) Storage capacity: 17 Gb	Exciting method of data storage that is already making a big impact ◆ Stores massive amount of data – up to 17 Gb. ◆ Excellent for showing video ◆ DVD players can read CD-ROM ◆ As with CD-R and CD-RW, there is a range of ways of writing (storing) data on DVD	◆ New technology, so number of DVDs, in use is smaller than number of CD-ROMs ◆ New technology, so prices of drives relatively expensive ◆ DVDs do not work in CD-ROM drives

Computers can be linked together in a network. Many schools, businesses and other organisations use networks because they allow computers to share three things:

◆ **Files**
◆ **Resources**, such as disk drives, CD-ROM drives, modems or printers
◆ **Programs**, such as word processing, a spreadsheet or a database

Networking also allows a network manager to control the activities of network users.

The most common way to link computers on a network is by cables. But some networks are linked by fibre optics, telephone lines, infrared waves, microwaves or radiowaves. The Internet is a vast collection of computer networks throughout the world, which involves all these different ways of linking computers (see pages 28–9).

Networks come in different sizes. A few computers, printers and large hard disks – usually on one site – can be linked in a small **local area network** (**LAN**), whilst many small and large computers, located on different sites spread over a large geographic area or in different countries, can be linked in a **wide area network** (**WAN**). Computers that are not networked are known as **stand-alone** computers. Data that is on a stand-alone system has to be transferred by e-mail or disk if it needs to be used on another computer.

To connect a computer to a LAN, you have first to insert a **network card** into which you plug the network cable. You then have to set up the **system software** which enables the computer to operate on the network. The computer is now ready to share files, resources and programs with other computers/users.

If you have a network in school, it is likely that the computers are connected by cable to a central device called a **hub** (Fig 2.21). This hub (or hubs if there is a large number of computers on the network) is then usually connected to a **file server**. A file server is a high-performance computer containing large hard-disk drives that are available to all network users. It is where application programs and data can be shared to all users on the network. A file server is not used as a normal computer terminal, as its job is dedicated (committed) only to the task of managing shared files. Some networks also use a printer server that is dedicated to managing all printers on a network. Where one powerful computer controls others, the network is called a **hierarchical network**.

Connecting computers in a LAN

To connect computers to a LAN, you need:
◆ network cabling
◆ a network card in each computer
◆ a hub (or hubs)
◆ a file server
◆ system software

Fig 2.21
*Layout of a typical
computer network*

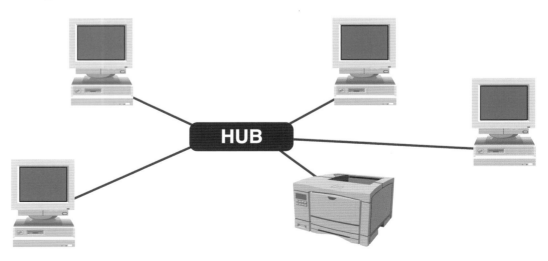

When a network does not have a file server, it is called a **peer-to-peer** network. In a peer-to-peer network, each computer acts as a server to the other computers – its peers – on the network. A peer-to-peer network also allows users to access each other's hard disks and peripherals.

Types of network

Careful planning of a computer network is essential. Most LANs use Ethernet as the standard way of networking computers using cables. There are three main types of layout (topology) of computer networks: **bus**, **ring** and **star**.

A **bus** network is the simplest type of topology, where the network nodes (computers) are in a line, as shown in Fig 2.22. Bus networks are cheap and reliable but if the cable breaks, the network is split into two unconnected parts. Bus networks are slower than star networks, with the speed of network traffic limited to 10 Mb per second.

A **ring** network (Fig 2.23) has no end to the line, as a bus network has. The last node (computer) is connected to the first node, forming a ring or loop. As with a bus network, if the cable breaks it will affect all the computers on the network. Ring networks are also slower than star networks, with the speed of network traffic limited to 10 Mb per second.

In a **star** network (Fig 2.24) all the nodes are connected to a central hub. This means that each computer has its own connection to the network and that a break in a cable will not affect the working of other computers. If the hub breaks down, then all the computers on the hub will not work. However, star networks, although more expensive to install than other types, are the quickest.

Fig 2.22 A bus network

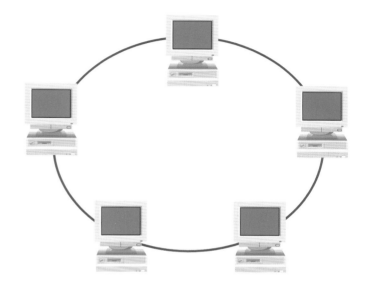

Fig 2.23 A ring network

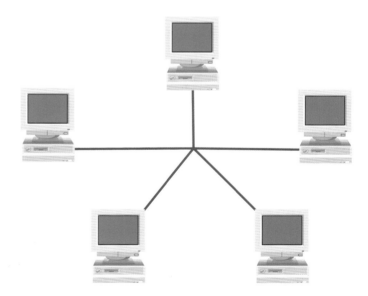

Fig 2.24 A star network

QUESTIONS

1 List three things that can be shared using a computer network.
2 Explain what is meant by LAN, WAN, topology, node and file server.

Cables are not always needed to connect computers to a network. Where a user has to carry a portable computer from place to place, the computer can be linked by a wireless method to a local area network (LAN). Wireless technology involves the use of infrared waves, radiowaves or microwaves. It is becoming increasingly popular as a way to transmit Internet data to **WAP** mobile phones. WAP stands for **wireless application protocol**.

Computers, located over a large geographic area or in different countries, are linked by **wide area networks (WANs)** using telephone lines, satellites or microwaves. For example, a chain of high-street shops throughout the UK may use a WAN to make a permanent link between each shop and the head office in London. Similarly, a branch of a bank may be linked through a WAN to other branches in several different countries.

The Internet

The Internet has been described as 'a network of networks'. It connects over 50 million computers worldwide. The Internet was started in 1969 in the USA to link up centres in the event of nuclear attack. Gradually, more networks joined, connecting thousands of commercial, government and educational networks.

To access the Internet, a user needs a modem, software (web-browser/e-mail package) and an **Internet service provider (ISP)**. Some ISPs charge for their services, whilst many now offer free Internet access. When users are connected to the Internet, they are said to be **online**.

Advantages and disadvantages of networked systems compared with stand-alone systems		
Type of system	**Advantages**	**Disadvantages**
Stand-alone computers	◆ Ideal for most home users ◆ No network card needed ◆ Can be dedicated to a specific task, e.g. composing music ◆ No need for network software licenses – only single-user license required ◆ Security from users on other sites	◆ Cannot easily share data, particularly large amounts of data, with others ◆ Data can be transferred only by disk or by modem. Copying on to disks can be slow, time consuming and unreliable
Networked computers	◆ Access to network from any workstation ◆ Share files with, and send messages to, other computers ◆ Share resources such as disk drives, CD-ROM drives, modems or printers ◆ Share programs (such as word processor, spreadsheet or database) which are stored centrally. Possible for network users to work on the same file rather than each user having own file. These programs are cheaper than one-off software for stand-alone computers ◆ Activities of network users and such things as amount of storage space available to users can be controlled by network manager	◆ Network cards, cabling, hubs and servers can be costly ◆ If the file server stops working (known as a 'crash'), it can stop everybody on the network from using a computer ◆ Poor security. With more users there is a greater risk of computer viruses and of unauthorised users (hackers) gaining access to network data ◆ Need for network manager to manage the system. This can be costly

Main services provided by the Internet

E-mail

Messages can be sent from one computer to another anywhere in the world.

Internet relay chat

Internet relay chat (IRC) allows users to go online at the same time and exchange text or audio messages in real time. Different ISPs have different names for this service, e.g. MSN Messenger Service.

World Wide Web (www)

The World Wide Web (www) – popularly known as the Web – is the main way of accessing information on the Internet. The Web is based on **pages** of information which are linked and viewed by a **web browser**, such as Internet Explorer. By clicking with the mouse on a **hypertext** link (links are usually underlined words displayed in different colours), you can jump to another web page or to another website. Millions of web pages are available on virtually every topic imaginable.

File transfer protocol

File transfer protocol (FTP) is the name given to the transfer of files across the Internet. FTP is the Internet equivalent of a file server, with files made available on thousands of the net's computers for downloading onto individual computers. Millions of users use FTP to download updates to popular software, such as Microsoft Word and Excel, although it can also be used to upload (send) files to websites.

Newsgroups

Newsgroups are online discussion groups where users with common interests, anywhere in the world, can share their views. Imagine a topic and there is usually a newsgroup on it!

Private communities

Some organisations or ISPs provide data and services only to fee-paying members. Many schools subscribe to private communities such as *Internet for Learning* and *AngliaCampus*, as they provide extra resources for both students and teachers.

QUESTIONS

1 Give two reasons why wireless technology is becoming more popular.
2 List two advantages and two disadvantages of using a networked computer.
3 List six services provided by the Internet.
4 Explain why the Internet is called 'a network of networks'.
5 List the three things needed for a user to access the internet.

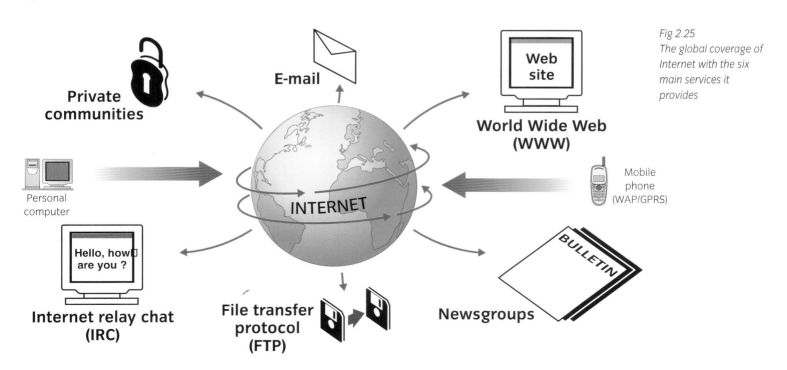

Fig 2.25
The global coverage of Internet with the six main services it provides

The process of starting a computer is known as **booting up**. The first thing a computer does when it is booted up is to check that it is working properly. It does this by following certain instructions held on a ROM chip known as the BIOS (see pages 12-13).

You can often see this happening as various lines of text briefly appear on the computer monitor. It will then look for an **operating system** (**OS**) – also known as system software – to tell it what to do next. The operating system is then loaded from disk to the computer's random access memory (RAM).

Stated simply: without an operating system a computer just would not work.

Learning to use a computer is made easier when you are using the same operating system as someone else. The most commonly used operating system is Windows, made by the Microsoft Corporation (Fig 3.1). When two different computers are both running Windows, important features – such as deleting and copying files and printing – will work in exactly the same way. Popular operating systems include Windows 98, Windows XP, Windows NT, Windows 2000, Mac OS X (Fig 3.2), LINUX and UNIX.

So what is an operating system? It is the software that controls the working of the hardware resources and all the other software.

Software control

The operating system controls how all software applications, games or other programs work on the computer, such as:

◆ File management – Saving, copying, renaming and deleting files.
◆ Multitasking – Allowing more than one program to

Fig 3.1
Microsoft Windows is the most commonly used operating system in the world.

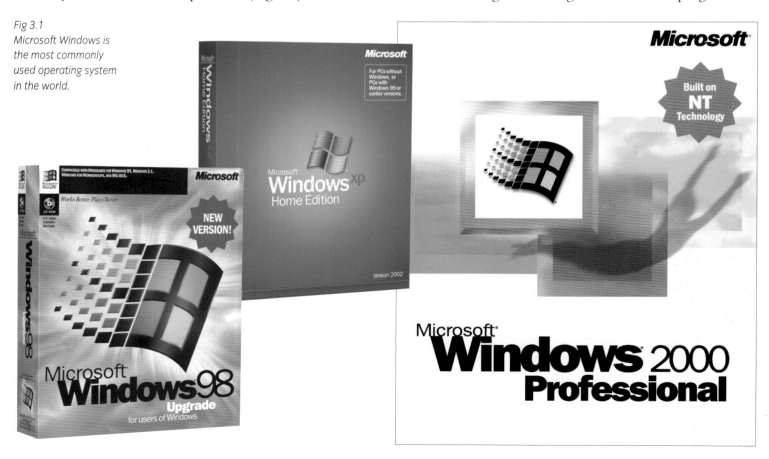

run (work) at the same time: for example, using a desktop publishing program while a graphics program is still running.

- ◆ Multi-user – Allowing more than one user on a computer network to access the same file at the same time.
- ◆ Security – When passwords have been set, allowing only those with the correct password to use the computer.

Imagine an operating system as a building block to which all other blocks (software applications) have to be added.

Hardware control

The operating system also sets the rules for controlling hardware resources such as:

- ◆ Peripherals – Controlling peripheral devices such as keyboards, printers and scanners.
- ◆ Memory – Controlling the amount of memory used.
- ◆ CPU – Controlling the time allocated to a task by the central processing unit (CPU).
- ◆ Disk space – Controlling the amount of disk space used.

In some hand-held computers – such as palm tops or personal digital assistants (PDAs) – the operating system is a permanent part of the computer on a ROM chip. However, in most PCs it is not. Instead, the operating system is loaded into the random access memory (RAM) from hard disk. There are two main reasons for this.

First, it is cheaper and easier for a company, such as Microsoft, to update Windows from disk rather than having to keep making new ROM chips and asking millions of computer users to fit them inside their computers. Second, by loading an operating system from disk, it allows some users to choose between different operating systems when they start the computer.

Operating systems are regularly updated to fix problems – known as **bugs** – and to add more features. Different versions of an operating system are given a number, or the year in which they were first produced, so that users can keep up to date: for example, Windows 95, Windows 98, Windows 2000, and Mac OS X.

Fig 3.2 Macintosh computers, although working in a very similar way to Windows computers, have their own operating system.

Summary of key features of the operating system

- ◆ Input/output control
- ◆ File management
- ◆ Peripheral management
- ◆ Resource allocation
- ◆ Command interpretation

QUESTIONS

1 Explain what is meant by each of the following terms: booting up, operating system.
2 Give four ways in which an operating system *controls hardware* on a computer.
3 Give four ways in which an operating system *controls software* on a computer.
4 List three different operating systems used on computers.
5 Why is operating system software loaded from hard disk rather than from a ROM chip?

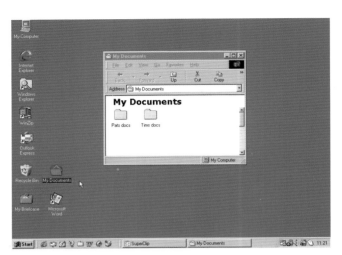

Fig 3.3 Windows 98 is an example of a graphical user interface (GUI). This screenshot shows the computer 'desktop', icons, the My Documents window and mouse pointer.

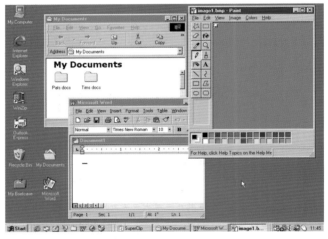

Fig 3.4 An example of two window-based programs (Word and Paint) open at the same time as My Documents window.

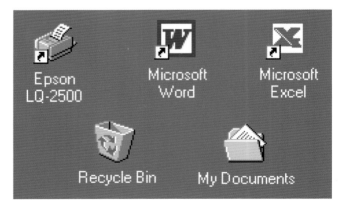

Fig 3.5 Icons have been designed to visually help the user to move around and control the computer. Here, there are icons for a folder, a printer, a recycle bin, and Microsoft Word and Excel.

How you interact with a computer and use it are controlled by the computer–user **interface**. After the computer has booted up and loaded the operating system, you will see the user interface (also known as the human–computer interface).

There are three main types of user interface: **command-line interface**, **menu-driven interface** and **graphical user interface** (**GUI**).

Command-line interfaces require users to type in commands using a special language. This special language makes command-line interfaces difficult to use, especially for new computer users.

Menu-driven interfaces were developed to try to make procedures friendlier and easier to learn. Users can control the computer by choosing commands and available options from a menu using the keyboard or a mouse.

Graphical user interfaces (**GUIs**) are provided by the Windows (Fig 3.3) and Macintosh operating systems. GUIs are presently regarded as the user interfaces which are easiest to use. As a result, all computers are now supplied with a GUI system installed. The best way to remember what makes up a GUI is to think of the word **WIMP**, which stands for **W**indows, **I**cons, **M**enus and **P**ointers.

Windows

A window is that part of the screen that holds its own document or message. Most computers now use window-based programs (Fig 3.4). A window can take up the whole screen or can be resized, moved or shrunk (minimized). Each time you open a folder, you see its contents in a new window. More than one window can be open at the same time. This is particularly useful for moving from one window to another or for copying files from one window to another.

Icons

An icon is a tiny picture of an object that is displayed on screen. Normally, you can use the icon in some way. For example, by using the mouse to double click on the icon of the Microsoft Excel spreadsheet program, you will start the program ready for use. Icons are designed to make things easier for computer users. Instead of having to remember commands, all you have do is to remember what the icons look like. Icons are not just for programs. There are icons for folders, the recycle bin (wastebasket), disk drives and printers (Fig 3.5).

Menus

A menu is a list of options from which you can choose what you want to do. Application programs use menus as an easy alternative to having to learn program commands. An advantage of using menus in Windows or on a Macintosh is that, for most programs, the first few menus are always in the same order. They also carry out the same functions, no matter which program you are using. For example, the file menu is first and enables you, among other things, to create, save and print a document (Fig 3.6).

Pointers

The most common pointing device is a mouse. As the mouse is moved, a pointer moves around the screen. The pointer is a very important part of GUIs, as it enables you to control the computer and to choose window items, to select text in a document or cells in a spreadsheet, and to create drawings and shapes (Fig 3.7). Other pointing devices include track pads, graphics tablets, joysticks and trackballs (see pages 14–15).

Improving interfaces

Software companies spend a great deal of time and effort trying to improve the interface so that the computer is easy to use. An important part of this is to design the system software and application programs to work *exactly the same way* each time they are used, as well as menus being *in the same place*.

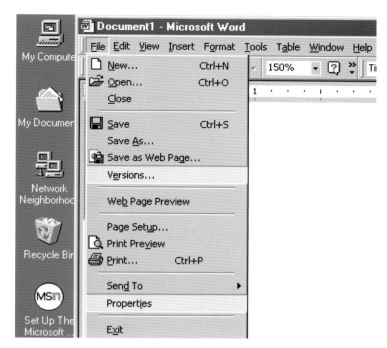

Fig 3.6 The file menu from Microsoft Word 2000

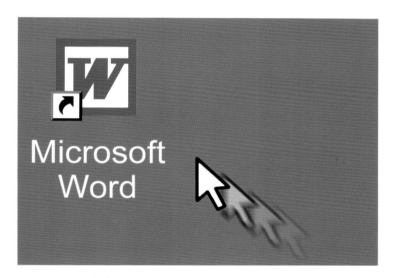

Fig 3.7 A pointer helps a user to navigate around the computer and to use application programs.

People use computers for many hours a day. Therefore, the screen design and screen colours must be visually pleasing and soothing. Also, some colours might be impossible for the visually impaired to see.

QUESTIONS

1 List three types of user interface.
2 Explain what is meant by a GUI and WIMP. Why do think GUIs are the most popular user interface?
3 Give two important factors that should be taken into account when designing a user interface.

Data transfer is the movement of information from one place to another. With computers this happens in three ways:

- within a single computer
- between a computer and other computers
- between a computer and external devices

Within a computer

The loading of the operating system when the computer is started is one example of data being transferred within a computer. This is because operating system data is transferred from hard disk to the computer's memory (RAM).

Data is also frequently transferred between software applications on a stand-alone computer. This can be done simply by copying and pasting or by the software itself opening or importing files that were created by a different software package. **Importing** is the term for transferring data from one program to another. For example, Microsoft Word will open web pages and documents created in other word-processing packages such as Word Perfect.

Between computers

Most computer users will, at some time or another, be involved in transferring files between computers. School students may need to transfer their work from a PC at home to the school network via a floppy or a Zip disk. Updates to software packages, such as Microsoft Office, can be downloaded from the Internet using file transfer protocol (FTP).

Sometimes, however, transferring data between computers requires a little preparation as not everybody uses the same software. For example, one person might use Microsoft Access as a database, whereas another might use Lotus Approach. The solution to this is to convert the file into a common file format that can be read by all software packages without changing or damaging the data. This process is known as **file**

conversion. In the example above, converting the file to **CSV (comma separated values)** would enable it to be read by other spreadsheets or databases (Fig 3.8). Text, too, can easily be converted. Saving text in **ASCII** (**A**merican **S**tandard **C**ode for **I**nformation **I**nterchange) format converts letters into binary code that can be read by any computer. There is a drawback, however, because saving a file as ASCII results in all formatting (bold, italic, etc.) being lost. To overcome this problem, files can be converted instead to **Rich Text Format** (**RTF**). RTF enables the file to be opened by other programs – even those on computers running different operating systems – as well as preserving all formatting. Another way of transferring data, made popular by the Internet, is by **HTML** (**HyperText Markup Language**).

Before transferring data, it is also sometimes necessary to reduce the file size. The process of reducing the size of a file for storage, or for sending via the Internet, is known as **file compression**. WinZip and Stuffit are popular

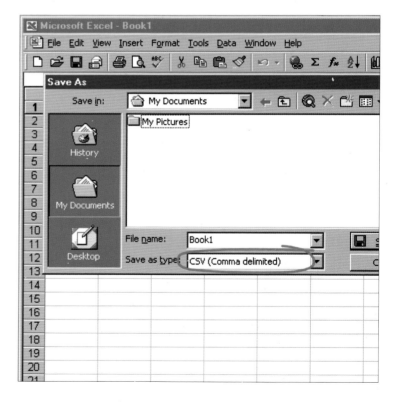

Fig 3.8 Saving an Excel spreadsheet in CSV format means that other spreadsheet or database programs can open the file.

programs for compressing files. File compression is important because some files, particularly picture, sound, video and animation files, can take up a large amount of disk storage space.

The larger the file size, the longer it takes to send via the Internet. This can mean that more money is spent on telephone calls. Users of the Internet will also know that web pages containing pictures can take a long time to load. Web designers try to get around this problem by reducing the file size of pictures – usually by saving them in **JPEG (Joint Photographic Experts Group)** format (Fig 3.9). When video is to be shown, this will be compressed using the **MPEG (Moving Pictures**

Experts Group) format. Music will be compressed using **MP3**.

Remember Compression of files can lead to a loss of quality.

Between a computer and external devices

Every time you instruct the computer to print something, data is transferred to an external device – in this example, a printer. Data can also be transferred to other devices such as disk drives (e.g. file servers on a network or a removable disk) or a robot.

Fig 3.9 Picture A was created in Photoshop and saved, uncompressed, in Photoshop format. Its file size is 7.8 Mb. The picture was then saved as JPEG (picture B), reducing the file size to 496 kb

Popular compressed file formats used on the Internet

Type of data to be compressed	Compressed file format
◆ Graphics	◆ JPEG (Joint Photographic Experts Group)
	◆ GIF (Graphics Interchange Format)
◆ Music	◆ MP3
◆ Video	◆ Versions of MPEG (Moving Pictures Experts Group)

QUESTIONS

1 List three ways in which a computer transfers information.
2 Explain what is meant by the terms file conversion and file compression.
3 Give one reason why many users need to convert files.
4 Give two reasons why you might want to use compressed files if you have a modem and access to the Internet.

We have seen that having an operating system such as Windows 98 is essential for a computer to work. This is because the operating system controls the computer's hardware resources and how all the other software works. Most of the software we regularly use has been created to do specific tasks – for example, word processing or desktop publishing. The term for software such as this is an **application program**.

An application program is defined as a program that enables the computer to carry out a specific task, or a range of specific tasks. The term program (or software) describes a sequence of instructions that are carried out by the computer.

Some application programs are written solely for a specific task – for example, the software used by air traffic controllers to manage the flights of thousands of aircraft. This software, which is known as **bespoke** or **tailor-made** software, is specific to an organisation or business and can be very costly to create.

Application programs

The most popular application programs, however, are those that are not specific to any organisation or business, and can be used by anybody (Fig 3.10). The programs that you use at school and home – word processing, databases, spreadsheets, presentation, drawing and painting – will be such programs. These programs are known as generic, or **content-free**, applications, because the user decides what to use the software for. For example, you might want to use a word processor to write a letter or curriculum vitae (CV), or to design a poster for the school play. Content-free software such as this is much cheaper than bespoke software and, because it has been used by millions of people over a number of years, is generally error (bug) free. Popular examples of application programs (software) are given in the table.

Remember An application program is a piece of software that enables the computer to carry out a specific task, or a range of specific tasks.

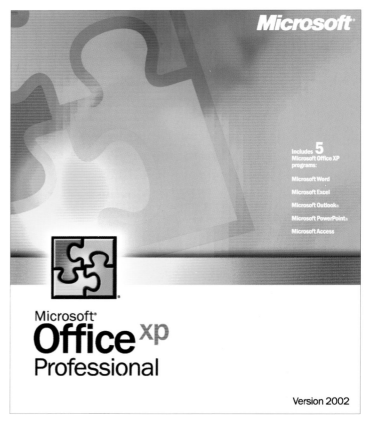

Fig 3.10 Microsoft Office XP contains five application programs: Word, Excel, Outlook, PowerPoint and Access.

Integrated software

Many computers are sold with **integrated software** already installed. Integrated software is the term for a program that includes all of the major types of application (word processing, spreadsheet, database) and brings them together into a single package. Microsoft Works is an example of integrated software. Some integrated software, such as AppleWorks, also includes presentation, drawing and painting features, making in effect six programs in one.

There are five advantages of integrated software.

- You get extremely good value for money, with up to six packages rolled into one.
- You have to learn how to use only the one package. The user interface is the same for choosing commands etc.

Type of software	Examples of application programs	Purpose
Word processing	Microsoft Word, Corel WordPerfect, Lotus WordPro	Writing letters, reports and other documents
Desktop publishing	Microsoft Publisher, Serif PagePlus, Adobe PageMaker, Quark Express	Producing newsletters, leaflets and posters
Databases	Microsoft Access, Lotus Approach, FileMaker Pro, Corel Paradox	Searching and sorting data
Spreadsheets	Microsoft Excel, Lotus 1-2-3, Corel Quattro Pro	Commonly used for finance, budgeting and so-called 'number crunching'. Also used for creating models, simulations and 'What if?' queries
Graphics	Microsoft Paint, Corel Draw, Corel Painter, Adobe Photoshop, Adobe Illustrator, JASC Paint Shop Pro, Macromedia Freehand	Painting and drawing
Computer-aided design (CAD)	AutoDesk AutoCAD, Viagrafix DesignCAD	Producing detailed plans or models, often in 3D. Used by engineers and architects, e.g. for plans of buildings or in the design of cars
Integrated software	Microsoft Works, AppleWorks	All the major application programs – word processing, spreadsheet and database – joined together (integrated) into just one program
Presentation software	Microsoft PowerPoint, Corel Presentations, Lotus Freelance	Delivering slideshows and presentations to an audience – normally using a large screen

Popular application programs

◆ Data can be easily transferred from one integrated application to another, using cut, copy and paste.
◆ It does not take up as much disk space as separate applications.
◆ It takes up less memory than separate applications.

There are two disadvantages of integrated software.

◆ Not all of the features of single applications are included. Therefore, the integrated software may not be up to the task(s) required.
◆ Some integrated packages do not include all of the applications that may be required.

Choosing software should be no different from choosing any tool for a job. Just as in DIY you decide whether to use a screwdriver or hammer to do a particular task, so with software you need to decide what it is you actually need to produce, and then choose the most appropriate program. This is very important when choosing programs to use for your coursework.

The large software companies (Microsoft, Corel and Lotus) sell their main application programs together in one package. For example, Microsoft includes Word, Excel, Access and other software as part of the Microsoft Office suite of programs (Fig 3.10). Although packages such as this are sold as integrated software, it is not true integrated software, as all of the programs are still separate applications.

QUESTIONS

1 What is an application program? Give three examples of application programs.
2 What is the difference between bespoke and content-free software?
3 What are the advantages and disadvantages of integrated software?

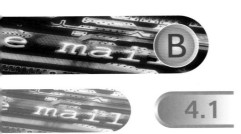
When it comes to presenting words, you have a choice of two techniques using computer systems: **word processing** programs or **desktop publishing (DTP)** programs. As word processing programs have become more sophisticated, they have been able do more of the things that originally only desktop publishing programs could do.

Word processing

How we used to do it

A word processor is the modern typewriter – and much more. It has many advantages over typewriters. You do not need to press the keys on the keyboard as hard, and you do not need to use correction fluid when you make a mistake. On a typewriter, when you get to the end of a line, you have to work out whether you have enough space to fit the end word in and then make the typewriter move to a new line. If you want to reorganise a piece of work, you have to retype it completely.

Making a document look good is quite hard on a typewriter. You need to press each key with the same amount of force to make the print even. You cannot vary the style very much – generally you have one kind of type-face. You can underline the text. You can centre headings but it is not easy to do. You cannot easily make complicated, formatted documents with a typewriter.

How we do it now

Word processing on a computer is simple. You start to type in your text and at the end of the first line the computer will automatically move down to the next line. You cannot make a line that is too long. Make a mistake and you do not have to correct it immediately. If you notice an error, you can position the cursor with

a mouse or cursor keys to delete or add letters, words, phrases, sentences or paragraphs – however much text you want to change. You do not have to do all the typing in one go. You can save your work on a disk and return to it later either to carry on or to make changes.

Making your words look good is straightforward, too. Unlike a typewriter, you can have different styles and sizes of the type-face in your document (Fig 4.1).

The Queen paid a rare public tribute to the man who has been her consort throughout her long reign, Prince Duke of Edinburgh.

The Queen and the Duke are not given to public shows of emotions. In customary Duke joked his way out of expressing true sentiments he may have felt on auspicious occasion. He said before 50 and colleagues at a reception in his "I'm not sure that I recommend being not so much the age but trying to survive these celebrations."

Fig 4.1 A word processor (right) gives better print quality than a typewriter (left).

What can a word processor do?

- It can save work to a disk, which can be loaded into the computer again to be edited.
- Mistakes can be easily corrected. Some word processors have the ability to search for every occurrence of a word and replace it with a different word.
- Parts of a document can be moved or deleted by highlighting the blocks of text in some way and using the facilities of cutting, copying and pasting to reorganise the work (Fig 4.2).
- Multiple copies can be printed.
- The document can be formatted in any way without the need for retyping.

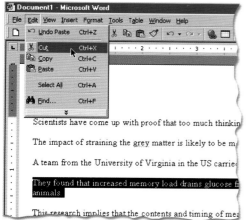

Fig 4.2 Using cut, . . .

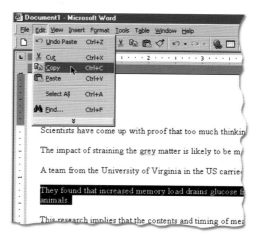

. . . copy . . .

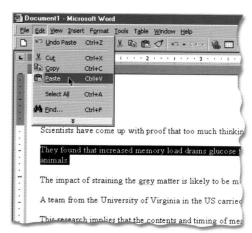

. . . and paste techniques to reorganise a document without having to retype it.

- Margins can be changed and the word processor will automatically alter the document so that the text fits between the new margins. You may even be able to put the text into columns, to make it look like a newspaper.

- Paragraphs can be easily aligned automatically in different ways. Paragraphs can be centred, ranged left or right, or justified (the last letter or punctuation mark in each complete line reaches the right–hand margin). The spacing between lines can be set.

- Different styles of text can be used on a page.

- Different type-faces can be selected, sizes of the letters can be set, and plain, bold, italic, underlined or a combination of these styles can be used.

- Simple tables can be produced. To align columns of text or numbers, use the tab key. To set up a tabulation, you need to know how to set the tab stops (Fig 4.3). Do not use the space bar to line up columns. When you change fonts or sizes, strange things will happen and your layout can become a mess!

- Headers and footers (such as the titles and page numbers) can appear automatically on every page.

The possibilities are endless. You can try lots of ideas to see which layout is best for your piece of work without having to retype the work – just alter the settings.

Rules for good-looking documents

An important thing to remember when it comes to making your work look good is not to use too many of the facilities at once. For example, a document that has several different fonts can be difficult to read.

Remember Who the document is for. Different sizes and styles should not be used without good reason. Make sure you use sizes and styles which help to communicate what you have written.

Fig 4.3 Lining up columns of information can be done using tab stops

Item	Colour	Code	Price
Shirt	Beige	SH173959	£18.95
Trousers	Blue	TR734669	£32.95
Shoes	Black		
Skirt	Green		
Jumper	Grey/Blue		
Blouse	Pink		

QUESTIONS

1 What are the advantages of using a word processor rather than a typewriter?

2 What for you and your work are the most important facilities offered by a word processor?

3 What advice would you give to a friend about producing a good-looking document?

Almost all word processors, however simple, should have the features listed on the previous page. More advanced programs, such as Microsoft Word, offer features to help you to make the 'perfect' document.

Check spelling

If you are not very careful, as you type you can easily hit the wrong keys and words become misspelt. You should always look at your work to check for spelling mistakes and use the editing functions to correct them. This can be difficult – imagine having to do it for this book! Many advanced word processors have a **spellchecker** built in. This will search out all the incorrectly spelt words and probably suggest the correct spellings. It will then let you replace the incorrect words with the correct ones.

While this is a very useful feature, it is not foolproof (Fig 4.4). Spellcheckers work by comparing the words you type with a built-in dictionary. This dictionary will only have a certain number of words to check against (not every word that exists). This means that a spellchecker will sometimes say that a word is incorrectly spelt when in fact it is correct!

Another limitation of the spellchecker is that it cannot tell you when a correctly spelt word is the wrong word to use. It does not read your work – it just checks your words against a list and warns you of any words that are wrongly spelt or that it cannot find. There is no substitute for reading your work carefully to make sure it makes sense when you have finished.

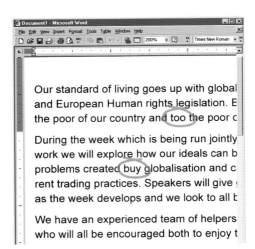

Fig 4.4 Spellcheckers do not spot all your mistakes. Look at the words 'too' and 'buy' in this example.

Fig 4.5 In a word processor, images can be placed on the same page as words. The words move automatically to make way for the images.

Include images from other programs

You can put information from other programs into word-processed documents. This is very useful if you are writing reports where some pictures, tables or charts need to be included. You do not have to leave gaps big enough to stick such images in later. You just insert the files from other programs (or copy and paste them) and the word processor will automatically create enough space for them (Fig 4.5).

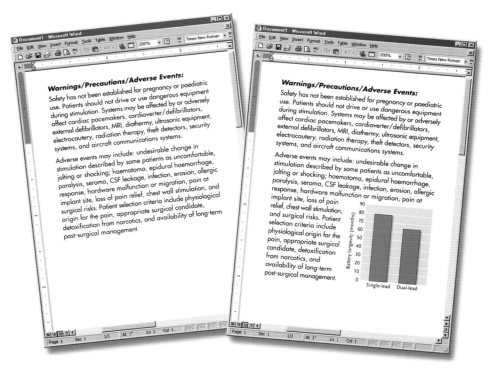

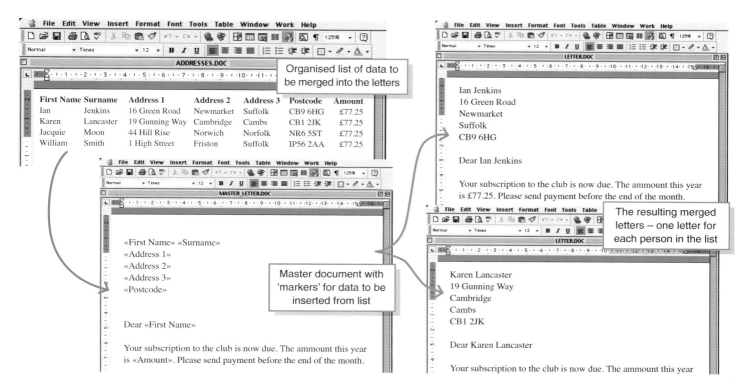

Fig 4.6 Mail merging lets you make many personalised letters from a list.

A limitation of some word processors is that they will not allow you to arrange the information in especially interesting ways. Remember: word-processing programs are not designed to perform complex layouts of combined information.

Mail merging

Sometimes a business will want to send a standard letter to a lot of people but each letter has to be slightly different in some way. For example, if a garage were sending out reminders for unpaid bills then the letters would be identical except for the customers' names and addresses and the amounts owing.

This could be done by typing the standard letter, saving it, and then making all the changes needed for each customer. The editing facilities would make this easy to do – delete the name and address and other details, and then type in the new information. But it would be a very tedious and repetitive job.

Mail merging (Fig 4.6) is a technique found in the more advanced word processors. Such programs automate this type of job and reduce the repetition. First, you type the list of details to be included in the

letter in a structured way – all the names in one column, addresses in the next column and so on. Next, you create a second document. This is the master letter. Instead of putting the actual names and addresses on this letter, you put a marker which refers to the list document and tells the word processor from which column the information is to come.

When these two documents are complete (and correct), you choose the merge function. This produces as many letters as there are people in the list by putting the appropriate information into the spaces marked in the master letter. This saves a lot of time.

With some word processors, it is possible to extract the list of customer details from a database to merge into the master letter. You may be able to do this later when you know how to use all the programs available on your school computers.

QUESTIONS

1 Write a paragraph explaining how reliable spellcheckers are.

2 Explain what is meant by mail merging, giving an example of its application.

To produce more complex layouts, you need **desktop publishing** (DTP) programs. These first appeared in the late 1980s and immediately revolutionised the way in which complex printed materials were produced. They came about mainly as the result of two advances. Computer operating systems were introduced which allowed programs to show on screen exactly what they were going to produce, such as different type styles. At the same time, a new form of printer was developed – the laser printer. This gave a much higher print quality than had been available previously. The combination of these two facilities was to give ordinary users the opportunity to produce high-quality printouts directly from the computer. There was concern that the printing industry might disappear.

Desktop publishing programs give flexibility over the arrangement of the words and pictures on a page. Contrary to some predictions, they have revolutionised the printing industry, not destroyed it. This book was produced using these techniques (as are most books and other printed material these days).

How we used to print

Books, magazines and newspapers used to be produced by a printing process called letterpress. In letterpress, the type was cast in a machine from molten alloys of lead, either as a series of separate letters, which were then assembled into words and sentences, or as a line (slug) of complete words and spaces. Each page was made up by placing this freshly-cast type in a frame. When the pages were complete and arranged in their correct sequence, the type was inked and paper pressed onto it to make the printed pages (Fig 4.7). Correcting mistakes was a troublesome, time-consuming and costly process that usually involved parts of pages being set and made up again.

As technology progressed, hot-metal composition became more mechanised but by the mid-1970s it had been overtaken by photo-typesetting. In this process, the copy comes out as continuous typeset text on film, ready to be made up into pages. At first, this was done by hand but later photosetting units included an automatic page make-up system. The pages of film, arranged in their correct sequence, are then used to produce metal printing plates.

By the mid-1990s, photo-typesetting had been overtaken by DTP.

Fig 4.7 Before composing machines became firmly established in printing works, each letter of every word was placed by hand in a frame to make a page. The type was then inked and the paper pressed onto it to produce the printed page. Today, the process is automated.

How we print now

Desktop publishing is different from word processing in that the text that you put on a page is not one continuous line. You can have several boxes or frames of text – each one separate from the other if that is what is needed.

Sometimes, the frames may need to be joined so that text flows from one frame to the next, like columns in a newspaper. The flexibility that a desktop publishing program gives is that you are in complete control of where the text appears and how it looks. You can even turn text round so that it goes down the side of the page (or at any other angle).

What can we do with a DTP program?

All the facilities you would expect to find in word processing programs are usually present in DTP programs. In addition, DTP programs give you greater flexibility when designing the layout of text. Usually, text is placed on the page in boxes or frames. The shape of the frames can be simple rectangles, or in more sophisticated programs like Quark Xpress, the shapes can be circles, ovals, polygons or irregular shapes. The position of each frame is up to the designer and text can be made to go in a range of directions. You could, for example, put a title along the side of the page instead of along the top.

If you want some parts of the page to be in newspaper column style, where the text flows from one column to the next, you simply arrange the frames in that way, side by side. The frames must then be linked so that the text automatically goes to the next frame (column) when the first one is full.

The visual effects that you can create with these programs are more varied and sophisticated than those you can achieve with most word processors (Fig 4.8). For example, you can apply colour to text and you can make all sorts of changes to a frame. You can produce the title as a bright colour on a dark background. You can decide what colour the frame should be and then choose a different colour for the text to make it stand out.

Sometimes, you might want the text to stand out in a frame. This can be done, and the thickness of frame and its colour can be chosen to add impact.

Fig 4.8 Desktop publishing programs give you the opportunity to create interesting layouts.

QUESTIONS

1   Describe how the pages of a book used to be produced using type cast from molten alloys.
2   Why is DTP more flexible than using a word processor?
3   What for you and your work are the most important features of DTP programs?

When using DTP, you can have more than just text on the page. You can add pictures, charts and diagrams created in other programs. Word processors do not allow much flexibility when it comes to arranging images on a page. For example, an image with text running down one side of it is only possible with the most modern word processors. All desktop publishing programs let you do this.

A facility offered in most DTP programs is **text wrapping** (Fig 4.9). This very useful feature ensures that images never hide any text. You can place (wrap) the text around them. The more sophisticated programs offer you several text-wrap options. The simplest programs let you create a blank line for the image or a simple rectangular box, around which to wrap the text.

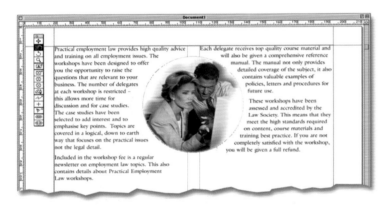

Fig 4.9
A DTP program being used to wrap words around an illustration.

The real strength of desktop publishing programs is that they let you bring together pieces of information from a range of programs and place them exactly as you want. This is the way that most professionals work with this type of software. They prepare the information with an appropriate piece of software and use DTP programs to assemble the information into one publication.

The range of paper sizes that you can use is also an asset of DTP programs. Many programs will ask you what sort of document and paper size you want when you start. When a booklet is to be produced on A4 folded to A5, getting the pages in the correct sequence can be

tricky. A DTP program can sort this out automatically, so that when you print on A4 paper the A5 pages will be in the correct sequence – all you need to do is fold the A4 sheets to make the booklet (Fig 4.10).

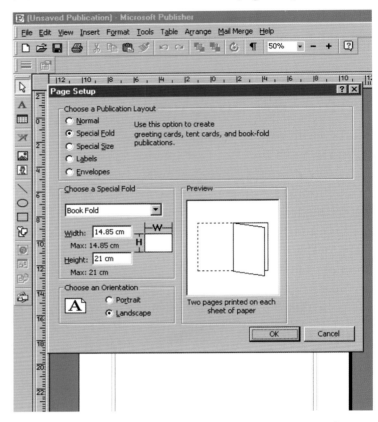

Fig 4.10 How a DTP program gets the proper sequence of A5 pages to be printed on A4 paper for folding into a booklet.

These programs can also make it easy to produce displays on large sheets. For example, if you want to make an A3 (or larger) poster but have a printer which will cope only with A4 paper, most DTP programs will produce your poster on as many A4 sheets as are needed to complete the whole image. The A4 printouts will have some overlap to help you to match them and stick them together to form the poster.

Rules for good-looking documents

The most important aspect of using a DTP program well is to plan your document before you start. If you do not have a clear idea of how you want it to look,

Text program	Advantages	Disadvantages
Word processing	◆ Easy to enter text ◆ Easy to edit and rearrange text ◆ Easy to format text – change the font and its position ◆ Most can check spelling ◆ Facilitates insertion of pictures and charts created in other programs	◆ Not very flexible for making interesting layouts ◆ Difficult to make booklet-type documents on anything other than A4 paper
Desktop publishing	◆ Easy to enter or import text ◆ Easy to edit and rearrange text ◆ Easy to format text – change the font and its position ◆ Most can check spelling ◆ Flexible arrangement of the elements on the page ◆ Text can flow around other elements ◆ Offers a wide range of page and paper sizes and document types ◆ Facilitates insertion and easy arrangement of pictures and charts created in other programs	◆ Sometimes more difficult to use ◆ Straightforward document layout can take more time ◆ An over-full frame of text will not show the end of the text and so make the document incomplete

you will probably find it difficult to create the effect you want. Start with the simple approach. Do not go overboard using many different fonts, styles and colours. Think about the readers of your document and make it easy for them to follow. (There is more on page design on pages 70–7.)

One thing that often happens with DTP programs, but never with a word processor, is that the user puts too much text into the text frame. The result is that the text stops mid–sentence and the user never sees the end of the sentence or paragraph. Look carefully at the printout to make sure it is complete – you might need to make the frame larger (Fig 4.11).

DTP programs do offer more flexibility in the arranging of the text and the illustrations, *but* think carefully about exactly what you want to achieve before choosing a DTP program rather than a word processing program. The question you must answer is: 'Does the word processing program have all the required facilities?' If the answer is 'No', you will have to use the DTP program.

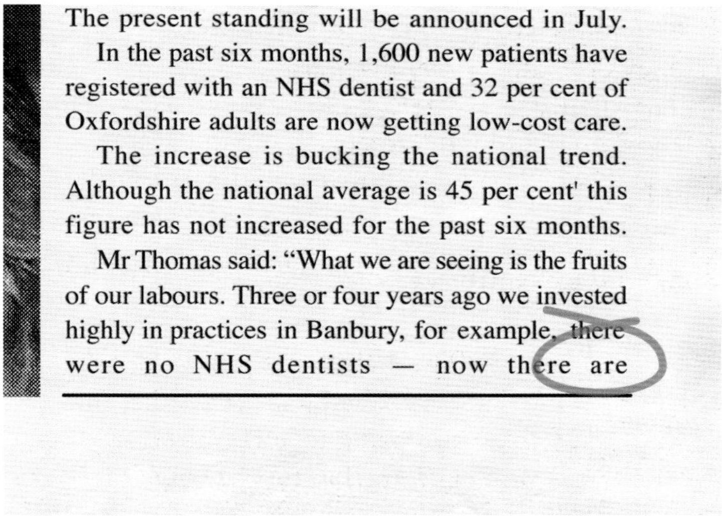

The present standing will be announced in July.

In the past six months, 1,600 new patients have registered with an NHS dentist and 32 per cent of Oxfordshire adults are now getting low-cost care.

The increase is bucking the national trend. Although the national average is 45 per cent' this figure has not increased for the past six months.

Mr Thomas said: "What we are seeing is the fruits of our labours. Three or four years ago we invested highly in practices in Banbury, for example, there were no NHS dentists — now there are

Fig 4.11 Always read carefully your final version to stop this happening. The frame was not big enough to hold all the text.

QUESTIONS

1 Show, with a drawing, how you might use text wrapping to make an interesting A4 page containing two pictures.
2 Give two further examples of the flexibility of DTP programs. Write a paragraph on each example.

To help you to save time on these two pages and on other pages, there is a range of different files that you can download from the Oxford University Press website, **www.oup.com/uk/ictforgcse**. The name(s) of the file(s) you need to download are given in each activity. There are text files which can be loaded into any word processor or desktop publishing program, and for some activities there are also picture files.

Sometimes, you will be told which type of program to use, but usually you must decide whether to use a word processor or a desktop-publishing program to do the work. Each activity has different things to be done. You should look at what you need in the final printout and match this to the features available in your programs when you choose which type of program to use. You should be able to explain why this is the most appropriate program for the job.

Task 1 Changing a document

Download the file **Text1.txt** (or one of the alternative files Text1.rtf, Text1.doc) from the OUP website. The text is continuous with no paragraphs and problems with punctuation. In the document, there is a title (centre top) that needs to be made to stand out. There are also section headings which need to be made to stand out in a common style.

1 Correct all the mistakes and present the document in a way suited to its contents. Explain why you have chosen to present it in this way.

2 When you read the text, you will see that it is not in the correct order. Which function in the word processor could you use to put the sections of text into their correct order? Next re-order the document.

When the final draft was presented to the group, they decided that they needed a name change. Pre-school and Family Group was too awkward, and they wanted it changed throughout to Children's Centre.

3 Describe all the ways you can think of to make these changes to the document. What do you think is the best way to do it and why? Make the changes using your best technique. When you have finished, comment on how effective you think it was.

Task 2 Listing TV programmes

The file **Text2.txt** (Text2.rtf, Text2.doc) is the text from one day's TV programmes, as listed in a newspaper. There are some problems with the order in the listing that you will need to correct. Then you will need to format the text, like the example in Fig 4.12, into five equal-width columns – one for each channel – to fit on to a single A4 sheet.

Fig 4.12
The layout of the TV listings that you are to produce.

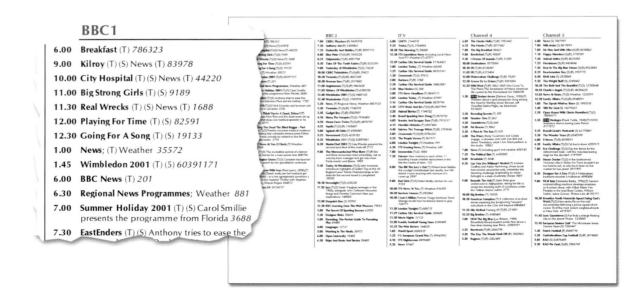

The time should be formatted with a full point between the hours and minutes. Each programme title should be bold and the VIDEOPlus+® code should be in italic. Subtitles, repeats and stereo programmes should use the abbreviations (T), (R) and (S), which are always inside brackets. Each film title should be highlighted by **FILM**

1 What do you think would be the best program to use for this task and why do you think it is the best?
2 Produce this page and then comment on any problems that you came across. For example, was it easy to format the text in the correct way? Was the program you used suitable? Did it have all the facilities you needed?

Task 3 Producing a menu

The file **Text3.txt** (Text3.rtf, Text3.doc) is the menu from Pasta@Paolo's, an Italian restaurant (Fig 4.13). The person who typed it did not know the best way to use a word processor to present the text. When you try to format it as Paolo wants it, you will find a problem.

1 Try to format this document as you see it in Fig 4.13, so that it will fit on to two sides of A4

Fig 4.13 This is how Paolo wants the menu to look.

paper. Can you identify what the typist did that is making it very difficult for you to do this? Can you correct it and use better methods to present this menu. What features of the program are you using that makes it easier to format the text?

2 Design and create a better format for the menu so that it can be free-standing on the tables in the restaurant (Fig 4.14). Produce some design sketches of what you intend to make (include some suitable pictures to give the menu more impact), choose the best program to do it and then make it. Describe how you created the improved format and any problems you came across.

Fig 4.14 Here are some ways in which you might make a free-standing menu. Think about whether printing over folds is going to make it easy to use or not. What else might you add to the menu now you are using both sides of the piece of paper?

Task 4 Checking your spellchecker

Load the file **Text4.txt** (Text4.rtf, Text4.doc) into your word processor. You are now going to see how good your spellchecker is.

1 Look at the text and you will find that not all the words are correct. How many words do you think are misspelt in this poem? (Perhaps you might like to print it out and mark all the 'misspelt' words.)
2 Spell-check the whole document and see how many words it says are 'misspelt'. Do you agree with the spellchecker? If not, can you explain why you do not agree with it?

There is so much software available which lets you create and edit pictures and other graphic images, that choosing the right one for the job is very important. The first question to ask is whether you need a **bitmap program** or a **vector drawing program**.

Bitmap programs

Bitmap programs (sometimes called **raster graphics** or **paint programs**) are those which generate a picture made up of thousands of dots or **pixels**. The dots are very close together and evenly spaced. In the simplest programs, the spacing will probably be 72 dots per inch (dpi), which means a picture which is a 1 inch square will be made up of 5184 dots (72 × 72). More complex programs may operate at 300 dpi or higher. Each dot can be a different colour and can probably be edited on its own by the tools in the program. The overall effect produces a picture in the same way as a mosaic does.

How do you create a picture?

To create a picture, you do not need to place each dot on the screen individually. Imagine how long it would take to create, say, a picture which is 6 inches by 4 inches! All bitmap programs have a range of tools to

help you, which are the computer equivalents of the tools you might use if you were painting with brushes or drawing with pencils. These tools put large numbers of dots onto the screen as you move a mouse or other input device.

The basic program tools consist of a paintbrush, a pencil, a paint bucket for filling areas with blocks of colour, and a spray can. These are all freehand drawing tools. You can also find tools that help you to draw regular shapes easily, such as circles and ovals, squares and rectangles. There is also likely to be an 'eraser' to help you to remove any mistakes! You can add text to your picture, zoom into the picture to make detail changes to the pixels, or select parts of the picture to rotate or distort. All of these tools will allow you to work in a variety of colours and patterns to create the picture you desire (Fig 5.1). Basic paint programs usually offer only a small range of colours – 16 or 256. More complex ones may give you up to 16 million colours!

Problems with bitmap

You will probably find it is quite easy to draw pictures with these programs but they do have their drawbacks. Just like real paint, when you put one colour on top of

Fig 5.1
This picture was created using some of the tools in a typical paint program. To fill a shape, there must be no gap in the outline otherwise 'paint' will spill out.

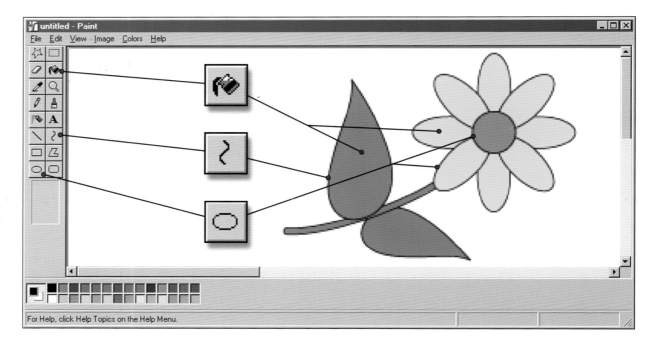

another which has dried, the second colour replaces the first. However, if you change your mind about the second colour and erase it, you will be left with a blank piece of screen – not the first colour.

Drawing a freehand sketch can often be disappointing. As the mouse is moved around, the paint program will record every movement while the button is pressed. However, it is difficult to draw with a mouse with the same precision as a real pencil or brush. Smooth curved lines are hard to achieve. Other input devices, such as drawing tablets, make it easier and more like using a real pencil or brush, but you cannot use drawing tablets with all programs.

Another problem with bitmap programs can arise in the printing of your work. The edges of objects on a picture can appear stepped or jagged. You can see this when you draw a straight line at an angle across a piece of artwork. Even if a straight-line tool is used, it still operates by putting dots on the page along the route of your line. So, the smoothness of your line depends on the number of dots per inch laid down by your bitmap program. The higher the **resolution** (more dots per inch) of your program, the smoother your line will be. For example, a line drawn at 72 dpi will not be as smooth as the same line drawn at 300 dpi.

Overcoming jagged edges

Current bitmap programs overcome the problem of stepped or jagged edges by using a technique called **anti-aliasing** (Fig 5.3). In this technique, the edges of the colours are blended to trick your eyes into seeing a continuous, smooth line.

Fig 5.2
More dots per inch (lower picture) gives better picture quality but they require a larger file to store on disk. Note especially the differences in the bow wave and numbers on the sails.

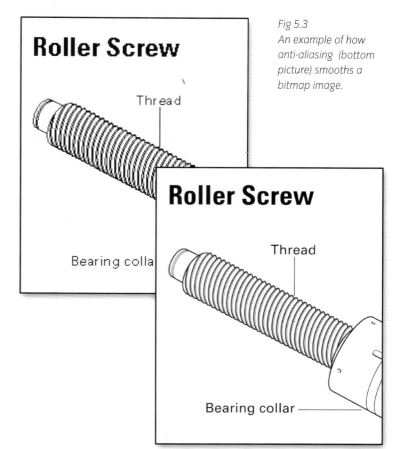

Fig 5.3
An example of how anti-aliasing (bottom picture) smooths a bitmap image.

QUESTIONS

1 Describe how a bitmap program generates a coloured picture, and the tools which are available in the program.
2 What determines the smoothness of outlines in a bitmap picture? Give a brief explanation.
3 What is anti-aliasing and how does it work?

Bitmapped images

Many devices which allow you to input images directly to the computer work only in bitmap mode. If you want to copy a colour photograph to use in a computer, then you may use a scanner. The scanner examines your photograph and breaks it down into a series of small squares called pixels. It then works out the colour and brightness of each pixel and sends that information to the computer. A digital camera takes photographs in much the same way, by breaking down the subject into pixels. Modern digital camcorders also work this way, and so it is possible to transfer still pictures from your videos to the computer.

High-quality photographic images require the great range of colours that only the pixel-based method of computer representation can give. The higher the resolution (dpi), the better the representation will be.

There are some very sophisticated 'artist' type programs which let you work as though you were using oil paints, watercolours, marker pens, pastels, chalk and so on to produce images just as an artist might do on paper or canvas. The subtlety of colour and tone can be achieved only by using bitmap programs.

Remember If you wish to create these sorts of image in your computer work, then you have to use bitmap programs.

How are bitmap programs used?

Photographic images can be stored as bitmaps. These can then be edited and changed before they are printed or incorporated into desktop publishing or other presentation work. Photographers and newspaper and magazine publishers increasingly use this computer technology to remove flaws from their pictures before they are published. (A common example is the removal of blemishes from models' faces, arms and legs.) Undoubtedly, many magazines you read have had photographs enhanced in this way (Fig 5.4). When a photograph gets scratched or damaged, a bitmap program can be used to remove the damage, so that the image is restored to its original state. Before bitmap programs became available, this would have been a very time-consuming task requiring a highly skilled technician to paint out the 'flaw'. Now, powerful programs allow the precise colours to cover flaws to be found very quickly.

Fig 5.4 Marks and blemishes on photographs can be removed by painting over them with the exact colour.

The more advanced programs can be used to produce all kinds of changes to your pictures. At the simplest level, you might just change the colour of an object. For example, fashion designers might like to know what a garment would look like made from different coloured fabrics. This can be achieved by simply replacing one colour with another.

Many programs will let you select just a part of a picture. For example, using the cut (or copy) and paste facility, you could put a suitable photograph of yourself into a picture of your favourite pop group. Then you can show your friends a picture of you with the group!

More difficult things can also be done – pictures can be distorted and changed (Fig 5.5). The more advanced programs will let you apply a range of effects. These can turn a photograph into something that resembles a watercolour or a Van Gogh oil painting (Fig 5.6). Images of objects can be distorted to give the impression that the objects are under water, and amusing distortions of, or additions to, photographs of people can be made. What you can do is usually only limited by your imagination or the power and sophistication of the program. Remember that distortions sometimes cause a loss of quality in the final picture.

There is a drawback to using bitmap programs. When a small picture is created and then has to be enlarged, the quality almost always suffers (Fig 5.7). When you make a small picture (such as a passport-sized photograph) larger, the final image becomes very fuzzy and jagged. If you make it too large, it will start to break up. This is because when you enlarge a picture, the computer can do nothing except enlarge the dots to fill the newly created space. That is, there are fewer dots per inch.

Remember Make sure that the picture is created at the correct size and quality (dpi) in the first place.

Fig 5.5 Distorting can be fun but the picture quality may suffer.

QUESTIONS

1　What are the advantages of storing photographic images as bitmaps?
2　Describe what happens when a small bitmap picture is greatly enlarged. What causes the effects?

Fig 5.6 Some programs can automatically change a photograph into a work of art!

Fig 5.7 Bitmap pictures do not enlarge very successfully. This picture has been enlarged up to 800% and is no longer clear.

Vector drawing programs create pictures in a very different way from bitmap programs. They do not build a picture as a collection of regularly spaced dots. They create it from a set of objects. Each object has a unique mathematical description which tells the computer its shape, size and colour, where it is to be on the page and which way around it is to be. This sort of program uses a grid (coordinate) system and stores the information as a set of numbers which describe all the properties of each object, such as the length of a line and its direction, the radius of a circle and where the object is positioned on the grid.

How do you create a picture?

Vector programs do not have the same sort of tools as bitmap programs. There will not be a paint brush, a spray can or an eraser. Vector programs enable you to draw straight and curved lines, boxes, ovals and regular and irregular polygons (Fig 5.8). The shapes can be filled with a single colour or, with more advanced vector programs, a range of colours known as **graduated fills** or **patterns**. It is difficult to get subtle colour changes (as in a photograph), and the effects of light and shade are hard to achieve.

A picture generated using a vector program is easier to alter than one generated from a bitmap program. You do not need an eraser because each object can be changed separately. To change or remove an object from a picture, first you select it (usually by clicking on it). Drag the object and you will move it to another place in the picture without changing any other object. If you use the delete key on the keyboard (or the delete command from a menu), you will remove the object. It is difficult to remove a part of a shape with simple programs. When a shape is too small, you can enlarge it without making it jagged. The program knows it is meant to be a larger version of the same shape. Bitmap programs have no information on the shape of objects.

Pictures created with vector programs are usually made up of a collection of simple shapes which together look like a more complex object or scene.

Advantages and disadvantages

Vector programs are very useful for producing diagrams. Producing artistic images in these programs is extremely difficult because there are no artist-type tools. Simple vector programs will let you draw lines and simple

Fig 5.8
Simple pictures can be made from elementary shapes. Changing pictures is easier than with a bitmap program.

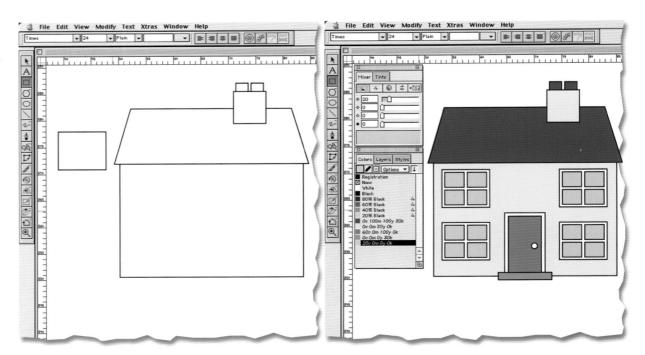

shapes, add text to your pictures. You may find that these objects can be rotated or transformed in simple ways. More sophisticated programs will let you draw freehand lines, and then they will smooth out your lines. (This is a very useful feature if you have difficulty in drawing with a mouse.) You will be able to move each object around your picture so that it is in the right place.

Objects can be grouped together so that when you move or change the size of part of your picture, all the objects move or change size together. Using the copy-and-paste facility, you can easily make exact duplicates of parts of your picture. When you have a picture that is made up of several identical parts, you do not need to repeat the drawing of each part. You draw it once and then copy it as many times as you need it (Fig 5.9).

Pictures can be made larger or smaller by any amount with no change in their quality (Fig 5.10). A small circle made into a large circle will still have a smooth circumference with no jaggedness. Also, any distortion applied to an object or part of a vector picture will not cause a loss of picture quality.

More advanced vector programs are able to produce accurate scale drawings and some have a wide range of distortions and other effects. They are also able to do interesting things with text. For example, you may be able to draw a shape and then get the text to flow around the outside of that shape. Some word processors have such features built into them to help you create attention-grabbing titles and headings.

As with bitmap programs, you will find that simple vector programs work with a limited number of colours while the more sophisticated programs offer many more colours (from 16 to several million colours). To help you to create accurate diagrams, some programs provide grids to draw on and/or rulers for drawing to a particular size.

QUESTIONS

1   In the creation of pictures, how does a vector program differ from a bitmap program?
2   Describe three advantages of vector programs.
3   What features in some vector programs would help you to draw accurate diagrams? Give an example of how you might use these features.

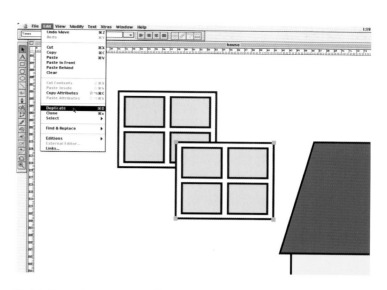

Fig 5.9 To create a picture quickly, you can replicate identical shapes rather than draw each one.

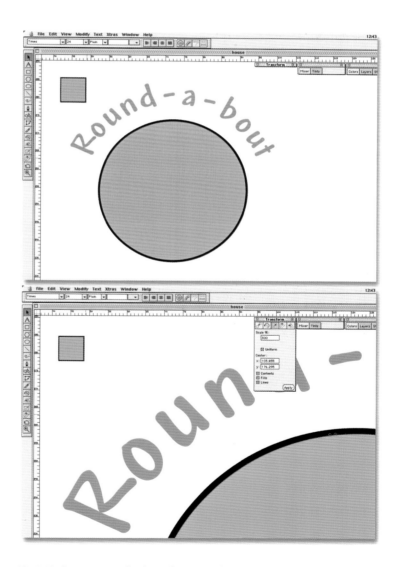

Fig 5.10 There is no quality loss when you enlarge a vector picture. Text can be made to flow around shapes to add visual interest.

Vector graphics are used particularly where diagrammatic images are required. When an architect wants to draw a plan of a housing estate, or details of the houses to be built there, the architect needs a program which can convey the information accurately to the builder. Scale drawings are used for this purpose and vector programs can produce these. This type of work is called **computer-aided design** (**CAD**).

CAD is used by a wide range of people and organisations. Some examples are:

◆ engineering companies which need accurate drawings of things to be made in their factories
◆ kitchen designers who need to plan the layouts of units in kitchens
◆ car designers who need accurate drawings of the many parts in a car
◆ sign-makers who need to create designs for signs over shopfronts and outside supermarkets
◆ fashion companies which need to draw the patterns used to cut out the pieces that make up garments.

Graphic designers also use vector programs. Most of the exciting colour effects, complex shapes, novel typography, and combinations of resized and distorted shapes can only be done to the high quality needed with a vector program.

How are vector programs used?

CAD programs are used when there is a need to produce very accurate drawings, usually to scale. Many manufacturers and design companies will build or buy a library of drawings of standard items, such as kitchen units or car parts, to speed up the design process. For example, a kitchen designer would have libraries of different sorts of cupboards, worktops, sinks and cookers predrawn accurately to scale (Fig 5.11). These would exist as files stored on a computer.

When designing a kitchen using a CAD program, the designer has only to draw the room to scale (including doors and windows) using the simple line-drawing tools of the program. To work out the layout, the designer simply inserts the required units from the library into the outline of the kitchen, puts them in place and uses rotate tools to turn them if they are facing the wrong way. When a unit will not fit, the designer can quickly rearrange the room by moving the units, deleting any unit which cannot be used. Such speed means that the designer can quickly produce several different arrangements for the customer to chose from.

The more advanced CAD programs can also put dimensions onto an object drawn to scale. This helps the person who is making the object to reproduce the design exactly. In

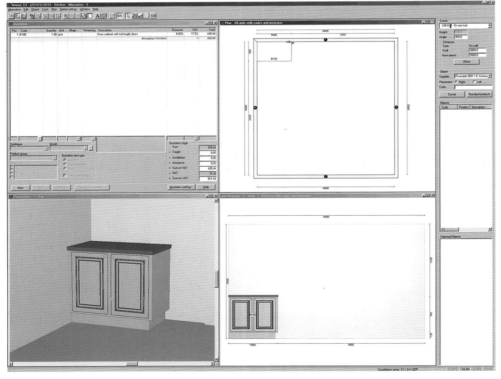

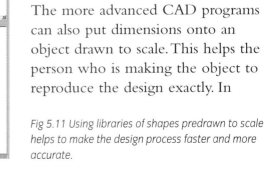

Fig 5.11 Using libraries of shapes predrawn to scale helps to make the design process faster and more accurate.

some factories, the CAD system is linked to machines which automatically make the objects. This is called **CAD/CAM (computer-aided design/computer-aided manufacture)**.

Graphic designers sometimes use CAD systems when they are producing the packaging for a new product (Fig 5.12). They would use different vector programs to produce the artwork that will be printed on the packaging. They want to be able to create interesting shapes or pictures, make the text stand out, include the manufacturer's name and put on a barcode. There might be a logo to include and this would probably be created with the same programs.

Vector programs offer designers a very wide range of colours plus the ability to produce some interesting effects. Sophisticated vector programs let designers blend shapes or cut holes in them so that what is behind the shapes can be seen through the holes. Some of these programs allow designers to colour shapes with complicated multicolour fills or fills which give the impression that the shapes are 3-D.

Graphic designers often use both bitmap and vector packages to produce artwork. This is because they may need the realism of high-resolution bitmapped photographs, combined with precisely created complex text or shape effects (Fig 5.13). You will find that in most vector programs you can import bitmap items. For example, if you were designing the packaging for a child's toy, you would probably design the net for the box with a vector program. You might then import some pictures to make the package attractive and to show what is inside the box. Finally, you would add the text on top of the pictures.

Fig 5.12 Packaging designers use CAD techniques to make sure the package is the correct size. The artwork may be created in another program. The designer selects the program for the features needed.

QUESTIONS

1 For what type of work is CAD used? Give four examples of its applications.
2 You are going to design a workshop which has units for the storage of equipment and materials. Outline in a paragraph how you would do it using a CAD program.
3 When might you want to use both bitmap and vector programs on the same piece of work?

Fig 5.13 An example of a graphic designer's work done without the use of CAD programs.

On the previous pages, we have been looking at programs that work in two dimensions. It is usually the case, however, that the objects being designed are three dimensional. Hence, many CAD programs have an element which will let you turn the plan view, side and end elevations of an object into a three-dimensional picture.

Most 3-D programs are vector programs. They store data which mathematically describes the three-dimensional shapes that make up a scene or an environment. The data describing an object will be: its shape; its height, width and depth; its position in the space; and possibly its colour. Some 3-D programs mix vector and bitmap processes to provide you with most realistic scenes. The vector part of the program describes the shapes of the objects and their positions, but their surfaces are bitmap images. For example, an architect designing a new building would create the shell of the building with the vector part of the program, but would use the bitmap part to apply brick, metal, glass and paint surfaces to give the client a good idea of how the finished building would look (Fig 5.14).

How do you create a 3-D picture?

At the simplest level, you would use a CAD program with a library of predrawn elements. You would place the elements on a plan view and move them to their desired positions. To see what the scene looks like, you would select a 3-D view from one of the program's options, and at once you have a 3-D picture (Fig 5.15). With some of these programs, you will get only one view but others allow you to move around the environment you have created and look at it from different positions. You are most likely to have come across this type of 3-D program for designing rooms in a house, such as a kitchen or a bedroom. There are also programs for garden design. First you place the flower beds, grass and paths where you would like them to be, and then put the flowers in the beds and the furniture and ornaments around the garden. Once you have designed the environment, you will then be able to look at it in 3-D to see whether you like it.

Fig 5.14 A frame structure can be shown as a series of connected lines. To give an impression of what the finished design will look like, surface textures are added.

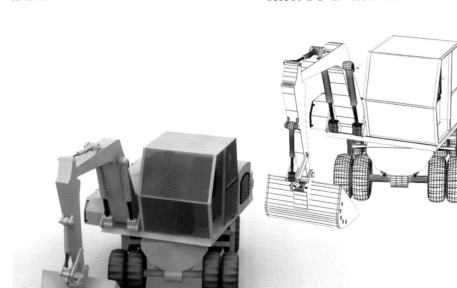

When you are designing a symmetrical shape using one of the more complex programs, you may find a program which asks you to produce a line profile (side view). It will then produce the 3-D shape by rotating or extruding the profile. You would draw the profile using simple vector drawing tools. To create the 3-D shape, you would choose the appropriate tool from a menu (Fig 5.16).

More sophisticated programs may also let you 'shine light' onto the objects you have created. This adds to the realism which can be created by the computer.

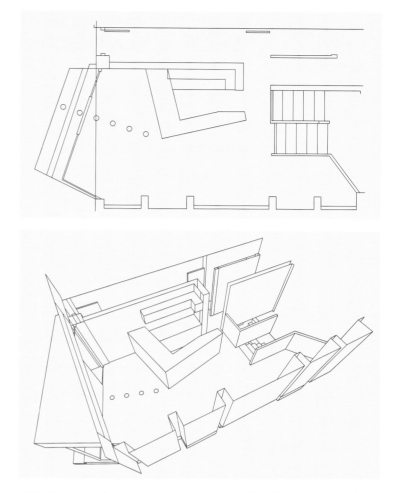

Why use 3-D graphics?

The major reason for using these programs is the speed with which a model of a design can be produced. Before these programs were available, designers had either to produce many drawings from different viewpoints, or to employ model–makers to build detailed scale models. Both of these methods require highly skilled people and take a long time to produce the results. Designers still need to be highly skilled to produce these models on a computer, but it is a much faster process. Also, if they make mistakes or change their minds, they can modify their designs and so change the models very quickly.

Fig 5.15 In many design programs you have to position the library elements in a plan view and then the program will create the 3-D view automatically.

Where are 3-D programs used?

The games played on computers and games consoles use programs which create real or fantasy 3-D environments in which the players then move around. Each new program published seems to use ever more realistic 3-D pictures. Games producers use 3-D graphics programs to create the scenes in which you play. Some games let you design and build new environments in which to play.

Designers of all types use these programs to save the time spent building models, so that they can quickly show clients what the final result will look like. Car–makers often use them to explore ideas for new cars. Architects use them to display the appearance of a new building. Town planners use them to show how an area can be improved.

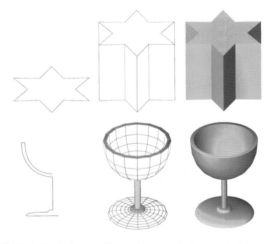

Fig 5.16 A simple line profile can be extruded or rotated to create a 3-D shape.

QUESTIONS

1 What are the advantages of using 3-D programs?
2 What sort of 3-D program would an architect use to impress a client who wants a visually exciting office block?

Film animators increasingly use computers to make still pictures move. For example, the Hollywood film industry now uses computer technology to make all animated films. *Toy Story* was one of the first films to use a wide range of computer techniques. The characters were first produced as 3-D models and then brought to life.

Creating an animation

At its simplest level, animation is just a series of still pictures called **frames**, which are shown quickly, one after another. Each frame is slightly different from the one before, so that the rapid change from one frame to the next results in a moving image (Fig 5.17). Early animators like Walt Disney had to draw each frame by hand. With simple computer programs, the illustrator has to do the same. Each frame of the film is drawn in a bitmap or vector program and saved. The frames are then imported into the animation program in the correct sequence and the animation program creates the moving effects by playing them in order. However, drawing each frame separately takes a long time.

The editing tools that are provided in even the simplest programs speed up the process of making all the frames you need. Using copy-and-paste tools, you can move objects around on the frame – you do

Fig 5.17 An animation is simply a series of still pictures played one after another to create the illusion of movement.

not need to redraw them each time. Some programs let you do simple distortions and rotations on parts of the frame, again speeding up the process of making the small changes from one frame to the next.

Animation programs often work with a mixture of bitmap and vector programs. The elements of the images are likely to be created with bitmap tools. However, each part of a scene could be a separate object, as in a vector program. The objects would be placed on the scene in layers and would be moved relative to one another to produce movement.

Advantages

As animation programs have become more complex, the speed with which animations can be produced has increased.

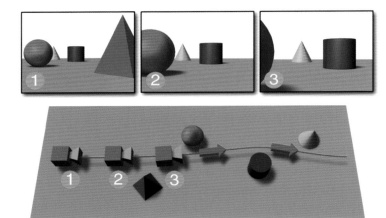

Fig 5.18 The views from a fly-through 'camera' in a 3-D modelling program. This type of animation is left to the computer to produce once the model has been created.

The feeling of moving through a landscape can easily be achieved by using a 3-D graphics program. Once you have created the scene, you draw a path for the 'camera' to fly along (Fig 5.18). Then you leave the computer to create each new frame for you. It does this by working out how the scene looks to the 'camera', drawing it and then storing it. The computer then moves the 'camera' to a new position and draws a new picture, and so on.

This way of making an animation needs a very powerful computer. The computer does take a long time to produce all the frames, but at least you do not have to draw each one.

Another way in which computers speed up the animation process is by **in-betweening** (Fig 5.19). The computer is given the position and shape of an object at the start and end of the sequence. The computer then works out all the in-between steps. For example, the computer can move the arms and legs of a person to create the effect of walking, running or jumping. Key frames in the movement are drawn and then the in-between frames are created by the computer, so that when the animation is played the movement seems smooth. In-betweening can also be used to transform one shape into another – sometimes called **morphing**.

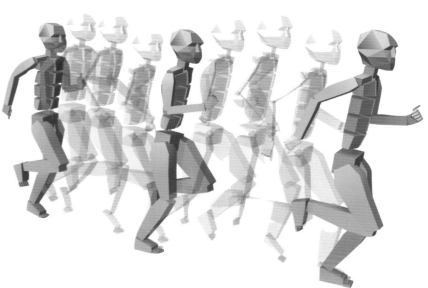

Fig 5.19 The start and finish positions are drawn and the computer creates all the In-between pictures to make a realistic movement.

QUESTIONS

1 Choose something that you would like to animate and sketch the first frame. Then describe briefly how you would complete the animation.
2 Explain the process of in-betweening, giving an example of how it might be used.

Summary of graphics programs

Program	Advantages	Disadvantages
Bitmap	◆ Good for artistic pictures ◆ Wide range of colours – shades and tones ◆ Wide range of artistic tools for creating effects	◆ Not easy to resize pictures and keep the quality ◆ Picture files can become very large, especially when working at high quality (high dpi). An A4, high-quality colour picture might need many Mb of disk space
Vector	◆ Good at diagrammatic pictures ◆ Shapes can be easily changed ◆ Objects can be easily duplicated ◆ Shapes and whole pictures can be resized with no loss of quality ◆ Wide range of effects possible	◆ Narrower range of shades of colour ◆ Difficult to produce 'photographic' pictures
3-D	◆ Many can take a 2-D plan view and create a 3-D view ◆ Often work with a library of predrawn objects which makes for speedy model making	◆ Simpler programs will give limited range of views (some only one view)
Animation	◆ Good at 'gluing' together a series of pictures to make a moving image	◆ Takes a long time to make an animation

Some of the activities here do not require you to create pictures but to work with files that you can download from the website, **www.oup.com/uk/ictforgcse**. For Tasks 4 and 5, your school may have some suitable software, or your teacher or parent may download software from a link on the OUP website.

Sometimes, you will be told which type of program to use, but usually it is up to you to decide which program is best. Each activity has different things to be done. You should look at what you need in the final printout and match this to the features available in your programs when you choose which program to use. You should be able to explain why this is the most appropriate program for the job. Choosing the right software tool for the job is a one of the keys to being successful with information and communication technology.

Make notes on why you have chosen the program. What facilities did you need for the job? Which programs had those facilities? If there was a choice of programs, why did you choose the one you used?

Task 1

For these activities consider whether a bitmap or vector program is the right one to use. Make some notes which show clearly why you have chosen the program. If you have time, it would be best to try all the activities. This will help you fully to understand the different ways of tackling drawing tasks. (If you are unsure which is the best program to use, you might like to do it twice – first with a bitmap program and then with a vector one – then decide which is the best program for the task.)

a   Draw a picture of a house for a young child's book.
b   Draw a diagram for one of the science experiments you have done recently.
c   Draw a map of your local area.
d   Design a logo for one of these: a local business, a club you belong to or another organisation.

e   Draw a net for a simple 3-D shape – a box to form the packaging for a new product. To see if your solution works, you will need to print it out, cut it out and make the box. (If you want to make this one harder, you might like to add the graphics to the net.)
f   Design and create a regularly repeating pattern that could be turned into gift wrapping paper or wallpaper.

1   While you are creating your chosen images, think about how easy it is to make changes to the images if you make a mistake or if you change your mind about part of the picture. Make some notes that will help someone else to understand how easy it was for you to alter your picture.
2   Which features of the program made it easy for you to draw your picture?
3   Which features did you find difficult to use?
4   Did you decide that one part of your picture needed to be made larger or smaller? How easy was it to do this in your chosen program?
5   Now you have finished your picture, do you think you chose the best program?
6   If you used a bitmap program to create the picture, do you think you could have used a vector program? If you had used a vector program, what would have been the differences in the end result? (If you used a vector program, how different would the picture have been had you used a bitmap program?)

Task 2

There is a selection of bitmap picture files available from the OUP website that all need some computer enhancement. In all cases, make some notes that tells your teacher which tools you used and how you used them.

1   The old black-and-white photograph (**Picture1.bmp**, Picture1.jpg) has some scratches and other marks on it. Use an appropriate program to restore the picture to perfect condition.
2   The school photograph (**Picture2.bmp**, Picture2.jpg) is being used by the teachers to show parents proposed changes to the school football kit.

Picture 1

Picture 2

Picture 3

The teachers want three different versions where the tops have been changed from red to blue, to green and to black.

3 The wedding photograph (**Picture3.bmp**, Picture3.jpeg) has unsightly signs on the wall above the bride's head and by the gueasts. Your job is to remove the signs to make the picture look more attractive.

Task 3

Use a vector program to build a library of simple elements in plan view (looked at from above), to a chosen scale, which could be used to design the layout of a room in a house, a classroom or a shop. Use these library elements to design a room plan to scale.

1 How did you set the scale with your program?
2 You want a particular item of furniture several times. Are there facilities which will save you from having to redraw the item every time you use it?
3 Why would a bitmap program not be the best one for this type of work?

Task 4

Build a simple brick house with a 3-D program.

1 How easy is it to work in 3-D on a computer?
2 How easy is it to make changes to your building after you have put the bricks in place. Can they easily be moved, changed or removed?
3 Does this program display features you would link with a bitmap program or a vector one?

Task 5

Animations are made up from a series of still images. Each picture in the sequence is slightly different, but when viewed quickly, one after another, they give the impression of movement. Design a simple animation (a ball bouncing, a ball spinning, a simple cartoon face making an expression). You will need to use a bitmap program to draw each of the frames. You may want to use some transformation tools or effects to speed up the process of making the pictures change. Each picture (frame) must be on exactly the same sized piece of 'paper', otherwise the animation will not work properly.

1 Use a program to assemble the pictures into an animation sequence. Then watch your animation.
2 How does using a computer to create animations make it easier than traditional methods? How does it not help or even make it more difficult?

The use of computer technology has made a dramatic impact on the music industry. Computers are regularly used to create the scores from which musicians play, to generate musical sounds, to record music and to distribute the recordings. Every stage of making music has been affected.

How we used to do it

Not so long ago, composers of both classical and popular music would mark the notes on manuscript paper ruled with staves. When they changed their minds about how the music should sound, they had to delete the original notes and put the new ones in their place. As you know from your own writing, this can make a mess. The editing tools that computers bring to writing can also be used in the composition of music (Fig 6.1).

Creating the parts for each type of instrument was a laborious process, which also usually involved copying at some stage. Here mistakes could be introduced, which sometimes were not spotted until the music was first performed.

How do we do it now?

At the simplest level, computers can be used to produce music scores by working like a word processor with notes instead of letters. Notes of different lengths are placed on a page in the right order with the other notation, such as key and time signatures. This is the equivalent of using different fonts and styles in a word processor.

The mouse is used to put the notes on the page since an ordinary computer keyboard is impractical for this operation.

Just as with a word processor, you can correct mistakes by deleting notes and other symbols until the music is just as you want it. Many of the programs now available will let you play back the resulting piece of music (as long as the computer has a sound card) so that you can listen to your composition. You no longer need musicians in order to hear your composition. Instead, you can improve it and get the effect you want on a computer.

Fig 6.1 Computer-generated musical scores are easier to read than handwritten ones.

Fig 6.2
Using computer technology, one person can make a sounds similar to those of a full orchestra or a band.

More efficient ways of getting the notes into the computer followed. Piano-style keyboards connected to the computer quickly became a more natural way of inputting the notes. Such keyboards are usually connected to computers by a **MIDI (musical instrument digital interface)** system. The music programs interpret the electrical contacts made by the switches under the keys as notes and the length of time each key (switch) is held down as the length of that note. The right note of the correct length then appears on the page. This is just how the letters appear on the page of a word processor.

A variety of different types of input are now available for music systems. Examples are drum pads, piano-style keyboards and synthesisers or sequencers.

Using these input devices we can 'record' music straight into the computer for printing either as a complete score or as individual musicians' parts. The chances of making a mistake are reduced and any mistakes that there are can be easily corrected.

How else are computers used in music?

The recording industry uses the facilities offered by computers to make and edit music recordings. You have probably seen the microphone socket on the sound card on your computer. This will let you record sounds directly to your computer. As well as electronic instruments, you can also record voices and acoustic instruments.

Computer recording cannot create a score – it is used only for recording and replaying sounds (Fig 6.2). It is also used to modify sounds before they are replayed.

Studios record the sounds from electronic and acoustic instruments and from voices straight into a digital format. This might involve recording to digital tape with a digital recorder but can also be directly to hard disk. To do this needs analogue-to-digital conversion.

The volume of a sound – that is, how loud or soft it is – is an analogue quantity. It varies continuously. So if a computer is going to be able to handle and process it,

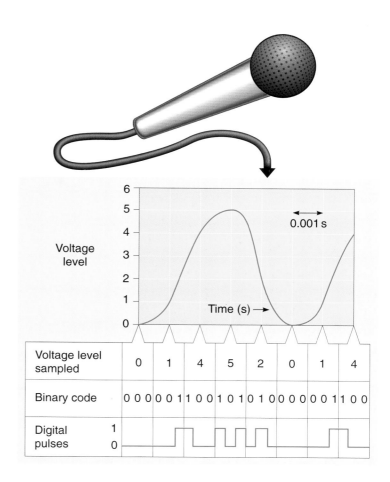

Fig 6.3 Sound waves are first converted into electrical signals. These are then turned into binary numbers – which the computer can read – by an analogue-to-digital convertor.

the sound needs to be turned into binary numbers to be stored on a disk. Once the sound is stored in this way, the computer can process the sound information and modify it as required.

What are the benefits?

Through this technology, music as a hobby or as a profession is made accessible to more people. No one has to be expert on an instrument to make music. The technology helps people to make the music they want.

QUESTIONS

1 Describe a simple computer system for composing a piece of music, giving its main advantage over the traditional method of composition.
2 Where would you use a MIDI system? Explain briefly how it works.

Once the original sounds are stored on a computer, there is a wide range of things you can do to them – rather like the changes you can make to pictures. Simple sound-recording programs let you highlight sections of music, and copy and paste them elsewhere. This means you can alter the order of the elements of a recording. You may also be able to apply some simple effects – like an echo – or to reverse the music so that it plays backwards.

What recording studios do

The music-recording industry uses these facilities in highly sophisticated ways. Parts of a piece of music, of a speech or of other recorded sounds can be organised in any chosen way. For example, a small section of a recording can be selected and played faster, slower, louder or softer. It can then be repeated, the length of the notes altered or the sounds distorted in a variety of ways. These parts can then be re-assembled into a new sequence of sounds to create the desired effect. This might be, for example, the sound effects for a drama production, the rhythm for a music track or a particular sound for a composition.

Each of these parts can be stored and played by a sequencer in any order, with more effects added to further manipulate or distort the sound. For example, it is possible for one person to become a whole band or orchestra by building up each instrument one at a time and using the computer program to join and overlay all the parts simply by using the copy-and-paste facilities with the effects.

Before we had specialised computer programs, this so-called **multitracking** was only possible using a tape recorder. The performer would record the first track and, while it was being played back, would add the second track to it, and so on. This was very time-consuming, and the continual re-recording of earlier tracks caused a loss of sound quality. Using digital recordings and adding them together to make a multi-track do not reduce the quality.

These facilities also allow recording engineers to balance the different sounds, making some louder and blending others.

Fig 6.4 Music recorded with MIDI instruments can be manipulated to create new sounds. Here, reverb is added to a sound, followed by chorus effect and then adjusting the sound with a filter and, finally, panning the sound to the right.

When a live recording is made with a computer system and there are a few wrong notes or other imperfections, the recording engineers can copy parts from a take that does not contain the imperfection and replace the defective sections. This is a lot easier than the methods they used to use of cutting and joining tapes to make the 'perfect' recording.

Manipulating printed music

Using a piano-style keyboard to input the notes for a music score may result in significant correction and editing if you are not very good at playing a keyboard. Here the tools in the program can help to smooth out the imperfections. For example, if you hold some keys down for too long, the notes will be too long on the score. So, you get the program to automatically adjust note lengths to particular values. This means you have less correcting to do later.

If necessary, you can easily make changes to the score. You can alter note lengths or delete notes. You can move individual notes or groups of notes up or down the stave. (This is often the case in orchestral scores, where some instruments might not play the same notes as other instruments.) You can move sections to other places in the score or just duplicate them. You can make notes or phrases louder or softer by inserting the correct commands, which you can also use to make phrases get gradually louder or softer (Fig 6.5). The number of changes that you can make without affecting the quality of the sound is endless!

QUESTIONS

1 What sort of sound effects can be achieved in a well-equipped recording studio?

2 Explain briefly how multi-tracking used to be done before the appropriate computer programs became available.

3 Give three examples of changes that can be made easily to an orchestral score being arranged on a computer.

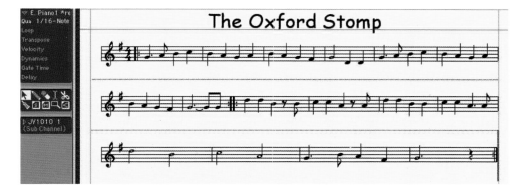

Fig 6.5 Once the notes have been captured from the instruments, the score can be edited for musicians to play. Keys can be changed to suit particular instruments by using a simple program command. Here, repeat signs and a title have been added. Below, the music score has been tidied up so that there are four bars to a line, which makes the score easier to read, and it has been transposed up a tone to put it in the right key for a B-flat instrument, such as a modern valve trumpet or a clarinet.

Digital recording to hard disk has one major disadvantage: the size of the sound files. One minute of CD quality recorded sound needs about 10 Mb of disk space. To record a whole CD needs a large amount of free space on a disk. The disk also needs to be able to record data quickly so that there are no breaks in the sound. It follows from this that a studio using this method of recording needs extremely large storage devices. The computer equipment also needs to be of a high specification to make the subsequent processing of the data as cost effective as possible.

Once the recording has been perfected, it is ready to be sold to the public.

Fig 6.6
Using computer systems to create recorded music is another example of capturing musical data, processing it to make the 'perfect' recording and then outputting it in a form which can be readily listened to. Here, EQ (equalisation) is added to a single guitar track, followed by (below) compression and limiting the music to a complete mixed track before burning it to a CD.

How is the product distributed?

There are a variety of ways to reproduce a recording (Fig 6.6). The most straightforward is simply to record the music from the computer to a cassette tape. The digital signals will be converted back to analogue signals for this process, and so a sound output from the computer is required. This is the reverse process of recording sound into a computer and will therefore need a digital-to-analogue converter. The sound card in a computer has this built in.

This is becoming a less common way of producing recorded music (Fig 6.7). At present, the CD has the largest share of the market, but there is also the MiniDisc and, increasingly, methods are appearing using the World Wide Web and files which can be downloaded from websites. **MP3 files**, as they are called, are based on a new file format which takes up much less space on a disk than the same CD track would. This type of file uses **compression methods** to make the file smaller: a typical file needs less than 1 Mb of storage space for 1 minute of music (although this does depend on the amount of compression and the quality of sound required). It is possible to get at least ten times more MP3 music on to a CD. There is a problem, however. Such a CD would not play on an ordinary CD player. It would have to be a data CD player, not a music one.

The relatively small size of MP3 files means that they can be easily stored on small disks. However, a 3-minute music track cannot be stored on a floppy disk. MP3 files can be fairly easily transferred over the telephone system from the World Wide Web.

You may have seen advertisements for MP3 players. To play your MP3 files, you need either one of these specialised players or a computer with an MP3 player program. MP3 player programs for computers are available on the World Wide Web (Winamp and Macast, to name just two). In future, the portable MP3 player may well replace the Walkman® and/or the portable

CD player. An MP3 player has no moving parts, so in theory its batteries will last longer. But the main advantage is that you will not get the 'Walkman®' wobble' of a tape that has been jogged, or the skipped tracks on a CD. If you run while listening to your MP3 player, the sound will not be affected in any way.

To get an MP3 file, you download it from a website and then play it on your computer or transfer it to your MP3 player by a wire connection. Some players use smart cards on which to store the music, so instead of carrying around tapes or CDs you will be carrying smart cards.

What will be the impact of all this?

The recorded-music industry is facing a tough challenge. How is it going to respond to the buying public? At the moment, you go to a record shop or mail-order company to buy your tape or CD. On the World Wide Web, anyone with a website, an interest in music and the ability to record and save it as MP3 files, will be able to distribute music. What will this mean for the future of the large recording companies and of the smaller groups trying to get recognised?

What about the listening public? They will be able to pick only the tracks they want to listen to rather than whole CDs. Once they have chosen the tracks, they will download them to their computers and on to their players. Customers will have much more choice.

QUESTIONS

1 What is the importance of MP3 files to the distribution of recorded music?
2 Give three advantages that an MP3 player has compared with other sound reproduction devices.
3 Write a paragraph on what you think will have happened to the recorded-music industry by 2010.

Fig 6.7 The technologies used in recorded music have changed dramatically from the first wind-up wax cylinder players to today's MP3 players.

Your school may already have some suitable programs to help you with this work, or your teacher or parent may download and install some of the programs following links in their area of the OUP website: **www.oup.com/uk/ictforgcse**

As always, there may well be more than one suitable program and it is up to you to make an informed decision as to which is the most appropriate for your needs. Always make some notes about why you have chosen to use that particular program – record the facilities it has that you need.

Task 1 Recording and storing sounds

Record and store sounds using the built-in recording software on your PC or Macintosh computer. You will find that the system software will let you use these sounds for particular effects.

What effects can you perform on your recording? Try some of them. Do they enhance the sounds or not? (See Fig 6.8.)

Task 2 Composing and performing a tune

Use a piece of score-writing software (such as that in Fig 6.9) to compose a simple tune.

1 Can you get the program to perform the music? If so, how can you alter the performance? Does the program let you choose and change the instruments?
2 How can you edit the music? If you have a phrase of the music you wish to repeat, does the program expect you to input it more than once or are there

Fig 6.8 A simple sound recording program (like Sound Recorder, which is available on all Windows-based computers) will let you record sounds via a microphone connected to the sound card. Once recorded, you can experiment with the sound: for example, speeding it up or slowing it down.

Fig 6.9
A simple music writing program that lets you create up to four 'tracks' of music. The score is created by selecting the appropriate note length from the palette and placing it on the score. A wide range of instruments is available and these can be changed at any time. You can play your piece of music to hear what it is like.

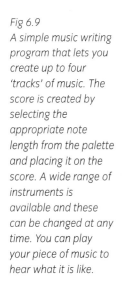

some functions which make a repeating phrase easy to put into the music? Are there other features that make this way easier than doing it by hand?

Task 3 Using sound clips

On the OUP website there is a collection of sound clips (**Sound1.wav** to **Sound6.wav**; or **Sound1.aif** to **Sound6.aif**). Your task is to assemble these clips into a unique piece of music. You may use a clip as many times as you like to create a repeating sound pattern. If the program you use can select just parts of a clip, you might like to use that feature (see Fig 6.10). Working in pairs, you might like to play to each other your 'composition' to see which you prefer.

1 Which program would be the best for this assembly task and why?
2 Describe how you went about putting your composition together. Did you have a plan of what you were trying to achieve before you started? If so, did you write it down (or make some sketches of the proposed structure)?
3 How close to your intentions was the final sound? If there are differences between the final result and what you intended, can you say why this happened? Was it a limitation of the program you used or some other reason?

Task 4 Creating a rhythm track

Create a rhythm track using a drum–machine program (see Fig 6.11). Create a track that you could perform to, or just recreate the drum rhythm to one of your favourite songs. You will sometimes find that each part of the drum kit will be a separate track, so you may find

Fig 6.10 Sounds can be recorded or imported and then stuck together using copy-and-paste techniques to form a new piece of music. Programs like this often allow you to apply effects to the whole or parts of a sound. Other programs may let you sequence the sounds using different techniques.

that some programs will limit the realism you can create.

1 How did you choose the instruments you wanted to use and was the range suitably wide for the sound you were trying to create?
2 How could you alter the speed of the rhythm?
3 Was there a limit to how long your rhythm could be?
4 Could you alter the number of beats in a bar of your rhythm?
5 How would you rate the program you used for the task you attempted? Did it have all the facilities you wanted? How easy was it to create the piece of music? Are there other methods that you know of that would have been quicker than the method you used?

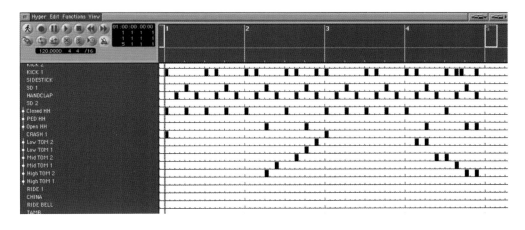

Fig 6.11 To make your drum track, you first select the instruments you want to have (Add Drum) and then add the number of bars you wish to make your track (Add Measure). A black rectangle means that the instrument will sound and an empty box means it will not play. Here, a four-bar track using 11 percussion instruments has been created.

When you require a printed document, the best tool you can use for mixing words and pictures (and other graphical information, such as charts and graphs) is a desktop publishing program. On pages 42–5, you saw that DTP programs are very flexible when it comes to complex layouts. Professional designers of page layouts use these programs mostly to assemble the elements of their documents, not to create the elements.

Designers know that, for drawing a picture, the tools in a graphics program are far superior to those in a DTP program. Similarly, they would prepare the text with a word processor because it will have more advanced facilities with which to check accuracy and format the text.

This unit (pages 70–7) looks at how to prepare files for importing or inserting into a DTP program. It contains some fairly advanced techniques and some technical jargon.

Preparing text and word processed files

With most current programs there are two ways in which you can transfer information from one program to another.

The most straightforward way is to have both programs open at the same time. Then, starting with the word processor, highlight the text you wish to transfer and copy it with the copy command. Transfer to the DTP program and paste the text into the DTP document. All the font, style and formatting settings should transfer with the text. All the setting up of the text done in the word processor does not need to be repeated.

The other technique, which professional designers use, is first to save onto a disk the individual files to be organised by the desktop publishing program, and then to use the insert–file command to import the information. This is the more flexible method, because you do not have to have both programs on one

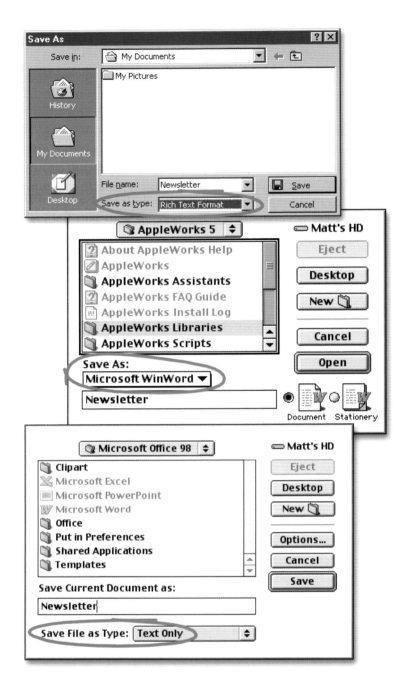

Fig 7.1 When you save your text to be used in a DTP program, make sure you use the right format. Here are just some of the popular saving formats.

computer and the two programs do not need to be running simultaneously. This is useful if your computer does not have enough RAM to run both programs at once. Sophisticated DTP programs are costly and so it may be that your school cannot afford to buy enough

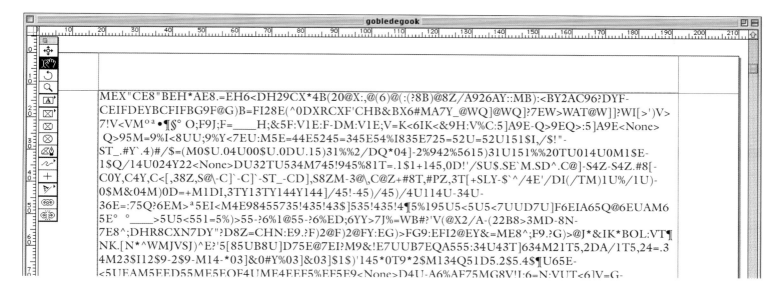

MEX"CE8"BEH*AE8.=EH6<DH29CX*4B(20@X:,@(6)@(:(?8B)@8Z/A926AY::MB):<BY2AC96?DYF-CEIFDEYBCFIFBG9F@G)B=FI28E(^0DXRCXF'CHB&BX6#MA7Y_@WQ]@WQ]?7EW>WAT@W]]?WI[>')V>7!V<VMºª•¶§º O;F9J;F=____H;&5F:V1E:F-DM:V1E;V=K<6IK<&9H:V%C:5]A9E-Q>9EQ>:5]A9E<None> Q>95M=9%I<8UU;9%Y<7EU:M5E=44E5245=345E54%I835E725=52U=52U151$I,/$!"-ST_.#Y`.4)#/$=(M0$U.04U00$U.0DU.15)31%%2/DQ*04]-2%942%5615)31U151%%20TU014U0M1$E-1$Q/14U024Y22<None>DU32TU534M745!945%81T=.1$1+145,0D!'/SU$.SE`M.SD^.C@]-S4Z-S4Z.#8[-C0Y,C4Y,C<[,38Z,S@\-C]`-C]`-ST_-CD],S8ZM-3@\,C@Z+#8T,#PZ,3T[+SLY-$`^/4E'/DI(/TM)1U%/1U)-0$M&.04M)0D=+M1DI,3TY13TY144Y144]/45!-45)/45)/4U114U-34U-36E=:75Q?6EM>ª5EI<M4E98455735!435!43$]535!435!4¶5%195U5<5U5<7UUD7U]F6EIA65Q@6EUAM65Eº º____>5U5<551=5%)>55-?6%1@55-?6%ED;6YY>7J%=WB#?'V(@X2/A-(22B8>3MD-8N-7E8^;DHR8CXN7DY"?D8Z=CHN:E9.?F)2@F)2@FY:EG)>FG9:EFI2@EY&=ME8^;F9.?G)>@J*&IK*BOL:VT¶NK.[N*^WMJVSJ)^E?'5[85UB8U]D75E@7EI?M9&!E7UUB7EQA555:34U43T]634M21T5,2DA/1T5,24=.34M23$I12$9-2$9-M14-*03]&0#Y%03]&03]$1$)'145*0T9*2$M134Q51D5.2$5.4$¶U65E-<5UEAM5EED55ME5EOE4UME4EEE5%EE5E9<None>D4U-A6%AE75MG8V!I-6=N:VUT<6]V=G-

---

Fig 7.2 If you do not use the correct file format, you may get this sort of thing happening when you import the text.

copies to make them available on all machines. This means you might compose the text in the word processor on one computer and arrange it on a different computer with the DTP program. You cannot use the copy-and-paste technique between two machines, so the insert-file method is the only way in that situation.

Professional designers use this technique because many companies compose their own text, but rather than buy all the DTP software and costly printing hardware, they send the files to a printing works for the DTP stage.

There is one most important thing to consider when you prepare material in one program to be used later in another. Will the information in the saved word-processed file be understandable to the DTP program?

How do you make sure that the information created by one program will be understood by a different program? When you save your work, you will probably give it a name and then click 'OK'. Look carefully at the box that then comes onto the screen and you will see a pop-up menu from which you can choose to 'Save File as Type'. So, you need to know what kinds of file your DTP program will import (Fig 7.1). This procedure is known as **file formatting**. At this point you may need to look in the manual or ask someone for help.

The simplest common file type is TEXT (.TXT is the file extension for PC-type computers). All word-based programs will be able to understand a TEXT file. There is a problem with TEXT files, however. They save only the words. They do not save the font, style and formatting information. Hence, the information does not look the same when you import it into a DTP program, and you have to repeat all the appearance settings.

Rich Text Format (RTF) was designed to overcome this problem. It saves the font, style and formatting information, as well as the words. When you import an RTF file into another program, it will look the same as it did in the program that created it.

There are many other file types which are specific to particular programs and you may well be able to import these also – but you will need to check before you try any of them (Fig 7.2). Microsoft Word files can be imported into most Apple Macintosh and PC DTP programs because Word is a very popular word processor.

QUESTIONS

1 Describe one method of transferring text from a graphics program to a DTP program.
2 What does file formatting mean and why is it such an important procedure?
3 Why was Rich Text Format introduced?

Preparing picture and graphic files for inserting and importing

Pictures are more complicated than words to put into a suitable file format for inserting or importing. This is because there are more types of graphic program – bitmap, vector, and three-dimensional. This means there are more file formats for pictures – and some of them are highly specialised.

If you have created the pictures in a graphics program, you can use the copy-and-paste technique as you would for text. Select each picture with the appropriate highlighting technique and use the copy command. Then paste the picture into the DTP program. This is not always a smooth process and you may experience some loss of quality in the transfer.

A better way is to save the pictures using an appropriate file format, and then to use the import-file command in the desktop-publishing program. However, there is a problem with this technique. The size of the file (in kb or Mb) can be too large to be saved on to a floppy disk. You would then need to find either a disk system that can store large files, or a different way of transferring the information. Generally, bitmap files will be larger than similar vector-based ones.

You may wish to use pictures taken with a digital camera or scan photographs with a scanner. You will need to know in which format to save these to allow you to import them into the DTP program.

The common file formats for pictures and graphics

Type of graphic program	Windows-based PC		Apple Macintosh	
Bitmap	PC Paintbrush	.PCX	MacPaint	PTNG
	Bitmap (Paint etc.)	.BMP	MacDraw/AppleWorks	PICT
	Digital camera programs, scanning programs and advanced programs, such as Photoshop, can save in a variety of formats	.GIF .JPG .TIF	Digital camera programs, scanning programs and advanced programs, such as Photoshop, can save in a variety of formats	GIF JPEG TIFF
	JPEG and GIF are formats which use file-compression techniques to make the file as small as possible		JPEG and GIF are formats which use file-compression techniques to make the file as small as possible	
Vector	CorelDraw	.CDR	MacDraw/AppleWorks	PICT
	Windows MetaFile	.WMF	Encapsulated Postscript from advanced vector programs such as Adobe Illustrator or Macromedia Freehand	EPSF
	Encapsulated Postscript from advanced vector programs such as Adobe Illustrator and Micromedia Freehand	.EPS		

You can see from the table that there are some file formats which are common across different computer types. However, it is harder to make sure that information created by one type of program will work with another when it is imported.

When you save your pictures, you need to make sure that you save them as a particular file type, just as you would for text. You might need to read the program manuals, or ask someone, to make sure that the DTP program will import that picture file.

Things to remember when creating pictures to be imported

When we considered creating pictures, we talked about what can happen when the size of the picture is changed. It is possible that the picture quality will be affected. When pictures are created for a desktop published document, they are usually not the right size for the spaces on the pages. This is particularly true for pictures taken with a digital camera or for scanned photographs. The camera or scanner will dictate the size and you have little control over this. When the images are too small for the space you wish to fill, you will be able to enlarge them when they have been placed on the desktop published page. As they are bitmap images, they will lose quality as you make the picture bigger (Fig 7.3).

If the picture is vector based, you will have no problem with resizing it. The quality will remain the same however large or small you make it to fit the space (Fig 7.4).

The design of your document – where the various parts are to go and how big they need to be – is a very important part of the process of good desktop publishing. Once you know how big the pictures need to be, you can look at the graphics creation programs to see whether they can help you to get the images just the right size. Only a small adjustment will then be needed when you bring them all together on the DTP pages.

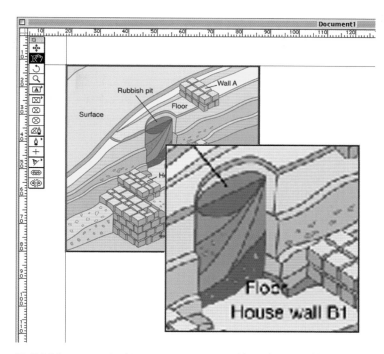

Fig 7.3 When you resize bitmap pictures, you could get distortion like this.

Fig 7.4 When you resize vector pictures, you do not get the distortion shown in Fig 7.3.

QUESTIONS

1 Write a paragraph about a method you have used to import pictures into a desktop publishing program, mentioning any problems you have encountered.

2 When you have enlarged images, what have you noticed about the quality of the image. Were the effects different for different file formats?

Once you have all the elements saved in a suitable format, you can start designing the document. You can design the layout before you prepare the files for assembly – there is no one correct way of doing this.

The design stage is essential if your message is to be communicated clearly. Just messing about with the text and pictures will usually leave you with a cluttered piece of work that is difficult to understand.

Choose the paper size (for example, A4) and which way the page(s) will be (portrait or landscape). Decide what information needs to be on the page(s), and, when there is more than one page, what information is going on which page. Think about the position and size of every element on each page. Will there be any elements common to every page?

Your next step is to sketch these ideas and add some annotation to give some idea of the size of each frame and what is to be in it – a short description or the name of the file would do. Where it is a frame of text, you might indicate the font to be used and any relevant formatting information, such as which are titles, captions and main text. The most obvious way of making the text fit the space on a page is to change the size of the frame or change the font, but there are other controls you may use (Fig 7.5). For example, you could adjust the space between the lines. This control is quite crude in a word processor and you may be restricted to just one, one and a half or two-line spaces.

DTP programs give you more control. In some programs it is called line spacing but in professional DTP programs it is called leading. This name goes back to the time when printers used to place blank strips of lead between the lines of metal type to adjust the spacing between the lines (see page 42).

In many desktop publishing programs, it is also possible to adjust the width of the letters (scaling) and the space between adjacent letters (kerning). If you look carefully at professionally printed material, you will see all of these are techniques used to improve the appearance of the pages and make the text fit easily into the available space.

Using too many different fonts looks unprofessional, and makes a page difficult to read. It is important to consider the position of the frames. Text that is placed close to the edge of a page can sometimes be difficult to read. When a frame has a visible border, the border should not be too close to the text as this can also make reading difficult. Never overcrowd a page! Guide the reader through the information. Professional designers will tell you that the use of empty space on a page is just as important as text and pictures when making a document clear and easy to understand (Fig 7.6).

Fig 7.5

designing and producing dtp pages
Standard setting with no special typographic effect

designing and producing dtp pages
Negative leading means that letters clash

designing and producing dtp pages
Adding extra space (kerning) between the letters

designing and producing dtp pages
Changing the width of letters (scaling) may mean having to reduce the text size

designing and producing dtp pages
*The headings in this book use two different **weights** of type*

designing and producing dtp pages
When reversing out type, choice of colour is important

Make sure that pictures do not distract from the main text. The size of the pictures is important and you may need to adjust this when you position them. Make sure that they balance the layout of the text. If text has to go over a picture, make sure that it is still legible.

For a newspaper-style document with several columns, make sure that there are not too many columns for the size of paper you are going to use. There is nothing more difficult to read than, for example, an A4 page with many narrow columns on it. When the lines of text in a column are too short, the eye cannot easily follow the text, and so fluent reading becomes impossible.

Should you create a magazine or booklet, you might want certain features to appear on every page – such as page numbers or a logo. Make sure these are in the same position on every page. If they appear in different positions from page to page, the reader will be distracted. If your program has a master-page facility, it will ensure that the positioning of repeated features is consistent throughout the publication. Finally, when you design a form which people are going to fill in, make the spaces large enough for them to write in.

QUESTIONS

1 Give some of the ways in which professional designers fit text into the available space.
2 To design a clean, elegant page, you must avoid doing certain things. What are they?

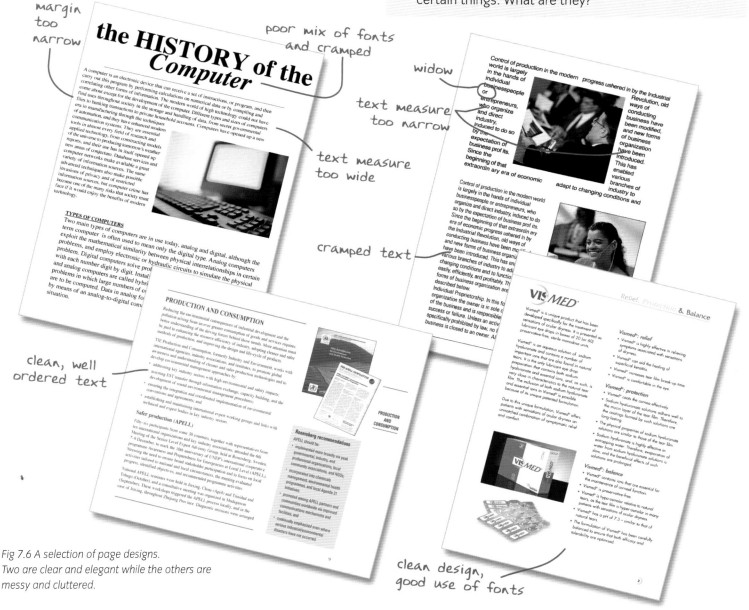

Fig 7.6 A selection of page designs.
Two are clear and elegant while the others are
messy and cluttered.

With these activities you need to plan your work carefully before you start. First, decide on the size of your publication. Next, decide what information needs to go on each page and how you will arrange it. Remember that you must decide on the essential information to be in the publication and on the relative importance of each piece of information. These decisions will affect the arrangement of the page(s). Then you need to collect and prepare the essential elements with the appropriate computer programs.

It is best to record every stage of the development of your project, describing clearly all the decisions you made along the way and why you made them. It is good to get used to doing this, because when you do your coursework, you will usually have to produce a report on how you solved a problem. Just handing in the printout of your solution will not get the highest marks!

When choosing the programs to prepare and assemble the page(s), think carefully about why you have chosen those particular programs. It is important that you choose those which have the right features for the things you need to do. Never choose a complex program just because you assume it is the best – it may be too hard for you to use well. Comment on those features which the programs have that you need.

Task 1 Producing a playgroup booklet

The committee of a playgroup want a booklet to be printed on a single piece of A4 folded to an A5 format. A set of files are available from the playgroup on the OUP website (**www.oup.com/uk/ictforgcse**).

Picture4.bmp (Picture4.jpg, Picture4.eps) is the group logo.

Picture5.bmp (Picture5.jpg, Picture5.eps) is a location map showing how to find the playgroup.

Picture6.bmp (Picture6.jpg, Picture6.eps) is a photograph of a playgroup session.

Text5.txt (Text5.rtf, Text5.doc) is a document containing general information about the playgroup and what it does.

Text6.txt (Text6.rtf, Text6.doc) is a document containing a list of the staff.

Text7.txt (Text7.rtf, Text7.doc) is a document containing a list of playgroup session times and costs.

These need to be turned into an information booklet for parents at the playgroup.

The playgroup would like the first page to be a title page and the rest of the information to be clearly laid out on the other pages. They would like you to make up a suitable caption to go with the photograph and include that in the final document.

1   Once you have looked at all the information in the files given by the playgroup, sketch some ideas showing how you could set the information on the pages.
2   What problems did you have making it all fit onto two sides of A4? How did you overcome these problems?
3   There was a choice of files to use – three for each document to be included. Which ones did you use and why did you choose them? Did you try different ones to see which might be the best to use? What decision did you come to as to which was the best to use? Give reasons for your choices.

Task 2 Creating a poster

Design and create a poster (or more if time permits) to advertise one of the following:
  a disco
  a sporting event
  a drama production for your school
  an event for your favourite club

Whichever poster(s) you create, you will need to prepare the text and the pictures that are to be included.

1   Briefly describe the programs you used to prepare the elements of your poster. Describe how you saved these files in the most appropriate way to make importing them into your final document as simple as possible.

2 Did you come across any problems with assembling the final poster? If so, what were these problems? How might you prevent these sorts of problems next time you need to do this type of work?

Task 3 Ticket and programme for a show

Design and create tickets and a programme for a school show.

If you have no ideas or do not have much time available, you may like to use the basic information contained in the files on the OUP website which you may want to include:

Text8.txt (Text8.rtf, Text8.doc) contains the name of the play, the dates and times of the performances and the cost of the tickets. You will need to add a venue to this information.

Picture7.bmp (Picture7.jpg, Picture7.eps),
Picture8.bmp (Picture8.jpg, Picture8.eps) and
Picture9.bmp (Picture9.jpg, Picture9.eps) are pictures that you may like to include of different aspects of the play.

Task 4 Creating an invitation

Design and create an invitation for a child's birthday party. Make sure you include a return slip for people to say whether they will be able to come to the party. This slip will need to be removed or cut from the invitation.

1 What would be the best size of paper to use?
2 Will it be folded in any way?
3 Why is clip art more appropriate in this activity than in many of the others here?
4 Can you always find suitable clip art for such a task? If not, can you think why this might be the case.

Task 5 Promotiing a new CD

Design and create the promotion material for a new CD featuring your favourite performer. There are several parts to this work. You may wish to try just some of them if completing the work is going to take too long. Do not forget that there will be some common elements that you could use on all the documents – for example, the record company logo.

A poster advertising the CD in record shops

Decide what size will be best to attract most attention and what information the poster needs to contain. Design the layout and create it.

The booklet to go with the CD in the case

This is usually a simple, folded and stapled book whose page size is 120 mm by 120 mm so that it will fit into the case. The number of pages will be 4, 8, 12, ...

If you want to be more adventurous, you might try to make a folded booklet that opens out to a larger format.

The information on the back of the CD case

The slip in the back of the case is a single piece of thin card folded into three sections. These are to line the fore-edge, the spine and the back of the case. More modern CDs have cases made completely of transparent plastic. For such a case, the fore-edge and spine of the slip have information and/or pictures on them. The back is 137 mm by 118 mm and the two folded strips for the fore-edge and the spine are both 7 mm by 118 mm.

The back will also include a barcode. A file containing this can be found on the OUP website (**Picture10.eps**).

The design on the CD itself

This is probably the most difficult part to do well because the disk is round and has a hole at its centre. The design has to include some essential information about the CD, one piece of which is the Compact Disc Digital Audio logo (Fig 7.7). A file containing this logo (**Picture11.eps**) can be found on the OUP website.

A CD has a diameter of 120 mm with a hole at its centre of 15 mm diameter. If you look at CDs, you will see that they do not always use all this space. Some have a blank central area, 35 mm in diameter.

Fig 7.7 Compact Disc Digital Audio logo.

It is possible to have as many different types of information in one document as you need. If you look at CD-ROMs or World Wide Web sites, you will find that many have words, pictures, sounds and animations or video clips all on the same page. To join all of these in this way requires a different type of program. DTP programs would not be of much use here, because they are designed to produce something on paper as the final result. It is not easy to look at and listen to animations and sounds on a page!

Programs that let you join all the media types into one file are generally referred to as **presentation programs**. The form of the final presentation will decide which sort of program you need to make the presentation.

Multimedia presentations

Programs used to create multimedia presentations will let you build in interactions with the presentation. On any 'page' or screen of information, there will be more than one way of moving on. They are not the sort of presentation where there is only one way to view the information held in the system. The user of the system takes the final decision about which information will be viewed and in which order this will happen. The designer of the system has quite a difficult task deciding how best to structure the information and its presentation so that users will be able to find what they are looking for (Fig 8.1).

An interactive CD-ROM is an example of a multimedia presentation. You will be aware of the wide variety of these now available. They are frequently used to present structured factual information. For example, some encyclopedias are on CD-ROMs. These programs are also widely used in other educational contexts, such as interactive stories and games for young children. You may also have come across interactive guides at tourist attractions, which have been created in this way.

Fig 8.1 A selection of screenshots from some multimedia products. Can you see how the designers have made it obvious where you can click to make something happen?

Preparing a multimedia presentation

As with desktop publishing, the design of a presentation is most important and so is the preparation of the elements that will make it up.

If you have never tried to build a multimedia presentation, do keep your first one simple. It takes a long time to successfully put together all the elements that make up the presentation. Remember, too, that just because you have the facility to bring them together on one 'page', this may not be the most helpful way of presenting the information for the reader.

In creating a multimedia presentation, the designer really needs to know who the readers will be, and to think carefully about the appearance and content of the presentation. The layout of the elements on each page is important. You will probably have words and pictures on most, if not all, pages but you may also have sounds and/or some form of animation. Will the reader have to do something to make the sound or animation play? If so, in what way will you make it obvious to the reader how to select this option? You may use buttons on the screen that the reader can click on. The layout of your page will need to have enough space on it for these buttons. You may also use buttons to move to the next part of the presentation, but how many ways forward (or backward) will be needed?

Fig 8.2 Creating your own video clips to include in a presentation will not be possible without a video-capture card in your computer. This is an add-on card and is therefore not a standard feature in most computers. You will also need video-editing software. Video files are huge, being many Mb in size.

Preparing the files

Just as with desktop–publishing programs, multimedia programs are best used as a way of assembling the various media parts. They are not particularly good for preparing these parts.

You will need to make sure that the way in which you save your files is the right one for bringing them together. Therefore, it is essential that you find out which file formats for words, pictures, sounds, animations and video clips the program will be able to understand.

Common file formats for the different media types		
Media type	**Windows-based PC**	**Apple Macintosh**
Words	.TXT, .RTF, Microsoft Word...	Text, RTF, Microsoft Word...
Pictures	.PCX, .BMP, .GIF, .JPG, .CDR, .WMF, .EPS, .TIF	Painting (PTNG), PICT, GIF, JPEG, EPSF, TIFF
Sounds	.WAV, QuickTime, RealPlayer	AIFF, QuickTime
Animations	Animated GIF, QuickTime	Animated GIF, QuickTime
Video clips	AVI, QuickTime	QuickTime

QUESTIONS

1 List the main features of presentation programs, and outline how you might use them.
2 Give some examples of the uses of interactive CD-ROMs.
3 You are designing a multimedia presentation on a subject of your choice. Describe how you would approach this task.

Working out the structure of the presentation is most important. The first thing that you need to decide is how many parts to the system there will be, and how these will relate and link to each other. Making a 'map' is a good way to help you to visualise this.

Once you have done this, you need to collect and prepare the elements that will go into the presentation. There are several things you will need to think about. These mainly concern how your choices will be limited by the computer and the programs you are using.

First, you will be constrained by the computer display screens. You will not have the great variety of page sizes to make your work look interesting, as DTP designers have. Most current computer screens are set at a resolution of 800 by 600 pixels. Visual display units, however, may work at 640 by 480 pixels for older computers and up to 1024 by 768 pixels for the most modern ones. So, you will be designing your presentation for one of these three sizes. Also, you cannot choose whether to have the page landscape or portrait, which will restrict your design quite severely.

Second, you will be constrained by the colour resolution of the display screen. This is something that you need to think about when preparing picture files. There is no point in preparing files in millions of colours if the display is going to be in only 256 colours. You will be creating files which waste disk space by being too big for the job that they have to do. You will

Fig 8.3 A possible structure for a multimedia presentation.

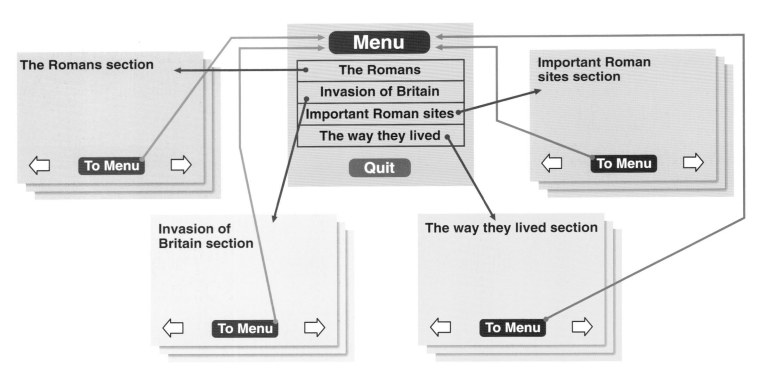

also want to think about the number of dots per inch for bitmap pictures. The screen is not a very high resolution device, so again you can make files too large by giving them too high a resolution (too many dpi).

Structure of the presentation

Once you have the basic structure, you can start to design the layout of the individual sections and then the individual screens. You may decide that to make it easy for the users to investigate your system, you will have a common set of controls which will always appear in the same place on your screens of information. You may want to have a different background for each section. Where will you put the pictures? Will you make them all the same size so that they fit the display easily?

A diagram of the overall structure is usually very helpful in making it clear what you are trying to achieve. Once you have this, then more detailed sketches for each section – down to the way the individual screens will be laid out – are also helpful. In the initial stages, you might want to explore different ways and try them out before you make your final decision. If you can, ask your users to help you finalise your designs.

Stages of design

How would you use such a program to build a presentation about the Romans as part of some history work?

Overall structure

You may have collected general information on the Romans, their invasion of Britain, the way they lived – buildings and clothes, and important sites and finds in Britain. One way of building this could be from a menu front page, with each section being like a part of a book but with ways of getting to any other section when you want to.

Once you have made these decisions, you will need to think about how each section will look and work. The structure diagram (Fig 8.3) shows a simple structure for navigating through the information. In this, each section is like a part of a book with 'page turning' controls which give the users a way to get back to the menu to choose another section or quit the presentation.

Finally, you will need to know how to make the actions work so that you can build your presentation.

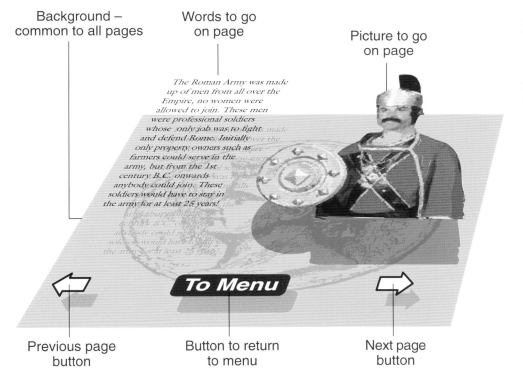

Background – common to all pages

Words to go on page

Picture to go on page

The Roman Army was made up of men from all over the Empire, no women were allowed to join. These men were professional soldiers whose only job was to fight and defend Rome. Initially only property owners such as farmers could serve in the army, but from the 1st century B.C. onwards anybody could join. These soldiers would have to stay in the army for at least 25 years!

To Menu

Previous page button

Button to return to menu

Next page button

Buttons play a sound to tell users they have clicked

Fig 8.4 The design for a page, showing the elements that need to be prepared for importing.

QUESTIONS

1 Give a reason why you cannot choose any page size for your presentation.
2 Why is it important to be careful in your choice of colour resolution?
3 Describe how the constraints on page size, on the shape of a page (portrait or landscape) and on colour resolution might affect your design ideas for a presentation.

The World Wide Web is one of the fastest growing areas of information presentation. New websites are constantly appearing and existing ones are being modified and updated. So how do you create and display a website? How you can find information on the World Wide Web is dealt with on pages 123–5.

To create a website, you will need a program which allows you to present the information in the desired way, and then to save it in a suitable file format for web systems to be able to interpret the information. There is a wide range of programs which will let you save in **HTML (HyperText Markup Language)** format (Fig 8.5). HTML is a universal language that all web-browsing programs understand. This means that people using a wide variety of computer hardware can all browse your information on the World Wide Web, regardless of the computer you are using to create it.

The most common browsers are Netscape and Microsoft Internet Explorer. But these programs only let you view (browse) HTML files, not create them. Website creation is one of the few computer areas where the users of the information do not need the same program on their computers as the creator used. To create a website, you could use a program such as Microsoft Word (a word processor) to construct your pages, and this same program will let you save the pages as an HTML file. Some DTP programs also have this option. There are specialist web-creation programs such as Microsoft Front Page and Claris HomePage. You can also write web pages using HTML editor programs.

With editor programs, you need some experience of computer programming, as your web pages are described in a programming language. All these methods produce pages of HTML code. The specialist programs do this hard work for you and so save time.

Fig 8.5
This web page has hypertext links (the coloured text) and picture elements. The pictures can be clicked on. The shape of the cursor gives a clue as to what can be clicked on. The HTML code is shown in the window inset on the right.

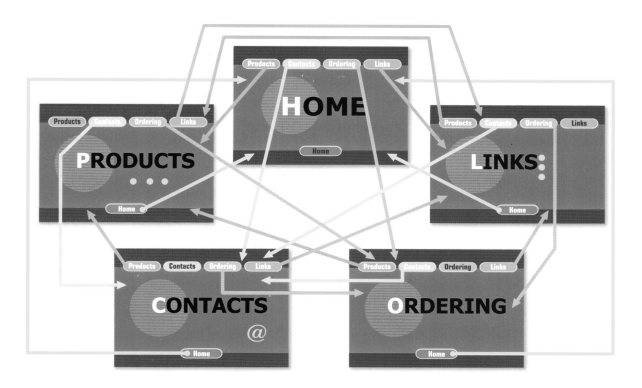

Fig 8.6 The structure of a website needs to be designed just like a multimedia presentation does. The design helps you to structure the way through the information, and to decide which elements go where.

Designing for the World Wide Web

The designer of a website (and the pages in the website) must think about the intended users. The material that will make up the pages of the site must be appropriate to those users. This is no different from DTP work or multimedia presentations. The structure of the site is important so that the users can easily find their way around the information (Fig 8.6).

The layout and linking of pages will need to be thought out right at the start. The same sort of graphical planning techniques you use for multimedia presentations are useful here. The actions on any page are made using hypertext links. These tell the browser software where on the World Wide Web the users are to go next. They will be defined usually by a website address **(URL)**.

Pages will not be restricted in size like multimedia pages. When a page needs to be larger than the screen it will be displayed on, the page will get longer and scroll bars will appear for the viewer to use. However, you do still need to make it easy for users to find their way around, so do think carefully about the size of each page.

As with DTP and multimedia, the files containing the information that you wish to present will need to be prepared in advance. You will use your web creation program to assemble the pages and the site. One important thing to think about is that all aspects of your web page will be transferred from the host computer to the viewer's computer. This will usually happen through a telephone connection to the viewer's computer. This is the slowest part of the interconnected system of linked computers that is called the Internet. To make the process of viewing the information as fast as possible, the files you use on your pages need to be as small as possible.

If you have used the Internet, you will already have seen that pages do not just appear but build up an element at a time. The words come first, pictures next and then the animated and sound components will appear. The larger each of these files is, the longer you will have to wait for them to appear on your computer.

QUESTIONS

1   For what purpose would you use HTML? Give your reasons.
2   What general advice would you give to someone who wants to design a presentation for the World Wide Web?

Preparing files for your website

Files need to be as small as possible. With text this is not a major problem – text files are usually quite small. Pictures need to be saved in a compressed file format. The most common of these on the World Wide Web are GIF and JPEG. Sounds can be saved in WAV, Real Player or QuickTime formats, and animations as animated GIFs. QuickTime and Real Player formats are also used for video files.

As the Internet develops, new technologies are appearing which allow the users to interact with the content. So you may come across Flash and Shockwave as technologies that you will need to install to take advantage of the latest developments. It is unlikely that you will need to understand these to create simple websites.

Making your website

Whatever program you use to make a website, you will end up with a collection of HTML files – one for each page of your website. You will also have a set of files that are the media elements which exist on your pages. If you use a background picture, you will have a file. Any pictures or graphics that appear on the pages will be separate files along with any sound and animation files. As you construct your website, it is important that you organise these elements into one place on your hard disk or network.

You will create your web pages in much the same way as you do DTP pages but there will be some different constraints. You may find that using unusual fonts will cause your users problems. If they do not have that font installed on their computers, they may not see the effect you are trying to create. So using standard fonts makes a lot of sense. You will also find that the range of type sizes you can use is more limited and that the sizes may not be measured in the usual way.

Effects that you would like to apply to the text need to be thought about carefully. Hypertext text links on a web page are usually coloured and underlined. You should therefore think twice before you underline text on your pages if you do not want to confuse your users. You might also need to think about which colours to use for text.

Some of the more straightforward web-creation programs might not let you rotate graphic elements on your page. If you want to have some interesting arrangements of pictures and graphics, you may have to create them in the rotated position with the graphics program you use to prepare these elements.

Try it out

Before going live, you should try out your website. Some creation programs will let you transfer to your browser program and try it out. If your program will not allow this, load your browser program and open your first HTML page with the 'Open' command.

Make sure that all the elements of your pages appear where you expect them to be, and that no elements are missing. Try out all the hypertext links to make sure that they go to where you want, and that any animations, videos or sounds play as you expect.

When you are happy with this, you are ready to transfer your website to the host computer.

Going live

The computer you created the website on is very unlikely to be the computer that serves your users. The host computer will most likely belong to your ISP (Internet service provider). This is the organisation which gives you a unique web address for your website and which will reserve you some disk space to store your site on. Host computers are on at all times and are permanently connected to the Internet.

You will need to transfer your web pages and all the files that are displayed on your pages to the host computer system, probably using an **FTP (file transfer protocol)** program. This is why you need to organise the files on your hard disk into one place. Your ISP will be able to tell you exactly how to transfer your website (and files) to make it live, so that other people can view it on the World Wide Web.

QUESTIONS

1 Give three examples of the constraints that you will meet when you try to create eye-catching webpages.
2 Describe what you would do before going live with your website.
3 What are the main services provided by ISPs?

Fig. 8.7
The process of creating a website and sending it to the host computer so that other web users can view it.

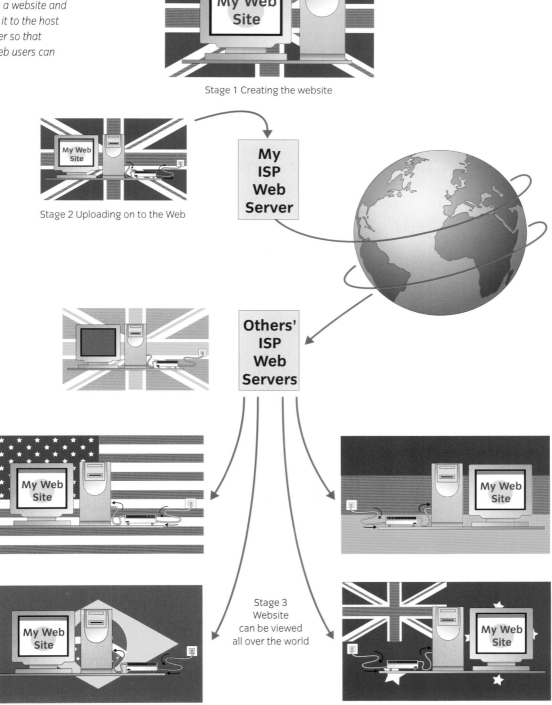

Stage 1 Creating the website

Stage 2 Uploading on to the Web

My ISP Web Server

Others' ISP Web Servers

Stage 3 Website can be viewed all over the world

In most business presentation programs, such as Microsoft PowerPoint the information needs to be presented in a specific order. These programs will normally be used to present highly organised information in a linear way.

This sort of software has replaced the showing of slides on a projector. Just like the other presentation systems described so far, these will let you display different types of information created with other programs. Again, the designer and creator should think about what needs to be presented. They will need to prepare the information in appropriate ways for bringing together in the presentation program.

Screen display size becomes an issue again. You will need to see all the information in a single screen so you will need to design the layout to fit your screen size. This means working at 640 by 480 pixels, 800 by 600 pixels or 1024 by 768 pixels. The most common size currently is 800 by 600 pixels.

These presentations are most frequently used in business presentations where a senior manager is reporting to the board on how well the company is doing, or a sales manager is giving a presentation to potential customers.

How might you use them?

At school, teachers find it very useful to keep a series of slides or notes on particular topics for a lesson. If you have a computer projection system, you may already have experienced this. Also, students often have to do a presentation for part of their coursework in English. They might therefore wish to organise a series of slides to illustrate what they are talking about. Such a system would allow them to present their information in a more professional manner. This could give the presentation more impact.

Designing the presentation

When designing a presentation you may wish to develop a 'house style'. This means that all the pages

Fig 8.8
A sales executive making a presentation to a group of customers.

could take a similar design format. The basic layout would be designed according to the types of information to be shown. In the case of a business presentation, you will usually find that all pages have the same background over which the information is displayed. This background will often contain the company name or logo.

The background will need to be created in a graphics program in such a way that the information to be displayed over it can be clearly seen. The size of the logo or company name cannot be too large, because it must leave enough space for the information. Also very strong colours should not be used, because they will distract the readers. If you want the background to be the same for every page of the presentation, you can set up a master page.

Many of these presentation programs (Fig 8.9) will use visual effects and animations as the presentation moves from one screen to the next. These effects will look similar to the way television news programmes present this sort of information. At the design stage, you can make decisions about how the information elements can appear and how you will move on to the next part of the presentation.

Building the presentation

These programs are again simply an assembly system. First, you can bring in the background image. You can bring all the parts onto page 1 in the program and decide their position. You will not usually import the text on such a presentation but type it directly on to the page. This is because the amount of text which will be displayed is usually not very large – important points will be displayed, not long descriptions.

Of course, most presentations will be more than one page long. You will build each page in the display order and put all the information onto it as you go.

Finally, you will select how items will appear on the page – the visual effects – and how you want to move on to the next page.

Now you are ready to try it out. Remember: when you use such a system it is not a replacement for the presenter. You will still need to do the talking. It is there simply to provide the prompts and display the visual information.

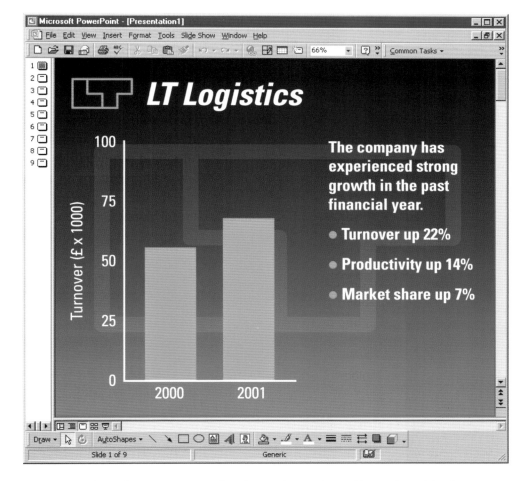

Fig 8.9 A typical page from a presentation that shows a clear, uncluttered layout. A graph has been imported to make the sales figures clear.

QUESTIONS

1 You are going to give a talk on a subject of your choice, which you will illustrate with a series of slides. Explain briefly how you would use a presentation program to organise your slides.

2 Describe briefly how you would design and build a presentation.

Your school may already have some suitable programs to help you with this work, or your teacher or parent may download and install some of the programs following links provided for them in their area of the OUP website: **www.oup.com/uk/ictforgcse**.

Task 1 Evaluating your own work

Evaluating your own work is something you may not find easy to do. So the first thing we want you to do here is to evaluate someone else's work. You are going to look at a piece of multimedia work done by a group of children as part of a presentation for History. It was aimed at 10–12 year olds. All the files that you will need to download can be found on the OUP website (**www.oup.com/uk/ictforgcse**). These are the presentation file (**Present.stk**), an animation file (**Anim.mov**), and a video file (**Video.mov**). Any sounds used with this presentation are stored inside the presentation file. You will need a player application such as MS Player.

You will also need QuickTime Player installed on your computer to view the video and animation files in this

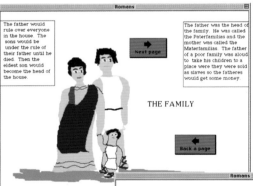

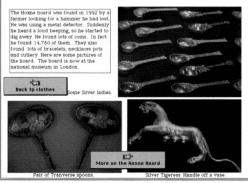

Fig 8.10
Two pages from the presentation on the Romans which can be downloaded from the OUP website.

presentation. (Of course, QuickTime should be installed *before* you start the presentation!)

Run the whole presentation and then think about the following aspects and make comments.

1 Is there a clear visual design to the presentation that guides the user through the information? How could this aspect of the presentation have been improved?

2 Is the presentation clearly structured? Does the information appear in a logical order? Are there any ways in which the structure of the presentation could be improved for the audience it was aimed at?

3 Could you design an alternative structure for this presentation? Make a sketch plan of how you would go about it. Include any written descriptions you feel are needed to make your intentions clear.

4 How would you change the visual look of the screens in the presentation?

5 The video sequence is shown as a very small window on the presentation page. Can you find out why this might be the case? If you have QuickTime Player available on your computer, you can play the video on its own. Try to make the video window larger and see what happens to the quality of playback. This may help you to answer the question.

Your evaluation of this presentation has so far only dealt with how the presentation was structured and designed. Another important aspect for any presentation that should also be evaluated is the content – the information being presented.

◆ Is the information presented clear and understandable for the people it is aimed at?

◆ Is the information accurate and factually correct?

6 Evaluate the content of this presentation from these points of view. Explain what you did to perform this evaluation. Did you find it easy to do all parts of this evaluation?

Why is it important that you consider the quality of the information?

Task 2 Putting together a multimedia presentation

You will need some multimedia authoring software to do this task..

Design and build a multimedia presentation which could be used in a primary school to help with teaching children to read.

1   First, decide on your content. (Don't try to make your presentation too complicated or too large. It will take you too long to do, and some of the tools we have made available to you will not let you build a large presentation.) What will you be trying to achieve and what elements will your presentation contain?
2   Draw a plan of the structure.
3   Design the layout of your first screen. Will all the screens be to the same layout? If the other screens are to be different, then also design these.
4   Do you intend to use any sounds on your pages? If you do, what is the purpose of the sounds? Where will you get the sounds from? Can you create your own easily?
5   Using animations should be considered if your presentation is to be for young children. What will be the factors that help you to decide whether or not to include animations?

Task 3 Creating a website

Create a website for an organisation that you know something about. Again, don't make it too large and ambitious. A simple structure will be sufficient to build your skills at preparing the information for display and building the site. You might like to use some software to create some simple animated GIFs to attract attention to important elements on your site.

1   Decide on the content for your website.
2   Draw a plan of its structure.
3   Design the layout of your index/menu page and any pages that will be linked to it. How will you move from one page to another? How will you get back to the index page? Will there be any links to other websites?

4   Explain how you will achieve all the linking across your website and how your design will not leave the user stranded, not knowing where to go next.
5   Prepare all the elements for your site and save them in suitable formats, and then build your site. Make notes about how this process went. Was it all plain sailing? Did it all go as you designed it, or did you have to make any changes along the way to overcome problems?
6   Once you have built the site, try it out to make sure that it works. You can do this by saving all the HTML pages, running the browser program on your computer and then opening your first page in the browser. If everything is working as intended, then all aspects of your site should do as you expect. Try out everything. Does it all work? If not, what are the problems and how might you put them right?

Task 4 Building a business presentation

As part of your GCSE English course, you will probably have to make a presentation on a topic of your choice to a small group of people. You will probably be encouraged to use visual aids to help you to make the presentation.

A presentation program such as PowerPoint could be used to help you with your presentation. So, choose a topic that really interests you and prepare a simple presentation using the program.

1   Design the presentation. How many 'slides' will you use? How will each 'slide' be laid out?
2   What pictures do you want to include on the 'slides'? Prepare these as files ready to include in the presentation. (Remember: save them in suitable file formats.)
3   Construct your presentation and try it out.
4   How easy is it to talk and use the presentation at the same time?
5   What do you feel are the advantages to presenters of using such programs?

Over the last few years, there has been a dramatic increase in the amount of communication that takes place using computer technology.

Communicating with fax

The first major advance was fax (facsimile transmission). This is a system that uses telephone lines and modems to transfer a facsimile (likeness) of a paper document to another person or organisation. The original document is scanned by the sending fax machine to create a digital image of the original. This digital information is then sent along telephone lines to the receiving fax machine, which converts the digital information back to an image and prints it on paper (Fig 9.1).

This first step in the communications revolution meant that documents could be transferred anywhere in the world almost instantly for the cost of a telephone call.

Fig 9.1 How information is transmitted between two fax machines.

Sending a fax is very similar to making a telephone call. The fax machine you are sending to must be free to receive the call. One disadvantage of faxing is that you can send your document to only one place at a time. So when you need to send a document to a number of people you have to make that number of telephone calls. Another disadvantage of faxing is the loss of quality in transmission. Usually, this is barely noticeable in the copy which is received – especially where the original document is good. Sometimes, though, the copy received is not very clear. Often this means that the quality of the original is poor. But sometimes even high-quality documents suffer serious loss of quality during faxing.

Many modern computer/modem combinations will allow you to send documents directly as a fax.

Communicating with e-mail

Although e-mail was in use over 20 years ago, it did not become as widely used as fax until the explosion of activities on the Internet and World Wide Web. E-mail has the advantage over ordinary postal services and faxing. Like faxing, it is very fast – an e-mail can arrive at its destination within a few minutes of being sent. But no one has to be available to receive an e-mail. An e-mail is received and stored by the service provider of the person it is addressed to until he/she is ready to read it on his/her computer (Fig 9.2).

You compose a message with your e-mail program, and give this message an e-mail address to send it to. You can attach documents to your e-mail if you wish. A file created by any program can be attached to an e-mail – for example, a word-processed file, a picture from a graphics program or from a digital camera, a spreadsheet file, etc.

Remember that the person receiving an attachment needs to have a program on his or her computer which will open the attached file. Remember also that it takes a long time to send a large file. Using file compression helps to keep telephone call charges down.

You can send a single e-mail to more than one person. This is because the place where you put the address on an e-mail can accept more than one address. Alternatively, you could use the address book feature of your e-mail program. Instead of putting each address on the e-mail, you can form a group of addresses and send the e-mail to the group. It costs you no more to send an e-mail to a group. You make one phone call to send it. Your service provider then copies your e-mail the right number of times and sends it to all the people you have addressed it to (Fig 9.3).

In school, you might use these techniques to pass work between yourself and your teachers. Once a piece of computer-based work is finished, you might e-mail it as an attachment to a teacher for marking. The teacher might then e-mail your work back to you with comments as to how well you have done.

Communicating with mobile phones

Modern mobile phones allow you to send messages as well as have ordinary conversations. The latest generation of mobile phones – WAP phones – have Internet capability. Using these, you can send and receive e-mails.

A mobile phone can be connected to a laptop computer so that you can send and receive e-mails from anywhere. Journalists use these connections to get news stories and pictures to their editors as quickly as possible.

All this work is both faster and easier as a result of computer technology.

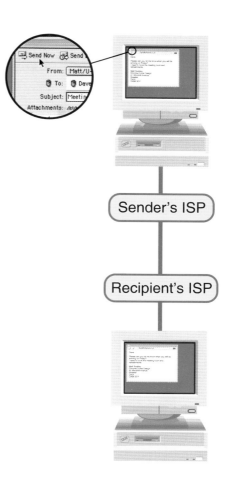

Fig 9.2
When you send an e-mail to someone, it first goes to your Internet service provider (ISP), from where it is then sent on to that person's ISP. It stays there until the person logs on to the ISP. It then goes to the computer to be read.

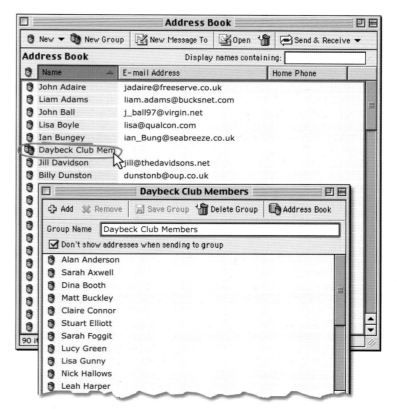

Fig 9.3 An e-mail address book with groups of addresses. Group addressing is one way of sending the same e-mail to several people at once.

QUESTIONS

1 What are the drawbacks of faxing?
2 You are the financial director of a building society. You need urgently to send a long letter with attachments to all your branches around Britain, all of which have fax and e-mail facilities. Explain what you will do.
3 You are about to buy a new mobile phone. Say which type you will choose, giving the reasons for your choice.

Video conferencing

In video conferencing, ISDN telephone lines are used to transmit live pictures and sound between two or more computers (Fig 9.4). As its name suggests, video conferencing is used mostly by businesses and in education to let people be in a 'conference' and discuss things of mutual interest. A school, for example, might link up with another school to do some work together – perhaps discussing things on a particular project. You can see what the other people at the 'conference' look like, as well as hear what they have to say, and you can show them pictures. The pictures are not of very high quality but when broadband communications are widely available, they will be much better.

Video conferencing allows people in various places around the world to talk about and discuss their work – to have a conference. When people need to work together on something, instead of travelling to a meeting to share ideas, they just organise a video conference.

Communications technology has brought to the workplace a variety of new ways of working.

Fig 9.4 Video conferencing helps people in different locations to work together.

Other examples of collaboration

Collaborative working does not have to involve people from around the world working together. It can be on a much smaller scale.

Networked systems in businesses and schools make collaboration possible. For example, a computer company help-line involves many operators answering telephone calls for help with computer and program problems. It is not possible for one operator to know all the answers to all the possible problems that users might experience. The company will have a database which contains answers to problems. When a help-line operator doesn't know the answer to a problem, the operator will ask the database whether it has an answer. When the answer is there, the operator can help the caller. When nothing is found on the database, the operator can request an answer from the company's technical department through the network system, and then telephone the caller when an answer has been found. This answer then becomes part of the database.

This is an example of a group of people using their skills in a collaborative way to increase the range of

information held in a database which helps the customers to solve their problems.

Producing a daily newspaper is a collaborative effort. Journalists find the stories and write them up using a word processor. Photographers take the pictures and get them into a computer format with a graphics program. The word-processed stories and the formatted pictures are transferred to the head office using e-mail systems (Fig. 9.5). Once they have been transferred to the network at the head office, the editors will decide which stories will be printed and which photographs will be used. These will be passed to the senior editors, who will decide which stories will go on which pages. Then the layout designers will create the newspaper. Once this process is complete, the newspaper will be transferred to the printing presses.

A newspaper could not be created by one person. The collaboration, over the internal and external network systems, of people with a variety of skills is essential to produce a newspaper.

You might need to work together across the computer network in your school. A group activity might involve you and your friends collecting information by doing a survey in different localities. If all of you each created your own database, the information that you had collected would be difficult to share. Also, it would be difficult to summarise what had been found out by the survey. To get the most out of the information which you have collected as a group, the information needs to be put into one large database so that you all can share it across the school network. You are collaborating with your friends by inputting the data you have collected. Then you all can look at the whole set of data to get the fullest picture about the outcome of your survey.

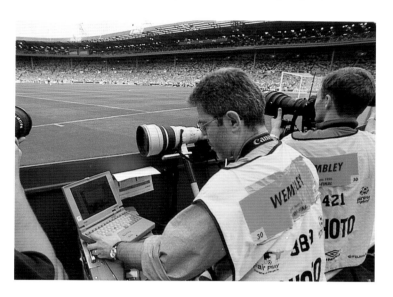

Fig 9.5 Newspaper journalists and photographers use modern communications technology to get their stories and pictures to readers as quickly as possible.

QUESTIONS

1 a) Explain what is meant by the term video conferencing.
   b) Give one example of how video conferencing can be used in business.
2 Give a brief description of one way in which ICT enables people to work collaboratively.

Communicating

To do the following tasks, you will need a computer which has access to e-mail services. Preparing materials for sending will not necessarily need access to these computers.

Task 1 Using the address book facility

The address book is a way of storing and quickly retrieving email addresses. Entering the correct e-mail address is important because an e-mail will not be delivered if the address has an error in it.

1 Using the e-mail program(s) available to you, build an address book which has all your friends' addresses in it.
2 Compose an e-mail message to a friend and put the address onto the e-mail using your address book. Encourage your friend to send you a reply.
3 Most e-mail programs will let you choose to reply to any message you receive. Try to use this facility rather than starting a new message when you reply to their replies.

Task 2 Building groups in your address book

Groups are a way of saving time when it comes to addressing e-mails to more than one person.

1 Using the people already in your address book, make some groups of people to send e-mails to. Think carefully who will be in which group.
2 Can a person be in more than one group?
3 Send some e-mails to your groups.

Task 3 Sending attachments

When you have files created in other programs, you may sometimes want to send these with an e-mail. You do this by sending them as attachments. To make a file easy to deal with, it needs to have the smallest file-size possible. Large files take a long time to send. There are two ways to make sure that the file is as small as possible. The first is to save it in particular ways. A graphics file saved as a bitmap is often large, but if you can save it as a GIF or JPEG file, it usually will be smaller. If you can't make the file small when you save it, then you might want to use programs which compress it after you have saved it. Programs like WinZip and Stuffit are compression programs.

1 Prepare some picture and/or word-processed files to send to a friend. Make some notes on how you did it so that if there is a problem you can help your friend to look at the attachments.
2 Send some e-mails with attachments to your friends and get them to send some to you.
3 How do you look at attachments? Write down the steps you go through to look at the e-mail and the attachments.
4 Did you get to look at all the attachments or were there some problems?
5 If you had problems, can you work out the reason(s) for the problems?

Collaborating

Task 4 Sharing GCSE information

This activity is concerned with students like yourself working together to share information that is of use to you during your GCSE years in school. If you visit the OUP website **www.oup.com/uk/ictforgcse**, you will see a link to a page which holds useful information about other websites which might be helpful to any student studying any GCSE subject. Each website in this list has been recommended by a student like yourself. We would like you to collaborate with other students by finding a useful website for any subject that you are studying for your GCSEs and e-mailing it to the website.

1   Use your skills at finding information on the Internet to search for information to help you with a topic you are studying in any of your GCSE courses. When you find something that you would like to share with other students, make a note of the URL.

2   E-mail the URL using the form provided on the OUP website.

You might want to visit this website when you are looking for information to help you with other GCSE subjects.

Task 5 Group work across a network

You are going to conduct a survey, collect information, input it into a database and then present your findings as a group. The survey is about what you and your friends in school are interested in, spend your money on and enjoy doing in your spare time.

Note You will need a database that works across the school network to do this activity. You need to be able to have more than one person at a time inputting data into the database file. Before you start this activity, you you will need to have the skills of creating and using databases covered in Unit 11.

In the first part of the activity, you have to work together to design and construct the survey.

1   Decide what questions you are going to ask your friends and design a questionnaire to collect that information.

2   Design a database structure that will hold the answers you collect on the questionnaire. Then build the database.

3   Hand out the paper questionnaires to a large number of people and get them to fill them in.

4   Decide what you want to know from the information you will collect and process. Each person or small group needs to take responsibility for finding out at least one thing from the database when it is complete.

Now you can work on your own but you will still be collaborating.

5   Share the returned questionnaires among the group. You can then share the data entry into the database file. Input your set of data.

6   When everyone has put their data into the database, you are ready to ask your questions. Ask your questions and present your findings in an appropriate way.

7   Can you answer the questions you set out to answer with this database? If not, can you work out why it is impossible to answer these questions?

8   Share your findings with the rest of your group by using a presentation of some sort.

A **spreadsheet** is an application program that allows text, numbers and formulas to be entered into a grid of rectangular cells. Spreadsheets are a particularly good choice of software when a task involves working with numerical data and displaying results in graphs. Spreadsheets are therefore widely used in finance-related tasks such as budgeting and forecasting (modelling).

Each year the governors of every school have to set a school budget. The budget will show how much money the school will receive and what the money will be spent on. A spreadsheet will often be used to do this. Apart from doing basic arithmetic – adding, multiplying, dividing and subtracting – the spreadsheet will easily allow governors to ask 'what if' questions. A typical question might be: 'What will be the cost to the school if we employ another teacher?' Spreadsheets can quickly, and easily, provide the answer.

An accountant works with figures. The first spreadsheet (VisiCalc) was designed to look, on screen, like an accountant's worksheet. This resulted not only in spreadsheets often being called worksheets, but also in the screen being divided into a grid of cells organised in rows and columns. What made a spreadsheet so special, however, was that hidden formulas could be put into cells to automatically calculate results.

How a spreadsheet works

A spreadsheet is a grid of cells organised in **rows** and **columns**. Each column is given a letter, and each row a number. This means that each cell has a unique reference identified by the column letter and row number. For example, B4 specifies the cell in column B and row 4. Look at the example in Fig 10.1. You will see how the spreadsheet is organised into rows and columns of cells. By clicking with the mouse, you can select individual cells or a range of cells. In this case, the single cell B4 has been selected.

The way spreadsheets are organised into rows and columns of cells is very similar to the way the game Battleships works when you are trying to identify the positions of your opponent's ships.

An extremely powerful feature of spreadsheets is the ability to enter formulas into cells. A **formula** is an equation that tells the spreadsheet what actions (calculations) you wish to take on any spreadsheet data. Normally, the data will be numeric, but formulas can also join text together. To enter a formula into a cell, you always have to type the equals sign. Formulas often calculate how one cell relates to another. For example, to add together the values in cells A1 and A2, and show the result in cell B1, you would type in cell B1 the following formula (Fig 10.2):

=A1+A2

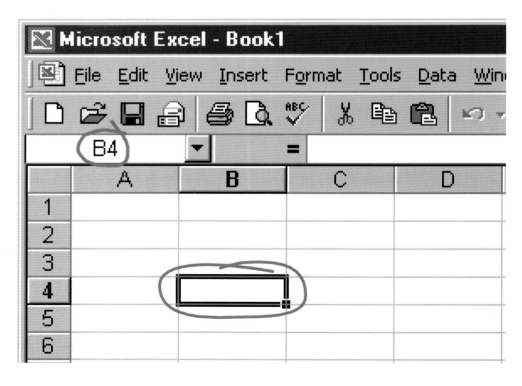

Fig 10.1 A spreadsheet is a grid of cells organised in rows and columns. Each cell has a unique identifier. In this case, cell B4 has been selected.

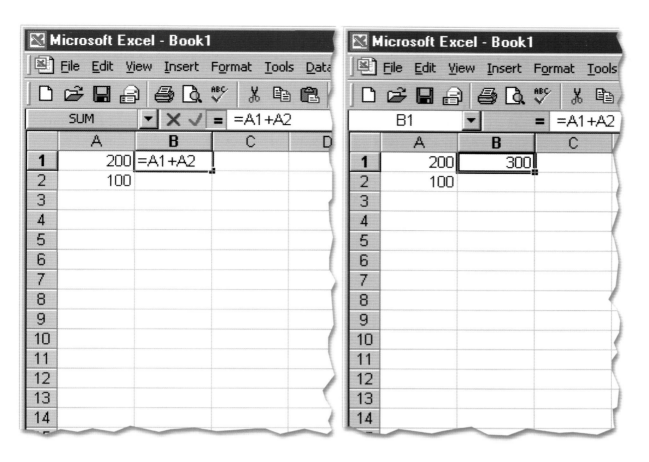

Fig 10.2
A formula is an equation that tells the spreadsheet what actions (calculations) you wish to take on any spreadsheet data. In this example, by entering the formula =A1+A2 into cell B1 the result (300) will automatically be calculated.

The beauty of a spreadsheet is that a formula needs to be entered only once into a cell. In the example just given, the formula was entered into the cell B1. The values in cells A1 and A2 can easily be changed without affecting the formula. In fact, the formula will automatically recalculate the result. For example, if the value in cell A1 is changed to 100 and the value in cell A2 to 800, the new result – 900 – will automatically appear in cell B1. By simply changing the values in cells, and having the program automatically recalculate the result, spreadsheets allow you to perform 'What if . . . ?' calculations.

When entering a formula, you tell the spreadsheet what calculation to perform (for example, adding, multiplying, dividing and subtracting) by using operators such as plus (+), minus (–), etc.

Spreadsheet programs are widely used in businesses and at home. The most popular spreadsheet programs are Microsoft Excel, Lotus 1-2-3, Corel Quattro Pro and the spreadsheet modules of AppleWorks and Microsoft Works.

Common arithmetic operators used in formulas

Operator	Meaning	Example
+	Adding	=A1+A2
−	Subtracting	=A1−A2
*	Multiplying	=A1*A2
/	Dividing	=A1/A2
%	Percentage	There are different ways to do this. One way is as follows: to add 8% to the value of cell A1, you would enter =A1*(1+8%)

QUESTIONS

1   Give two reasons why you might choose to use a spreadsheet program.
2   Give an example of when you might use a formula.
3   If £120 was entered into cell A1 and £33 entered into B1, what formula would you put in cell C1 to
    a) find the total of cells A1 and B1
    b) multiply cell A1 by B1
    c) multiply A1 by 9 per cent?

An extremely powerful feature of spreadsheets is the ability to use formulas to make calculations on values in cells. To try to help us use formulas, some programs, such as Microsoft Excel, contain functions. **Functions** are ready-made formulas that have been built into the spreadsheet.

The most frequently used function is the SUM function, which is used to add the numbers in a range of cells. For example, if you want to add together the numbers in cells A1 to A10, you could use the + operator in the formula to add the cells as follows:

=A1+A2+A3+A4+A5+A6+A7+A8+A9+A10

It is much quicker and easier to use the SUM function:

=SUM (A1:A10)

Note the colon (:) in the formula. This tells the spreadsheet to apply the SUM function to the range of cells (A1 to A10). To enter a function, you can either type in the function name (in this example SUM) or choose a function from the function box. The table at the bottom of the opposite page shows some common functions and how they can be used.

Once a formula has been entered into one cell, it can be copied to other cells. In Excel, this is done by using the

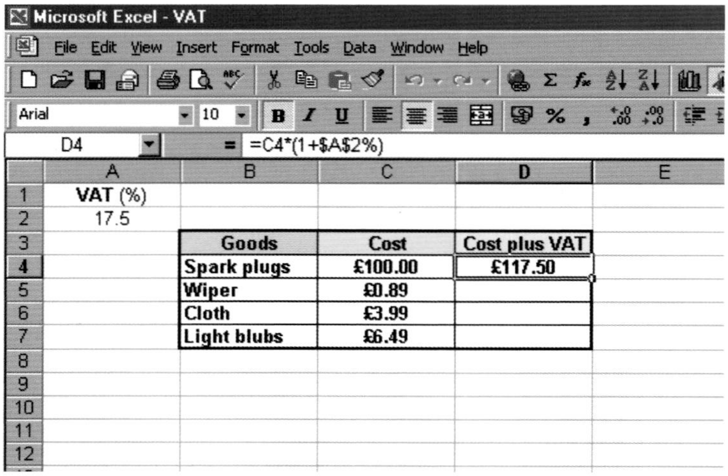

Fill Down command from the Edit menu. This saves having to retype the formula cell by cell. Other spreadsheet programs copy formulas in different ways.

Relative and absolute references

Copying formulas can be extremely useful, and happens because the spreadsheet is using relative cell references. A **reference** is the term used to describe a cell, or range of cells, in a spreadsheet. A reference tells the spreadsheet where to look for the values or data you want to use in a formula.

Relative references are references to cells relative to the position of the formula. For example, if you put the formula =A1 into cell B1, A1 is the reference and the spreadsheet will automatically enter into cell B1 whatever value is in cell A1. This is an example of a relative reference. It is important to remember that a relative reference *changes when a formula is copied or moved*. For example, if the formula in cell B1 is copied to cell B2, the cell reference will change. This means that the formula in cell B2 will have changed to =A2.

If you do not want the cell reference to change in this way, you can use an absolute reference. **Absolute references** are fixed references that *do not change when a formula is moved or copied*. To make a formula contain absolute references, a dollar sign ($) is inserted before the column or row reference that you do not want to change: for example, A2 (see Fig 10.3).

Value Added Tax (VAT) has to be paid on most goods and services. At present, VAT is set at 17.5%. If you created a spreadsheet to automatically work out the price of goods with and without VAT, you would use an absolute reference for the cell containing the VAT amount of 17.5%. This is important if you want to copy the formula to other cells and keep the VAT as it is. Without an absolute reference, the formula might not work or the VAT might change when copied – not a good idea!

Fig 10.3 By using an absolute reference ($) – in this example to cell A2 – a formula can be copied without the cell reference changing.

Comparison and reference operators	Meaning	Example
Comparison operators allow you to compare two values		
=	Equal to	A1=A2
>	Greater than	IF(A1>60, "Grade A","") In this example, the greater than operator(>) is used with the IF function to give a grade A to a student who scores more than 60 in a test
<	Less than	IF(A1<20," Sit the test again","")
> =	Greater than or equal to	A1>=60
< =	Less than or equal to	A1<=60
Reference operators join ranges of cells for calculations		
:	Range of cells	A1:A175

QUESTIONS

1 What is a function? Give three examples of functions and explain their purpose.

2 What is the difference between relative references and absolute references?

Common functions used in Microsoft Excel

Function	Meaning	Example
SUM	Adds all the numbers in a range of cells	=SUM (B1:B175) If you wanted to add together the numbers in cells B1 to B175 you could use the + operator to add the cells (B1+B2+B3 etc.). This would take you a long time! It is much quicker, and easier, to use the SUM function
AVERAGE	Calculates the average of a range of cells	=AVERAGE (B1:B3) If you had three tests in a term, and the results were entered into cells B1, B2 and B3, the AVERAGE function can be used to calculate your average score
COUNT	Counts the number of cells that contain numbers	=COUNT (C1:C30) Suppose you and other members of your class are collecting money for charity. You enter the amount collected into cells C1 to C30. Then you can use the COUNT function can be used to count up the number of students who have paid in money.
IF	Spreadsheet makes a choice depending on what it finds. It returns one of two values depending on the condition that you set	= IF(D1<=2,"Ask Mum for a loan!","Money OK") In this example, cell D1 contains a formula showing how much pocket money you have left. If D1 is less than or equal to £2, then 'Ask Mum for a loan!' is displayed. If you have more than £2, then 'Money OK' is displayed.
COUNTIF	Counts the number of cells that meet the given criteria.	=COUNTIF (D1:D30,"=A") In this example, cells D1 to D30 have exam grades. To find out how many students got grade A, you could use the COUNTIF function.

When you have a task that involves calculations, you must first compare the different features of the software available to you. You can then decide which software is best for the job. Some word processors and databases can also include spreadsheet–type features and you must decide, having analysed your task, which software to use. If the task is for GCSE coursework, you will need to justify your choice of software for the examiner.

Below is a table showing some of the main features available in the popular spreadsheet program Microsoft Excel. Compare these features with other programs that are available to you.

Aspect	Feature	Example
Design	On-screen grid	Text, numbers and formulas to be entered into a grid of rectangular cells
	Different fonts and font sizes	Choice of font is important if people are to use a spreadsheet without straining their eyes! Ten is the standard font size, although you can change this to whatever you want
	Different styles	Just with word-processed documents, presentation can be improved by appropriate use of bold, italic and coloured data
	Alignment of data	Data can be aligned to the left, right or centred in a cell. It is also possible to centre data across a range of cells and to display text at any angle
	Cell format	Cell formatting allows you choose the right format for your data. For example, the number of decimal places or whether a £ sign is automatically displayed
		It is also possible to create your own 'custom' formats. For example, if you wanted centimetres (cm) to appear in a cell in Excel, you would format the cell(s) using the custom format 0.00 "cm"
	Use of colour shading	Colour can make the spreadsheet attractive. However, too much of the wrong colours can make the spreadsheet difficult to look at
	Use of borders	Borders can be put around a cell or cells to improve the appearance of a sheet or to draw attention to key data
	Column width	Changing the width of a column – by dragging the right-hand column boundary – enables data to be fitted into one column, rather than appearing to spread across neighbouring columns
	Column headings	Column headings can be 'frozen' in place so that the headings always remain at the top of the screen, even when you scroll down a spreadsheet
	Multiple sheets	Not all of the data has to be displayed on one sheet. Different sheets can be kept together in one file and easily accessed via sheet tabs

Common functions used in Microsoft Excel

Aspect	Feature	Example
Input/Output	Import data	Data can be imported from other software in, for example, CSV format. Also graphics can be imported from drawing or painting programs
	Page break preview	This allows you to see what the printed page will look like. By dragging the page borders, you can fit your data on to one or more pages
	Print whole or part(s) of spreadsheet	Sometimes you may want to print print part of a sheet, not the whole thing
	Page orientation	Landscape (horizontal) or portrait (vertical)
	Graphing	Graphing (charting) data can be very important in showing patterns, comparisons and trends in data. A wide range of graph types are available in Excel
	Export data	Data can be exported to other applications. 1 Via the clipboard using cut, copy or paste. 2 Using different file formats (e.g. in CSV format). 3 Being linked directly with other programs such as a word processor
Other features	Auto fill	By dragging the 'fill handle' with the mouse, the time, days of the week, or months of the year can be entered automatically (the 'fill handle' is a small rectangle found at the bottom right of a selection)
	Spell checking	Checking spelling is as important in spreadsheets as in any other application
	Macros	There are times when you have to do the same task: for example, sorting then printing a list of names. To help you do this, Excel enables you to record macros. Macros are a series of commands that a spreadsheet can perform automatically. You record macros in a similar way to using a tape recorder to record music.
	Data validation	Data validation ensures that only the correct data is entered into a cell or cells
	Functions	Functions are ready-made formulas that have been built into the software: for example, SUM, COUNTIF, MATCH, VLOOKUP
	Conditional formatting	Conditional formatting allows the colour of cells, or their data, to change automatically when certain conditions are met. For example, the cells of all students scoring less than 30% in a test can be shaded red
	Sharing the spreadsheet	Sometimes on a computer network it is necessary for more than one user to use a spreadsheet at the same time. This is possible if 'sharing' is turned on
	Security	It is possible to password protect a whole file, or even individual cells, so as to stop anyone else changing or entering data
	Lookup tables	For quick data entry, as well as data validation, lookup tables can be used. For example, by entering a product code, say 2, the details of product 2 will be displayed. See the file **Example functions in Excel.xls** from the OUP website (www.oup.com/uk/ictforgcse) on how to do this

QUESTIONS

1   Using the computer file **Choosing the right file for calculations** – available from the OUP website and CD-ROM – compare two programs that are available for you to use if you were to do a task involving calculations.

2   Explain the advantages of using the following features in a spreadsheet:
    a) Data validation
    b) Lookup tables
    c) Macros.

Graphing (charting) data can be very important in showing patterns, comparisons and trends in data. Instead of having rows and columns of data, a graph can make a strong visual impact. This often makes the data much easier to understand.

We are surrounded by information in newspapers, magazines and television. These media help us to understand the figures they use by presenting them graphically. Spreadsheets are ideally equipped to do this but we need to choose the appropriate graph style with care. It is possible to draw graphs that show us nothing at all or give us misleading information.

Month	Average sunlight (hours)	Temperature (°C)				Discomfort from heat and humidity	Relative humidity (%)		Average precipitation (mm)	Wet days (+0.25mm)
		Average								
		Min	Max	Record min	Record max		am	pm		
Jan	5	6	14	−3	22	*	83	72	39	8
Feb	6	6	15	−4	23	*	82	70	34	6
Mar	6	8	17	−1	24	*	81	69	51	8
Apr	7	10	19	1	26	*	77	66	32	6
May	10	13	22	5	31	*	77	67	29	5
Jun	10	17	26	8	37	Medium	70	65	17	3
Jul	11	20	29	12	39	Medium	70	65	3	1
Aug	10	20	29	11	37	Medium	75	65	25	3
Sep	8	18	27	4	35	Medium	79	69	55	5
Oct	6	14	23	1	31	Moderate	83	71	77	9
Nov	5	10	18	1	26	*	83	72	47	8
Dec	4	8	15	−1	24	*	82	72	40	9

How to make a graph

The numerical information needs to be laid out on the spreadsheet so that the items to be graphed are in one group of adjacent cells. This means that you need to think about what you are going to do *before* you set up the table of information.

A piece of graphical information that you often see is the average monthly temperatures and the average monthly rainfall for holiday resorts. The table above right shows the weather data for Palma in Majorca. As this table is presented, it may not be possible to produce a chart that shows the monthly averages of hours of sunshine, maximum and minimum temperatures and rainfall. This is because the yellow columns of data are not all next to one another. The data might need to be laid out as shown in the table on the right.

Now the data in the spreadsheet can be highlighted as a continuous set of data, and the graph can now be produced (Fig 10.4).

Month	Average sunlight (hours)	Min average temperature (°C)	Max average temperature (°C)	Average precipitation (mm)
Jan	5	6	14	39
Feb	6	6	15	34
Mar	6	8	17	51
Apr	7	10	19	32
May	10	13	22	29
Jun	10	17	26	17
Jul	11	20	29	3
Aug	10	20	29	25
Sep	8	18	27	55
Oct	6	14	23	77
Nov	5	10	18	47
Dec	4	8	15	40

The graph in Fig 10.4 is not very easy to understand because the range of rainfall is large (3 mm to 77 mm) and all the bars are drawn on the same scale. You might be able to change the graph type so that there are two different scales. In the example shown in Fig 10.5, the

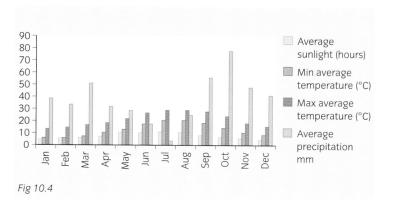

Fig 10.4

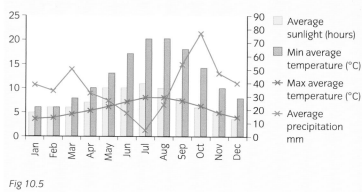

Fig 10.5

average hours of sunshine and the minimum average temperature are shown as bars measured against the left-hand scale, and the maximum average temperature and the average rainfall are shown as lines graphs measured against the right-hand scale.

If you do not look carefully at the scales, the minimum temperatures look as though they are larger than the maximum temperatures. You can see how easy it is to mislead people with graphical information. If you made separate tables, from which you drew separate charts, it would make it easier to understand the information (Figs 10.6 to 10.8).

Now each piece of information can be quickly understood. The best month for sunshine is July with an average 11 hours a day. July and August are the hottest months, when the maximum average temperature is 29 °C. The wettest month is October, and the driest is July.

Once you have produced understandable charts, they can be imported into other documents using copy-and-paste techniques. Before you make the final presentation of the information, you might want to alter the colours of the bars, lines or pies, and label axes. Most spreadsheets allow you to do this.

Remember Choose the type of graph carefully so that it shows the information clearly with little chance of misinterpretation.

For further information on different types of graph, use the OUP website (**www.oup.com/uk/ictforgcse**).

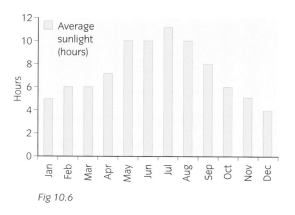

Fig 10.6

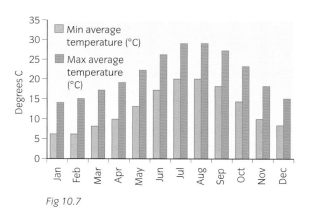

Fig 10.7

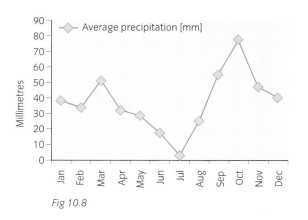

Fig 10.8

Task 1 Entering formulae

First, you will download from the OUP website (**www.oup.com/uk/ictforgcse**) the file **Spread1.csv** (or the equivalent Excel file, **Spread1.xls**).

Open the file and:

1 Enter the formula =B2★7 into cell C2
2 Copy the formula in cell C2 down to cell C8. If you are using Excel, do this by dragging the 'fill handle' – a small rectangle at the bottom right of the cell.
3 Work out what formula has to be entered into cell D2. Remember: the formula has to calculate the cost of milk over a year. When you have done this, copy the formula down to cell D8.
4 Work out what formula has to be entered into cell E2 to calculate the cost of milk over 50 years. When you have done this, copy the formula down to cell E8.
5 Now enter a formula into cell B9 that will add the values of cells B2 to B8. Use the SUM function to do this. When you have done that, copy the formula to cells C9, D9 and E9.

Task 2 Recording students' marks

Download the file **Spread2.csv** (Spread2.xls). Your task is to enter functions and formula into a spreadsheet that records student marks.

Open the file and:

1 Work out which function should be used (in cells G3 to G8) to total students' marks.
2 Use the AVERAGE function to work out the average mark for each student.
3 Enter a formula that would work out students' total marks as a percentage of their three tests.

With more advanced spreadsheet programs (like Excel), you might consider using the following functions:

COUNTIF: To count the number of boys and girls in the class (cells B11 and B12).
VLOOKUP: In the file Spread2, you will see a table showing GCSE grades and the equivalent points score. Enter the VLOOKUP function into cell K3 so

that when a GCSE grade is entered into cell J3, the correct point score is entered. When the function is working, copy it down to K8.

GCSE GRADE	POINTS
A*	8
A	7
B	6
C	5
D	4
E	3
F	2
G	1

The file **Example functions in Excel.xls** has worked examples of all the main functions. Use this for reference if you get stuck.

Task 3 Calculating VAT

Small and large businesses need to send invoices to their customers so that they get paid for the goods or services they provide. Most goods and services that can be purchased attract Value Added Tax (VAT). If you look at invoices or receipts, you will often see that the VAT payable is shown as a separate amount for each item and as a total amount, which is added to the total pre-VAT cost to give the grand total that you have to pay.

Invoices will often be created using a spreadsheet-type program. To save time and to make sure that the amount of VAT to be paid is correct, the program can calculate the VAT.

Download the file **Spread3.csv** (Spread3.xls) and load it into your spreadsheet. It is the framework for an invoicing system for G & T Electronics – a company that sells TVs, videos, hi-fi equipment, as well as washing machines, refrigerators etc. The spreadsheet only shows the layout of the invoice that G & T want. It includes the basic pre-VAT prices of some products but does not have any formulas or functions on it to calculate the final prices the customer is going to pay. Currently, VAT is charged at 17.5% of the basic price.

1 Work out a formula that would calculate the amount of VAT to be paid on the product on row 7 of the spreadsheet and place that into the appropriate cell.

2 What is the quickest way to copy the formula you have created for the VAT on row 7 to help you to work out the VAT for the products on rows 8 to 10?

3 Create these formulae so that your spreadsheet has VAT calculated for all products on the invoice.

4 Column F on this spreadsheet needs to work out the total price (including VAT) for the number of products that have been bought, and in cell F16 there needs to be a formula that calculates the grand total that the customer has to pay. Design the formulas that will be needed to do this and put them into the spreadsheet.

5 When it comes to doing your coursework, you will need to show the examiners and your teachers that your spreadsheet does really work. It is often helpful to printout the answer as well as a formula view printout. Produce both these printouts and then give a brief description of how your spreadsheet works.

So far, you have probably used relative references throughout this task. Now we are going to look at another way of doing this task, which may save businesses a lot of time if the government decides to change the rate of VAT.

Download the file **Spread4.csv** (Spread4.xls) and load it into your spreadsheet. You will notice that it is very similar to the previous spreadsheet except that the VAT rate of 17.5% has been entered into cell D3. G & T Electronics would like you to modify the spreadsheet so that if the rate changes to 15%, all the company has to do is to type the new VAT rate into cell D3 and everything alters automatically. (**Hint** You will need to use absolute cell references in some of your formulae.)

6 What formula could you use in cell D7 that would involve a reference to cell D3 when calculating the VAT due on the refrigerator?

7 How could you copy this formula to other cells in column D so that they all use the information in cell D3 to calculate the VAT?

8 Now you have referenced all VAT calculations to cell D3 to find the rate of VAT, see if this works. Change

the VAT rate to 15% and note the effect on the totals. Does it work? Try other rates of VAT (10%, 20%, . . .) and check that you get the answers you would expect.

9 Again, print out formula views along with your answers and annotate them to help another person understand how you built this invoice system.

Task 4 Booking theatre seats

A play will be performed for two nights. You must produce a spreadsheet which will book seats for a small 50-seat theatre.

You must produce:

1 A spreadsheet showing which seats have been booked for each night.

2 A plan of the seating, using one cell per seat. The seats should be arranged in five rows with ten seats per row, making 50 seats in total. The first two rows (20 seats) are priced at £2.50 and the remaining three rows (30 seats) at £2.00.

3 A graph showing ticket sales for the two nights.

Set the spreadsheet up to analyse:

4 The % of seats booked each night.

5 The total income per performance and over the two nights.

6 The average attendance over the two nights.

With more advanced spreadsheet programmes (like Excel), you might consider using facilities such as:

◆ Conditional formatting to get the cells to change colour when they are booked.

◆ Data validation to ensure that only X can be entered to book a seat.

◆ AVERAGE, COUNTIF (to find the total number of seats booked) and SUM functions.

When you have finished your spreadsheet, show it to your teacher or a friend, as they will want to check that everything is working properly! You should also print out the spreadsheet data and the formulae used. Annotate and make notes on your printout(s) to explain how your spreadsheet works.

A computer can be used to quickly search and retrieve information or data that has been collected and specially organised. The application software that does this is known as a **database**. Databases have four main properties: information can be stored, quickly found (retrieved), changed and deleted.

Databases are in widespread use, as they help people quickly to find the information that they want. For example, if you want to find a person's telephone number, BT's Directory Enquiries will be able to search their database of millions of customers and tell you the number in a few seconds.

Databases vary in size and use depending on what is required. A small database, such as one that keeps information about a CD collection, can be run on a personal computer at home. Larger databases now play an important part in how our society works. Industrial, commercial and public organisations use databases to maintain their businesses and services. Examples of these large databases range from booking holidays and airline tickets through to the Police National Computer

database, which gets 65 million requests each year from police officers who want information about criminal suspects or stolen cars.

Geographic information systems (GIS) are another example of how databases are used today. What is so special about a GIS is that data is presented in the form of some kind of map. One way in which a GIS can be used is to hold grid references, street addresses or postcodes in a database, and then – when requested – to show a street at exactly the right location on a map. Geographic information systems play an increasingly important part in many organisations. For example, a GIS can be used in weather forecasting, or used by the emergency services to plan quick routes for their vehicles.

A **database management system (DBMS)** is the term for programs that handle the storage, modification and retrieval of data, as well as controlling who has access to the information. Database programs, such as Microsoft Access, Lotus Approach, FileMaker Pro, and Corel Paradox, are available on personal computers and provide an opportunity for people to create their own databases at home, school or at work. It is also possible to set up a database in spreadsheet programs such as Microsoft Excel.

In schools, the collection and organisation of student information is a good starting point when you are trying to understand how databases work. Before the widespread use of computers, student information was kept on

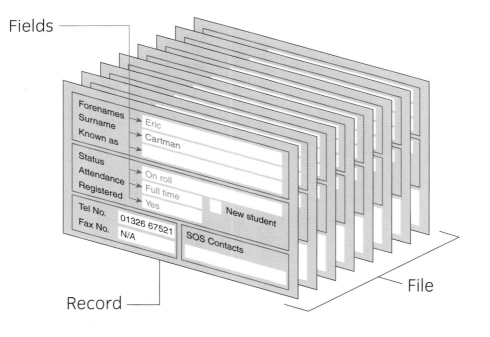

*Fig 11.1 A good way to understand the structure of databases is to think of a card index. All of the cards constitute a **file**, each card of which is a **record**. On each card is a number of **fields** that contain information.*

pieces of paper in boxes or filing cabinets. If you and a small group of friends each put your personal details, such as name, address and date of birth, on a record card, then it might not take too long to find those of you whose birthday is in April. However, if everyone in your school filled out a card, then it would take very much longer! Furthermore, changing information, such as addresses, could also take a long time.

Databases are organised in **files**, which consist of a series of **records**, which in turn consist of a series of **fields**. Once you have understood this, you will be well on the way to understanding databases. A collection of data or information that has been given a name is called a **file**. For example, information about all of the students in a school could be saved in a file called *Students*. This *Students* file would be a collection of **records** about every student in the school. Think of every student in your school as each having his or her own record. In a paper-based system, each student would have his or her own record card. A database is organised in a similar way – but not on paper (Fig 11.1).

A record usually contains a number of **fields**. A field is a space for one item of information. In our example, the information on each student record, such as forename, surname, gender, address, etc, would appear in fields. This means that there would be one field for your forename, another field for your surname and so on. Each field has its own name. This is known as the **field name**.

The power of a database is that information contained in fields can be found, grouped, sorted, exported – often in a matter of seconds.

QUESTIONS

1 What is a database?
2 Give two examples of large databases that might be used to help members of the public.
3 Explain what is meant by: file, record and field.
4 Look carefully at the table below. Do the advantages of a database outweigh the disadvantages?

Advantages and disadvantages of a database compared with a paper-based system

Advantages	Disadvantages
◆ Can save enormous amounts of paper as well as filing space	◆ The computer(s) and peripherals required can cost a lot
◆ Data can easily be entered by keyboard or scanners	◆ If the computer, or computer network, is not working, then the database cannot be used
◆ Speed – data can be found, calculated and sorted very quickly	◆ Security is very important as some people may attempt to get access to confidential information. Sometimes this may involve illegally hacking into the program or data
◆ Data can easily be changed and updated	
◆ Data needs to be entered only once, yet can be presented in many different ways. A whole range of different reports can be produced	◆ The database file can become corrupted or infected by a computer virus. This can lead to the file not working properly. In some cases, the database may not work at all. Making a back-up copy of the database is therefore essential
◆ Data can be checked on entry	
◆ Passwords can be set to allow access only to those with permission to use the database	◆ There is often a limit to the size of a database file
◆ The data structure of a database can be changed, with new fields added, even after the database has been created. A paper-based system would have to be restarted from scratch.	◆ Some databases can be complicated to use
	◆ Some databases require much time to be spent on staff training, which can be costly
◆ Data can be imported and exported to other programs	◆ Data held about people may be incorrect
◆ A database file can be automatically linked to others	
◆ Databases can be shared with other users if the computer is part of a local or wide area network. This includes the Internet	

Creating a database – getting the structure right

You saw on pages 106–7 that a **field** is the place where a particular type of data can be stored. There are different types of field for different types of data. For example, students' names would obviously be text, but their ages would be numbers. These are known as **field attributes**.

When you create a database, you will have to choose field types based on the kind of information you want each field to contain. The field type determines what kind of data can be entered as well as what operations the database can perform with the data. *Before* creating a database, it is important that you have worked out the field attributes for each field. The most common field types are shown in the table.

Another important field attribute is **field length**. Not all databases require you to set a maximum field length, but many do. This is because, by deciding in advance the maximum length of a field, file size can be kept as small as possible, as there is no wasted storage space. Also, the time taken to process data is kept to a minimum.

Field length is measured in characters. A character is one letter or number. Setting the right field length is important. Think what you would have to do when setting the field length for a surname field. A field length of 5 characters would be right for those whose surname was Smith (5 characters) but not suitable for Rushbrook (9 characters). Some databases allow **fixed** field lengths – for example, 30 characters. The field stays 30 characters long even when the name Smith (5 characters) is entered. To overcome this, and to save space, it is also possible to have **variable** field length. For each surname this stores only the characters in that surname and changes (is variable) depending on the length of each surname.

When constructing a database, it is also important to plan to have a field that will always have a unique value, regardless of how many records there are. This field is known as the **key field**. The key field's unique value therefore applies to only one record.

The need for a key field becomes clear when you think of what might happen if you wanted to search a students' database for John Smith. Smith is a common surname and you may find that there are lots of Smiths

Fig 11.2
*Many schools have a database of all of the students in the school. Here you can see a student **record** clearly showing the **fields** into which student information can be entered. How many fields are there?*

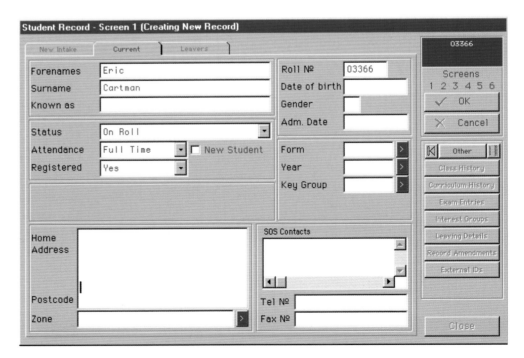

in your school – and more than one John! It is better, therefore, to have a unique reference (key field) on which to search.

In relational databases (see page 114), the key field (also known as the primary key) is used to link different database tables.

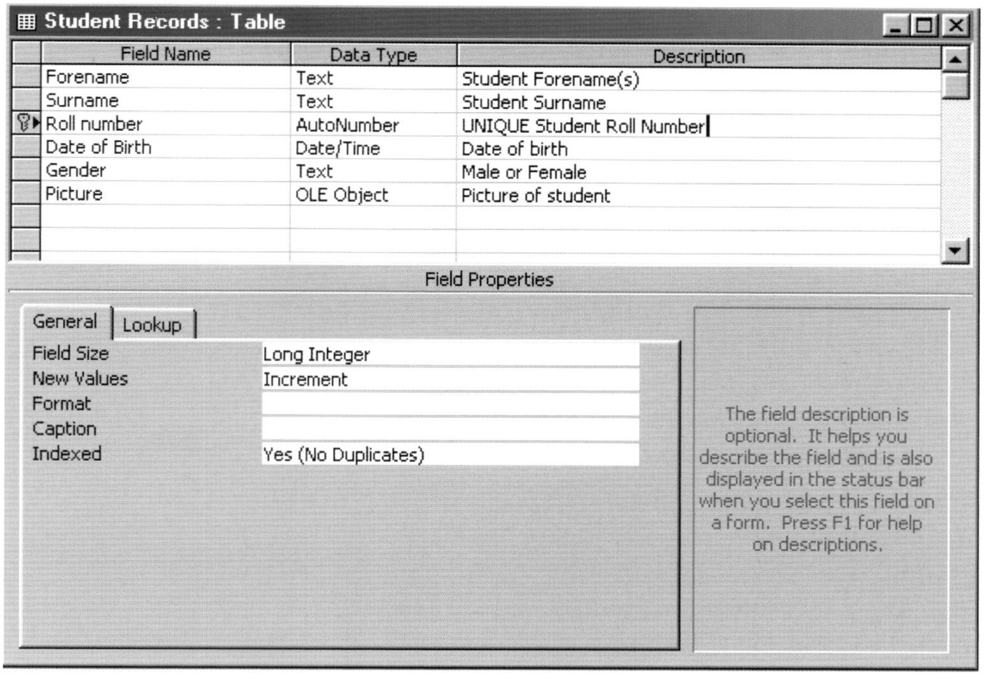

Figure 11.2. Shows a screenshot of a student record in a school's students database. You will see a field called Roll No. This field gives each student her or his own unique number on the school roll, so this is the key field. School students in England have been allocated a **unique pupil number (UPN)** that will stay with them throughout their school career. This makes the UPN field a key field in any students database.

When you design any database, it is worth remembering that screen design (sometimes known as **forms**) is important. Some databases allow you to move the position of fields on a record to where you want them, and to add colour etc. to improve the visual appearance of records. Most databases also allow you to design different layouts and views of the data.

Fig 11.3 When creating a database, it is important to set the correct field data type.

Common field types found in databases

Use this field type...	When the field's data is...
Text	Text (usually up to 255 characters)
Memo	Large amount of text (usually up to 64000 characters)
Number (also known as a numeric field)	Numbers, for example 12345
Date	Dates, for example 21/04/55
Time	Time, for example 16:31
Currency	£ or $
Autonumber	Automatically generates a number every time a new record is created
Container	Picture, video clip, sound file or OLE object from another program (Windows only)
Yes/No (also known as a Boolean or logical field)	Yes or No
Calculation	Result of a formula, for example Balance = Field 'money in' – Field 'money out'

QUESTIONS

1. Explain what is meant by the following terms: field attributes, fixed field length, variable field length, key field and form.
2. Give two reasons why choosing the correct field type is important.
3. Give two reasons why setting the maximum length of a field can be important.

Capturing data

The collection of data into a suitable structure for processing by a computer is called **data capture**. The most popular input device on PCs is a keyboard. However, entering large amounts of data using a keyboard can be slow. Also, mistakes can be made when typing. So other input devices are used. For example, barcode readers used in libraries and retailing are a highly accurate and quick method of data capture. Barcodes, though, are only suitable for capturing pre-printed information. (For the full range of input devices, see pages 14–17.)

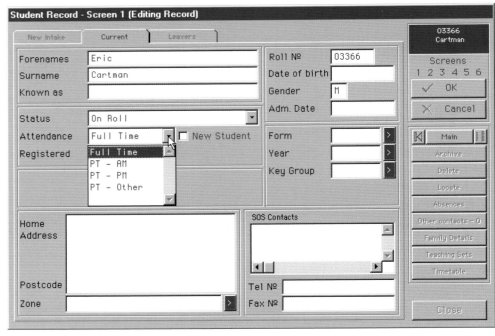

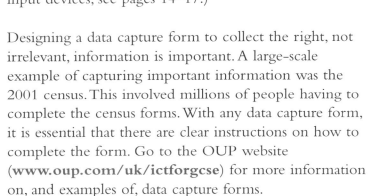

Fig 11.4 Value lists are a quick and accurate way to enter data. In this example, student attendance can be Full Time or Part Time (PT).

Designing a data capture form to collect the right, not irrelevant, information is important. A large-scale example of capturing important information was the 2001 census. This involved millions of people having to complete the census forms. With any data capture form, it is essential that there are clear instructions on how to complete the form. Go to the OUP website (**www.oup.com/uk/ictforgcse**) for more information on, and examples of, data capture forms.

Entering data

Data entry should be as straightforward and quick as possible. This is particularly important if a database has hundreds, or thousands, of records. Data also needs to be accurate (see Data validation opposite). To help with this, you can set the entry options for fields.

One entry option is to get data to be automatically entered into a field. For example, if all students in a school live in the County of Norfolk, then it is possible to have Norfolk automatically entered into the County field.

In most databases, you will need to enter the same values into a field repeatedly. For example, all students in Year 11 will be in forms or tutor groups. It is much quicker and more accurate to choose a student's form/tutor group from a list, rather than having to type it in each time. A **value list** (or **combo box**) lets you do this by choosing a value from a list (Fig 11.4).

Other entry options include a **check box**. This can be useful because, instead of putting Yes or No into a field, you can have a check box, where a tick equals Yes and no tick equals No. Another option is to have **radio buttons**, also known as **option buttons**.

These methods of data entry reduce the possibility of error when inputting data.

Data validation

It is important that only the correct data is entered into fields. **Data validation** is where the software checks that what is being entered into a field (or cell in a spreadsheet) is allowed. There are several different checks that the software can make.

The six main ones are:

- **Type** That the data is in the correct format: for example, a number in a numeric field.

- **Empty** That the field is not left empty. The user is asked to enter data if it has not been entered. This is used for important fields where you must have an entry: for example, a person's surname or National Insurance number.

- **Value list** Only allows values to be entered from a pre-defined list.

- **Range** Only allows values to be entered from a certain range: for example, from 1 to 10

- **Check digit** That numbers have been entered correctly. An extra number (the check digit) is added and a calculation is made which shows whether the numbers have all been entered correctly. This type of check is used to verify such things as product codes in shops.

- **Check length** That data entered is of a certain length, i.e. number of characters.

Data verification

Data verification is the term used to describe the checking of data, usually by a person. Data is often keyed into a database from forms, where mistakes in keying do occur. So someone should check what has been entered into the database against what is on the forms.

There are several advantages of using a database over a paper-based system (see pages 106–7). A major one is that, apart from the data being quickly found and retrieved, it can easily be changed and updated. This happens in the following ways:

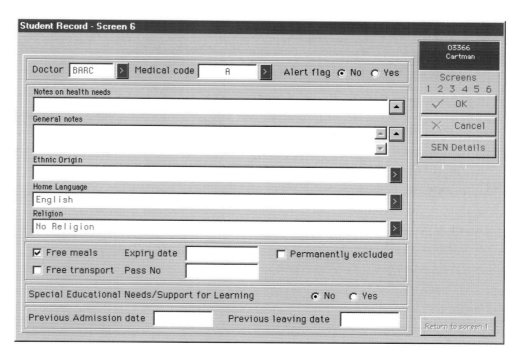

Fig 11.5 Five fields in this screenshot have been set as check boxes and radio buttons. Which fields are they?

- **Adding records** A new record can be added to the database file: for example, when a new student joins the school.

- **Deleting records** An individual record can be deleted from a database: for example, when a student leaves the school. A group of records can also be deleted at the same time: for example, the whole of Year 11 after finishing their GCSE examinations. Moreover, data in individual fields can be deleted.

- **Changing (amending) records** A record can easily be changed: for example, when a student's family moves house, the new address and telephone number can be entered into the address and telephone fields.

QUESTIONS

1   In creating a database, when would you choose the following entry options: auto enter, value list (or combo box), check box?

2   What is data validation? What are the six main data validation checks?

3   Explain how data verification is different from data validation.

111

You saw on pages 6–7 that computers have important advantages over manual systems. They can work extremely quickly, and automatically, to make calculations and to retrieve and sort data into some useful form. All these functions are known as **data processing**.

Searching a database (sometimes called interrogating or querying data) is reasonably straightforward once you realise that you must tell the program precisely what to search for. You do this by giving clear criteria (conditions) for the search. You might know what you want to find, but the software does not – until you tell it.

Searches (queries) can be as simple or as complex as you like. To search a database, you must first enter the search criteria into a field or fields, or find it in a dialogue box. Then you instruct the program to go off and find all of the records that match the conditions that you have set. For example, to find all the Smiths in a school, you would enter =Smith into the surname field.

Many database systems require you to make requests for information in a special query language, known as **SQL (structured query language)**. An example of SQL is the query

    SELECT ALL WHERE age > 13 AND name = "Smith"

This searches for all records in which the name field is Smith and the age field has a value greater than 13. SQL is the main language for database management systems running on minicomputers and mainframes but now is increasingly used by PC database systems.

The secret to searching a database – including those on the Internet – is to try to be as specific as possible in your search. If you want to find the record of John Smith, not all of the Smiths in the school, then you could search the forename field (=John) and surname field (=Smith) *at the same time*. By searching on more

than one field, you can narrow down your search. If you enter search criteria in more than one field, you perform what is called a logical AND search.

It is also possible to use OR and NOT in your searches (see pages 118–19). You can search for records that meet certain criteria and then temporarily hide (omit) those records. For example, if you want to work with all the students in the school except those in Year 11, you can specify Year 11 in the find request and then omit those records.

Operators used in searching databases		
Operators	**Meaning**	**Example**
=	Equal to	= Smith. Searches the surname field and finds all those named Smith
>	Greater than	> 15. Searches the age field and finds all those whose age is greater than 15
<	Less than	< 14. Searches the age field and finds all those whose age is less than 14
>=	Greater than or equal to	> = 11. Searches the age field and finds all those whose age is greater than or equal to 11
<=	Less than or equal to	< = 6. Searches the age field and finds all those whose age is less than or equal to 6
*	Asterisk, known as a wild-card character, can be used to represent one or more characters	=T*m will find Tim, Tom and Tristram

After conducting a search, you end up with a set of records (or a record). This is known as the **found set**. (When you find all of the records in the database, the found set is the entire database.) For example, if you searched a student database for all the girls in Year 11 (Year Group = 11 AND Gender = F), then the records found will be the found set. However, you might find that the girls' records are not in alphabetical order. You will therefore have to sort the records.

Sorting records temporarily reorders the database file. Sorting allows you to browse, update, export, or print records in a particular order (Fig 11.6). It is possible to sort text in ascending (A to Z) and descending (Z to A) order. It is also possible similarly to sort numbers, dates and times in ascending and descending order. Being able to sort records quickly is one of the advantages of using a database.

You can also import data from another database file, or from another application, into an existing database. For example, a primary school could send a database file to a secondary school with details of all the Year 7 students who will be joining the school in September. This data can be then be imported into the secondary school's database. It is also possible to **merge** (combine) two or more database files.

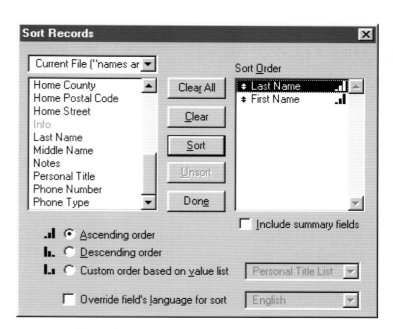

Fig 11.6 *Databases allow you to quickly sort data according to the criteria you specify*

Fig 11.7 *By searching on more than one field, you can narrow down your search. This example shows a search in the* County *and* Balance *fields for companies in Norfolk with a balance over £1000.*

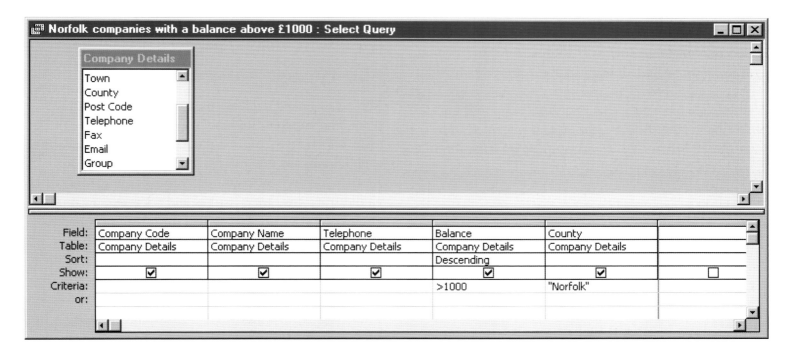

Graphs are often the best way show patterns, comparisons and trends in data. Some databases have built-in graphing facilities. For those that do not, data can be exported into other programs that can produce graphs. This may involve saving the data as Tab-Separated Text (.TAB), as Comma Separated Values (.CSV) or as a text file (.TXT), in order for it to be recognised by the other program.

1 Give two other terms for searching data.
2 Explain what is meant by: search criteria, sorting, merging.

A **database management system (DBMS)** is the term for programs that handle the storage, modification and retrieval of data, as well as controlling who has access to the information. A DBMS organises information in a number of different ways.

Flat-file databases are used on personal computers. A flat-file database can only work on one file at a time, and this must store all the data. Although easy to use and create, flat-file databases are not suitable for large databases as they can be slow, have a large file size and use a lot of memory.

In contrast, **relational databases** have links (relationships) to more than one file. These links allow data from another file to be shown, used, and edited – but not copied – in a current file. Whenever the values in the other file change, the data displayed in the current file also changes. In some databases, data is stored in containers known as **tables** (rows and columns of data) and then relationships are made between tables.

A simple example of a relational database could be where your school stores school-visit information in a *Visit* file, and then uses it with student information in a *Student* file, and with parents' billing information in an *Invoice* file.

One advantage of relational databases over flat-file databases is that by having a number of related files, instead of one, data is accessed only when needed. This results in less data being stored in memory, smaller file sizes and faster access. Another advantage is that data need only be changed in one file. If there were two flat-file student databases – one for the school office and another in use in the ICT department – and a student leaves, the student's record would have to be deleted from *both* flat files. In a relational database, it would need to be removed from only the single student file.

In large organisations, there is a need for the relational database to be used on local or wide-area networks. These are called **distributed databases** and can be accessed by hundreds of users simultaneously.

File types

In a set of linked database files, there are various file types. The **master file** is the chief file that keeps the main information, summary data and key fields in the data. The master file accesses and displays data from another file. In a business, for example, the master file would store customers' names and addresses, account numbers and so on. Any orders that customers make would be recorded in the business or transaction file, noting, for example, what items were ordered and their cost. The **transaction file** then updates the master file.

There also is a file, known as the **change file** or **transaction log**, which keeps a record of changes to the transaction file. This is important, as many businesses need to record the history of what transactions have taken place – not just the latest one.

File organisation

Files can be stored and organised in two main ways. In a **serial file**, records are not stored in any particular order.

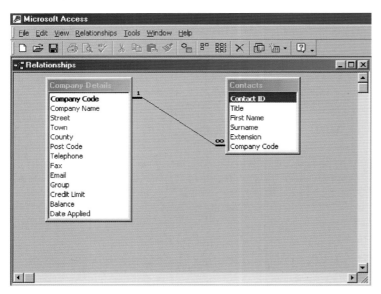

Fig 11.8 In a relational database, files or tables are linked together. In this example, the **Company Code** key field in the **Company Details** table has a one-to-many relationship with the **Company Code** field in the **contacts** table.

In a **sequential file**, records are sorted into some kind of order: for example, students may be sorted by their unique pupil number (UPN).

Accessing files

Serial files are accessed (and read) by a program which goes through each record until the required record is found. In contrast, in **direct access (random access) files**, the required record is found straight away (directly) without first going through the other records.

Backups

Making **backups** (copies) of files is always important. For businesses and other organisations that depend on databases, it is essential. Files can become damaged, corrupted or even lost. Think what would happen to travel agents if they couldn't use a database for booking flights (Fig 11.9) or to doctors who couldn't access patients' details. To prevent situations like this happening, the regular backing up of files occurs. If a file does become damaged or corrupted, then the files, and the data they contain, can be restored from the backup copy and business can continue as normal.

QUESTIONS

1 What is a database management system (DBMS)?
2 Explain what is meant by: flat-file database, relational database, distributed database.
3 List four advantages of a relational database over a flat-file database.
4 Explain what is meant by: master file, transaction file and change file.
5 Give three reasons why it is important to make backup copies of files.

Fig 11.9 Databases are in widespread use in all sorts of organisations. Here a booking is being made for a holiday.

Task 1 Database structure

It is important to carefully plan the structure of a database before you start creating one. Using the following table you must:

1 Choose the most suitable field type for each field.
2 Set the maximum field length for each field. (See different field types on page 109.)
3 Identify the key field that must be a unique identifier. Why have you have chosen this particular field as the key field?

Field	Field type	Field length (In characters)	Key field (Tick the field that should be the key field)
Surname			
Forename			
Date of birth			
Gender			
Form			
Roll number			
Admission date			
Photograph			
Address			
Postcode			
Telephone number			

4 Design and produce a data capture form to collect this information from new students as they enter the school.
5 What techniques have you used on the form to minimise errors in collecting the information?
6 Test the form on a friend to see whether he or she gives the information you would expect. If there are problems, how would you modify the form?

Task 2 Creating a file

1 Start a database program and create a new file called *Students*.
2 Using the structure outlined in Task 1, create the 11 fields, making sure that you give each field a proper field name.
3 Set the field length for each field according to the table (if your database program will let you).
4 Now set the field type for each field. This can be difficult in some databases. Don't panic! Either use the program's help menu, or ask a friend or your teacher for help. If possible, set the role-number field as Auto Number so that the database automatically assigns a unique number to each student.

Task 3 Students records

Download the file **Data1.csv** from the OUP website (**www.oup.com/uk/ictforgcse**). The file contains student records. The fields in the file **Data1.csv** that contain data are: Surname, Forename, Date of Birth, Gender and Form.

1 Import the data in **Data1.csv** into the database you created for Task 2. Different databases do this in slightly different ways. So check with your teacher how to do this.
2 The records are not in alphabetical order. Sort the database by surname. Then print out a copy.
3 A list of students has to be printed showing the students in Form order, followed by Gender and then by Surname. Sort the database to achieve this and then print out a copy.
4 Some of the data is incorrect. Students in Form 11 BZ should in fact be in 11 RC. Rather than correct each record record-by-record, most databases include a Replace feature. Use this Replace command to replace 11 BZ with 11 RC *in one go*. Ask your teacher for help if you do not know how to do this.
5 Search the database to select just the students in Form 11 RC and print a list of these students in alphabetical order.
6 Describe how you produced this list, including how you set the search criteria for the database.

Task 4 Interrogating census data

Download the file **Data2.csv** from the OUP website. The file contains information from the 1851 census about people living in the parish of St George, Colegate, Norwich.

Import the data in Data2.csv into your database program. Different databases do this in slightly different ways. So check with your table how to do this.

Note that the OUP website also has the same file in different database formats, such as Microsoft Access, so use one of these files if it is easier.

Interrogate the database to find the answer to these questions.

1   What was the total number of residents in Colegate in 1851?
2   How many:
    ■   males (Gender = M) are there?
    ■   females (Gender = F) are there?
    ■   servants are there? (Occupation = servant). Are most servants male or female?
3   What is the name and age of the youngest live-in servant? To find out, sort the current list of servants in order of age.
4   What was the youngest age for marriage for girls? Search for people who are female, married and less than 24 years old. (Marital Status = married, Gender = F, age < 24).
5   Search for all the residents of household 260. (Survey Order = 260). What is the occupation of George Bell?
6   Search for all who are the same age as you. How many of them are obviously not at school?

Note For each search you do, it is very useful to annotate the printouts with the way you set up the search – the search criteria. This sort of evidence is very helpful with coursework to show that you really do know how to search a database.

Task 5 Mail merging

Mail merging is the process of combining names and addresses stored in a data file with the main document (usually a form letter) created in a word processor.

1   Download the file **Data3.csv** from the OUP website.
2   Using this data, create a mail-merge document in your word processor. This should be a letter addressed to the parents/carers of the students, informing them of a forthcoming parents' evening. (An example of how to do this is given on the OUP website.)

Ask your teacher for help if you do not know how to mail merge.

The four steps to successful mail merging are:

◆   Open/create the word-processed document you want to use.
◆   Open/create the data file.
◆   Create the main mail-merge document with the field to be merged.
◆   Merge the data.

Data systems are in widespread use at school, at work and in the home. When you use the Internet to access online encyclopaedias, such the *Encyclopaedia Britannica* (www.britannica.com) or use an encyclopaedia on CD-ROM or DVD-ROM, such as *Encarta, World Book* or *Grolier*, you are using a data system (Fig 12.1). These encyclopaedias allow you to browse and search articles

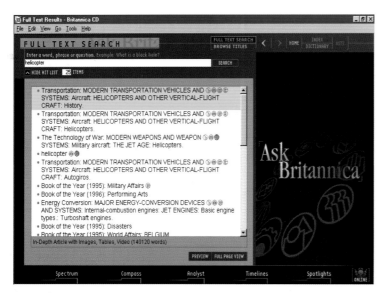

Fig 12.1 Modern encyclopaedias on CD or DVD-ROM allow you to quickly search thousands of articles to find the information that you want.

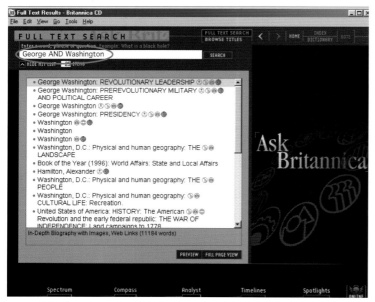

Fig 12.2 Using the boolean operators AND, OR, NOT helps you narrow or expand a search.

(text), pictures, maps, sounds, animations and videos. Most of these encyclopaedias also have links to relevant websites.

When using the Internet, you can often use online data systems without realising it. Some families regularly shop via the Internet using home-shopping services such as those offered by supermarkets (for example, Tesco's, www.tesco.com). Data systems such as this arrange things by subject – for example, buying a videotape. You start with this heading, and then work your way down through menus until you find the product you want to buy.

Most data systems allow you to carry out keyword searches. The secret to quickly find the information you want is not to search on a single word but to make your keywords as specific as possible (see pages 120–3).

Boolean operators

When searching an encyclopaedia or the Internet, you can use what are called **Boolean operators**. At first, these operators seem very difficult to understand, but are in fact reasonably straightforward when you actually use them. Time spent experimenting with Boolean operators is time well spent, as using them will save you a great deal of time when searching (Fig 12.2).

Boolean operators help you to narrow or widen a search. They allow you to combine several words in one search or to exclude certain terms from your results. There are three Boolean operators available:

◆ The AND operator searches for entries which contain all your search terms. For example, searching for 'cat AND mouse' would find articles that only contain both the term 'cat' and the term 'mouse'.
◆ The OR operator searches for entries which contain one or more of your search terms. For example, searching for 'Hitler OR Germany' finds entries containing either one word or the other, or both words.

◆ The NOT operator searches for results which do not contain your search term. For example, searching for 'Apple NOT Computer' would find articles about apples, but not about Apple computers.

AND and NOT operators can also be used together. For example, 'coffee AND NOT biscuits' finds all entries which contain the word 'coffee', but not the word ' biscuits'.

Wild cards

A **wild-card character** is a special symbol that stands for a letter or a number. It can also stand for more than one letter or number. Wild-card characters are used in word processing programs to search for text, as well as for searching in data systems. Popular wild cards are the asterisk (★), which can be used to represent one or more characters, and the question mark (?) for a single character. Examples of the uses of wild cards are:

◆ Searching for 'sol?' finds all four-letter words beginning 'sol'. For example, sold and sole.
◆ Searching for '???on' finds all five-letter words ending in 'on'. For example, bacon and Devon.
◆ Using ? as a wild-card search in the middle of a word is also helpful if you are not exactly sure how to spell what it is you are looking for. For example, type 'Dick?ns' if you are unsure whether the author's name is spelt Dickins or Dickens.
◆ Searching for 'shop★' matches all words beginning 'shop', including shop itself. For example, shop, shopping, shopkeeper, shoplifters.
◆ The pattern '★ion' matches all words ending 'ion'. For example, billion, cushion, fashion, lion, onion.

In most encyclopaedias, it is also possible to search and browse by media type (animations, movies, pictures, sounds) and topic (art, geography, history, science etc). By browsing or searching in this way, you can quickly focus in on the information that you want to find. In Fig 12.4, you can see how easy it is to find details of all the geographical maps of Europe in an encyclopaedia. This is done by entering Europe in the word search box, then selecting map as the media type and geography as the topic.

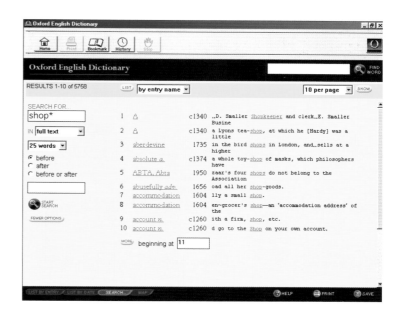

Fig 12.3 A wild-card character is a special symbol that stands for a letter or number. This screenshot shows a wild-card search of the Oxford English Dictionary for all of the words beginning 'shop'.

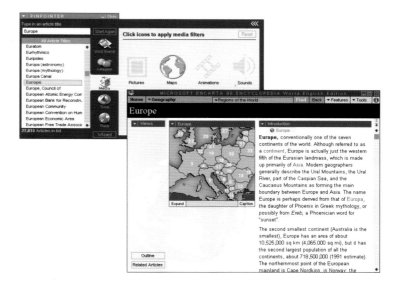

Fig 12.4 You can also search most encyclopaedias by media type and topic.

QUESTIONS

1 What are the three types of Boolean operator? Give an example of how you could use each one to help you search.
2 What are the two most popular wild cards used in searching? Give an example of how you could use each of these wild cards to help you to search.

The World Wide Web (www) is based on millions of pages of information linked together and viewed by Internet browsers. An Internet browser is a software application that allows you to go to resources and websites on the Internet. Popular browsers include Microsoft Internet Explorer and Netscape Navigator.

Every site on the Internet has an address known as a **URL (uniform resource locator)**. In order to access a site, you enter its address (URL) into the Internet browser. There is a space at the top of the screen (called Address) for you to enter the URL. For example, typing www.bbc.co.uk would find the BBC.

You will see addresses that start http://. The http tells you that it is a website. To save you time, most browsers today do not require you to type the http://. You just type www followed by the rest of the address. Sometimes you may also see an address that starts ftp. Ftp sites are not websites, but sites that allow you to transfer files across the Internet.

If you don't know the URL of the site you want, you can use a search engine. A search engine is a software application that finds websites using keywords. Search engines have their own websites. A list of some of the most popular search engines is shown in the table opposite.

Understanding Internet addresses

//	A double slash (//) in an address gives you the path to the computer (server) on which the resources are stored	.uk	.uk in an address indicates that the country is the United Kingdom: for example, www.bbc.co.uk
/	A slash (/) in an address shows the path (route) to where resources are stored on the server. In other words, the exact location	.edu	.edu in an address indicates a US university: for example, www.harvard.edu
		.ac	.ac in an address indicates a UK university: for example, www.uea.ac.uk – the University of East Anglia
http	This tells you that it is a website. Http (hypertext transfer) is the set of rules (protocols) used to show web pages on a computer that have been retrieved from web servers	.org	.org in an address indicates an organisation of some kind: for example, www.literacytrust.org.uk
ftp	File transfer protocol. Ftp sites are not websites, but sites that allow you to transfer files across the Internet	.gov	.gov in an address indicates a government department or organisation: for example, www.ofsted.gov.uk – OFSTED inspects schools
.com	.com in an address indicates a commercial organisation: for example, www.microsoft.com	.sch	.sch in an address indicates a school: for example, www.cns.norfolk.sch.uk – City of Norwich School (CNS) in Norfolk
.co	.co in an address indicates a company or commercial organisation: for example, www.amazon.co.uk	.html or .htm	.html will often appear at the end of an address and indicates that it is a file which contains hypertext: that is, a web page

Whenever you find a site that you think you would like to visit again, you can 'bookmark' it, by adding it to your list of favourite sites. By opening your list of favourite sites, you can go straight to any site you have bookmarked without typing the URL or using a search engine.

There are two distinct approaches to searching the Web – directories and keyword searches – although most sites offer both. Directories, sometimes known as channels, arrange things by subject, like the *Yellow Pages* telephone directory (see also www.yell.com). You start with a general heading, and then work your way down. For example, to find the University of East Anglia using the Yahoo! search engine, you would choose: Education>UK>Higher Education>Colleges and Universities>University of East Anglia.

Other search engines index the words on tens of millions of web pages. This indexing is undertaken by software robots (also known as spiders) that continually search the Web for new sites or changed web pages. Indexing web pages in this way allows you to search using keywords.

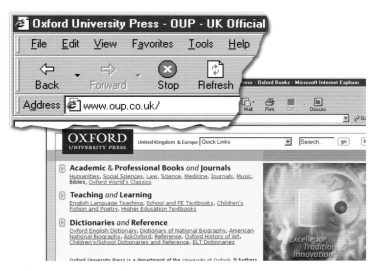

Fig 12.5 To move around the Internet, type in a web address

Fig 12.6 You can choose from a range of search engines to help you to search the Internet

Popular search engine	Address (URL)
AltaVista	http://www.uk.altavista.com
Ask Jeeves	http://www.ask.co.uk
Excite	http://www.excite.co.uk
Google	http://www.google.co.uk
Hotbot	http://www.hotbot.lycos.com
Infoseek	http://www.infoseek.com
Lycos	http://www.lycos.co.uk
Mamma	http://www.mamma.com
UK Plus	http://www.ukplus.co.uk
Yahoo!	http://www.uk.yahoo.com
Yell	http://www.yell.co.uk

QUESTIONS

1 What is a URL? Why are URLs important when using the Internet?
2 What information about country, county and organisation can you find out from the web address www.cns.norfolk.sch.uk?
3 What is a search engine? Give three examples of popular search engines.
4 What are the two main approaches to searching the World Wide Web?

A popular way to search the Internet is to carry out keyword searches. To do this, you must enter some keywords and then instruct the search engine to start searching (Fig 12.7). Clicking on a search button with your mouse usually does this.

The search engine will list all the sites that match the keyword(s) you have typed in. Sometimes there will be thousands, or even millions, of these. To help you, the search engine will show you what it thinks are the best sites that match your search request. These sites will be in a ranked order, with the search engine deciding what it thinks are the closest matches to what you want to find (Fig 12.8).

Clicking on a website in the suggested list takes you to that particular site. When you have finished looking at the found site, clicking on the back arrow returns you to the search engine screen. Most websites include **links** that will take you directly to other sites. Links are shown as coloured or highlighted text. Clicking on a link takes you to that site. In this way, you can move from site to site without using the search engine or entering a series of URLs.

Remember Whenever you find a site that you think you would like to visit again, you can bookmark it, by adding it to your list of favourite sites. By opening your list of favourite sites, you can go straight to a site you have bookmarked without typing the URL or using a search engine.

There is a number of choices available to you when you get to the page(s) of information you want. You can print the page, copy and paste text and pictures to another application, or save the whole web page or its separate elements (text, pictures, sounds etc.) to your own computer or on to a disk.

Advanced (complex) searches

Most search engines allow you to conduct more advanced searches. Advanced searches quickly allow you to focus in on what you want to find (Fig 12.9). Mastering how to use advanced searches is well worth the effort, as it can save valuable minutes – even hours! – in getting to the information you want.

Fig 12.7 When entering the keywords for your search, try to be as specific as possible.

Fig 12. 8 The search engine shows you what it thinks are the best sites for your search. Note: it has found swimming clubs as well as pool (bar game) clubs.

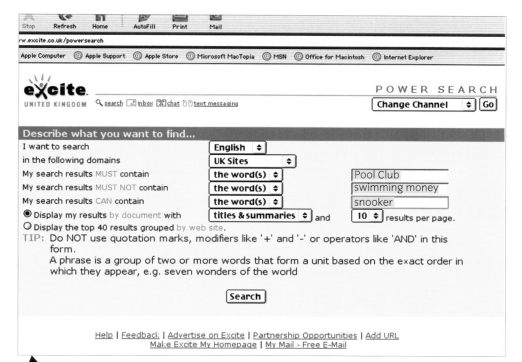

Warning Because you find information on the Web, it does not mean that that information is correct. Be critical of what you find. Check whether the source of the information source is reputable. If you can, compare the information found with that from other sources.

Tips to help you search

◆ Try not to search on a single word.

◆ Make your keywords as specific as possible.

◆ Look for a specific name or a phrase by putting it in quotes: for example, "Norwich City Football Club".

◆ Make your search more specific by using Boolean operators (see pages 118–19). Boolean operators, represented by the words AND, OR and NOT, allow you to look for certain words whilst ignoring others. AND will narrow your search. For example, 'science AND museum' only looks for documents with both words in them. You can use OR to find websites with either one word or the other. Some search engines use the plus sign (+) before a word to include the word in a search, and a minus sign (-) before a word to exclude it.

◆ Use wild cards. For example, entering 'educ★' finds education, educational, educated. Symbols used to represent a wild card vary from one search engine to another, the most common ones being ★ and ?.

◆ When you have difficulty finding what you want, try a different search engine. Search engines can index different websites, or different pages, and they each conduct searches in slightly different ways.

Have a go at using different search engines and decide which is best for you. Try the same search in different engines and see what they do. Remember that the way you search might depend on which engine you use. For example, AltaVista uses Boolean operators whilst Google does not.

QUESTIONS

1 What is a keyword search?

2 Why might you want to bookmark a website?

Task 1 Searching an encyclopaedia

This task involves your going online and using the Internet. You may find that access to the Internet can be slow at certain times of the day. This is nearly always caused by the very large number of people using the Internet at peak times. To avoid this, a good time to access sites (such as the site mentioned in this task) is in the morning. That is, before people in the USA and Canada get up and go to work!

1 Go online and type in the URL **www.britannica.com** to go to the *Encyclopaedia Britannica* website.

2 You are going to search for an article about CD-ROMs: enter the keyword CD-ROM into the search box.

3 The website will now search its databases looking for all mentions of CD-ROM. On the results screen, you'll see the outcome from searching *Encyclopaedia Britannica*, the World Wide Web, magazines, and books. You can also click on hot-linked titles to learn more.

4 Now narrow your search by choosing the Advanced Search option. You can then choose whether to search the encyclopaedia, the Web, magazines or books. Click Encyclopaedia.

5 Now set the search conditions to: Searching for documents for which each entire document contains the exact phrase CD-ROM.

6 Submit your request.

7 Go to the article on CD-ROM. In what year was the first audio CD introduced? When was DVD introduced?

You now have four options:

◆ To save the page as text (with no formatting) or as a web page (HTML).

◆ Copy the article and paste the text into a word processed document.

◆ Print the article.

◆ e-mail the article.

Choose one of these options.

Task 2 Comparing search engines

Your task is to compare four different search engines available on the World Wide Web. A list of some of the main search engines is on page 121. For the purposes of this task, use the following four web sites. (If you wish, you may change one to your own favourite search engine and choose others from the list on page 121.)

Yahoo!
www.uk.yahoo.com/
AltaVista
www.uk.altavista.com/
Google
www.google.co.uk
Ask Jeeves
www.askjeeves.co.uk

The Crucible is a popular play by Arthur Miller, based on the witchcraft trials of 1692 in Salem, Massachusetts. *The Crucible* is often studied as part of GCSE and A-level courses. Your task is to find suitable resources on the Web that could be used by students who are writing essays or doing a project about the play. Using your four search engines:

1 Do a keyword search for *The Crucible* using the first search engine.
   ◆ How many hits on *The Crucible* did the search engine make?
   ◆ How easy was it to find information about the play *The Crucible*, rather than anything else with 'crucible' in it?
   ◆ How close are you to finding the information you want?

2 Now repeat your search using the other three search engines and answer the above questions for each one.

3 Look at your answers for all four search engines. What in your opinion was the best search engine to use? Give reasons for your answer.

4 Does using other keywords, such as *Arthur Miller's The Crucible, Salem, Salem and witchcraft*, help in your search? Can you think how else to search for this information using Boolean operators?

Task 3 Using Boolean operators

For this task, you will search for articles about the so-called Great Depression in the world economy that started in 1929. The Great Depression led to widespread unemployment in industrialised countries.

1 Go online and access the *Encyclopaedia Britannica* website (**www.britannica.com**) or use an encyclopaedia on CD-ROM that you have access to.
2 Conduct a search using the keyword *depression*.
3 When you get the search results, you will notice that they include depressions to do with the weather, depressions to do with history and mental depression (feeling very unhappy). In other words, your search has been too wide.
4 To narrow your search, enter *depression AND 1929*. What has happened to your search results?
  Tip There is a shortcut to using the Boolean operators AND, OR, NOT. This is to use the plus sign (+) for AND and the minus sign (-) for NOT.
5 Conduct another search using the keyword *depression*. Look carefully at the search results.
6 Now search using the keywords *depression NOT mental NOT weather*. Better still, replace the NOT operator with a minus and enter the keywords: *depression -mental -weather*. Look carefully at the search results. What has happened?
7 Which method of searching was the best in getting you to the information about the Great Depression that started in 1929?
8 Can you think of any different ways in which you could have searched for this information?

Task 4 Finding maps of places

GIS systems were mentioned on page 106. There are several such systems which are freely available for you to interrogate on the Internet. They have information of a geographical nature which you can access by searching in a range of ways.

If you want to find map information about any place in the United Kingdom, you could visit any of the following websites:

www.multimap.com/map/places.cgi
www.streetmap.co.uk/
www.ordsvy.gov.uk/getamap/getamap_index.htm

1 To locate a map of a place, how do you think you might need to search the website? What would your criteria be?
2 Visit these websites to see how many different ways you can find a map of a particular place. Which method do you find easiest?
3 Can you find a current map of the location of your school or home and an historical map of the same area from any of these websites? When was the historical map made? How different is the area around your school/home now? Produce a report that includes these maps along with your observations about how the area has changed. (You will need to use your copy-and-paste skills, together with word-processing or DTP skills to complete this.)

The following two websites let you find map information internationally:

www.mapblast.com/myblast/index.mb
www.mapquest.com/

4 Choose two very different places in the world and see how detailed a map you can find about these places.
5 Is the detail on the maps of these two places as good as that on the maps of the UK place you found? If it is not as good, can you think why this might be?
6 Do these websites work in exactly the same way as the UK map websites? Do you give the same information to find a place or is different information needed? Why do you think this is so?

You are surrounded by computer control systems but probably don't know it. If you think that a computer system has to have a keyboard, a screen and a big box, then think again. There are more computer systems in the world that don't possess these features than those that do, and such computer systems are mostly control systems. Control systems, such as pedestrian crossings, are met in every aspect of your daily life (Fig 13.1).

Fig 13.1
Control systems are around us all the time.

Control is all about making devices do what we want them to do, in the right order and under the right conditions (Fig 13.2).

At home

In the kitchen, microwave cookers, washing machines and tumble dryers all have control systems inside them to make them do their job at the press of a button. In the sitting room, remote control televisions, video recorders and audio systems have built-in control systems.

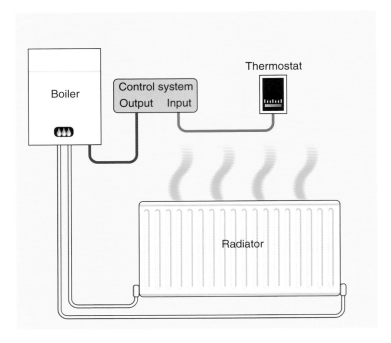

Fig 13.2 The control process is like any other information system process. Information from sensors feeds a processing unit, which in turn tells output devices what to do. For example, in a central heating system, the heat generated by the radiators is fed back to the input sensors to stop the rooms getting too hot.

The central heating system comes on at a particular time of day and goes off later. While the system is on, it automatically makes decisions about the temperature in your house. When the house is too cold, it will turn the boiler on. When the house is too hot, it will turn the boiler off. Do you want only the hot water to be on, or the radiators as well? The system is collecting such information all the time and responding according to what the inputs tell it. This is a control system which works automatically.

Out and about

All modern cars have a management system which tells the engine what to do. This controls the flow of fuel to the engine and stops the engine from going too fast. Remote-control locks respond to a signal from the key to lock the doors.

Traffic-light systems respond to traffic passing over sensors in the road and change the lights accordingly or stop all the traffic to let pedestrians cross the road. Rail-crossing barriers come down automatically to stop the traffic to let trains pass.

Buildings with air conditioning have sensors which detect the temperature and humidity inside the buildings and turn on the heating and/or the humidifiers when needed.

In the high street

A cash dispenser is a complex control system which is part of a wide area network. It detects your customer information from the card you put in, but will not let you have any money until you give the correct PIN code. The display then asks how much money you want. The system selects the appropriate number of notes and passes them out of the machine to you.

A security system in a shop detects the tag on a stolen item as the thief passes through the screens. This sends a signal to the control system to make an alarm sound. The sensors on automatic doors detect when people are near and make the doors open. The doors also have sensors which tell the system when a person is still between the doors, so that the system will not close them onto the person.

In the factory

You have probably seen TV advertisements showing computer-controlled robots welding or painting cars on a production line. There are many other uses for computer-controlled systems in factories. They are most frequently used in situations where the work is tedious and repetitive, or where the environment is potentially dangerous to humans.

CNC (computer-numerically-controlled) machine tools are linked to computer design systems to streamline the design-to-make process (Fig 13.3). This is called CAD/CAM. First, the product is designed very accurately on a computer with some design software. Then the design is transferred into a file which will tell a CNC machine tool what to do. For example, if the machine is a lathe, the instructions will set the speed of rotation of the workpiece, and tell the cutting tools

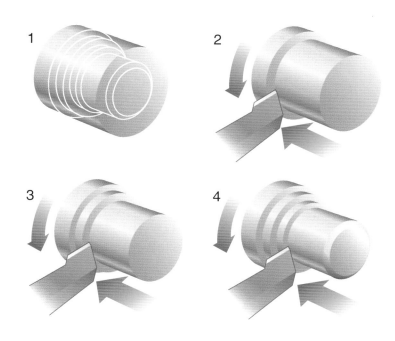

Fig 13.3 A computer-numerically-controlled machine tool is used to make the same product over and over again. CNC machine tools are used for repetitive, tedious tasks which require high accuracy. Here, a rotating workpiece is being cut to form a stepped spindle. The workpiece starts as a cylinder (1). Its diameter is reduced in a series of steps (2–4) by a cutting tool whose position and rate of movement are computer-controlled.

where to move, in what order to make the cuts and how fast to cut the workpiece. The lathe will produce as many precise copies of the original computer design as are required.

In entertainment

Computer control of lighting systems is used in clubs, theatres and other places of entertainment. Varilights® are the most obvious example of controlled lights but a whole lighting rig can be controlled by a computer, where the sequence of lighting effects is stored and replayed as required. Other stage and scenery effects can also be computer-controlled.

QUESTIONS

1 Give three examples – one each from your home, a supermarket and a factory – of things which have control systems. Describe briefly how one of your examples works.

2 You are creating a rock musical for a large stage. Describe some of the lighting effects you would like to have and how you might control them.

A control system consists of some sensors which input information, a processing unit (computer) which decides how to respond to the inputs, and output devices which do what is required (Fig 13.4). A control system also needs an interface unit between the computer and the input sensors and the output devices. This unit turns the signals from the sensors into something that the computer can understand, and the signals from the computer into something that will work the output devices.

Another major reason for having an interface unit is to get the correct voltages to work the various electrical parts. For example, if you are controlling lights on a stage show, they need 240 volts and large currents to work at their full brightness. The electronics in computers work at 5 volts in most systems. If you were to connect a stage lamp directly to the computer electronics, there would be no light and probable damage to the computer.

The same is true for sensors. Some are analogue sensors which need to have their analogue signals changed into the digital signals that the computer can understand (Fig 13.5). This is done by an electronic analogue–to–digital

converter. There could also be voltage differences between the sensors and the computer that the interface unit needs to deal with. The purpose of the interface is to make all parts of the system work with each other.

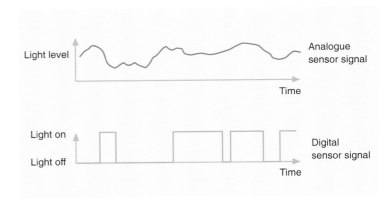

Fig 13.5 Digital light sensors can only tell the system whether the light is on or off. Analogue light sensors can tell the system how bright the light is.

The processing unit in a control system will be a computer which has a program built into it. It will usually not be like the computers that you use, where you change the program by loading a new program from disk. The processing unit has a resident program in its electronic circuits. Such a system is called an **embedded controller**. Embedded controllers have only one program in their electronics to do the job they were designed to do. This makes them much cheaper to make because they do not need disk storage devices, a keyboard, a mouse or a screen. Once the system has been tested to make sure that it behaves as it should, these elements are not needed. The outputs will be the things that are being controlled, not the screen.

Controlling things

Control systems are **real-time systems** which rely on feedback from the environment in order to work. They need to be able to respond immediately to the current conditions as described by the sensors and to let the processing unit take the appropriate action. A railway-crossing control system would not be very useful or safe if it did not respond immediately to the oncoming train and stop the traffic!

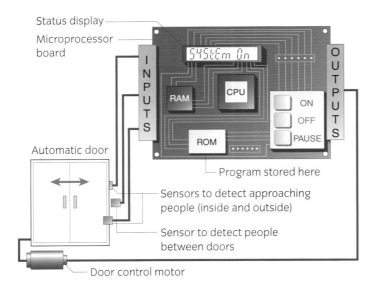

Fig 13.4 A typical control system looks like this. Note that it does not have a screen, disk or keyboard. The program is stored in ROM.

To do this, there has to be a computer program which is constantly looking at the data from the sensors and making decisions about what the output devices should do.

Controlling something often involves identifying sequences of events and making sure that they happen in the right order. This is often represented as a flow chart or flow diagram (Fig 13.6).

What is the impact of control?

On the previous pages, the impact of computers on our lives at work and at leisure was mentioned. Computer manufacturing systems are doing many tedious and repetitive tasks. In electronic circuit production, the components are automatically put in the right place on the circuit boards and then automatically soldered into position. The speed and accuracy at which these machines work are greater than those of skilled workers. The danger to the workers from the heat generated by soldering is removed by having automatic soldering systems.

Automatic railway signalling and barrier systems have replaced crossing keepers. On minor branch lines, crossing keepers used to wait for long periods between trains. When a train did come, they would have to set the signals and open and close the crossing gates. Now this can be done automatically and monitored from a central control centre by a small group of railway workers.

The number of people needed in such areas of work has changed and usually been reduced. The skills the workers need have also changed. Rather than doing the repetitive tasks themselves, they now keep the machinery running.

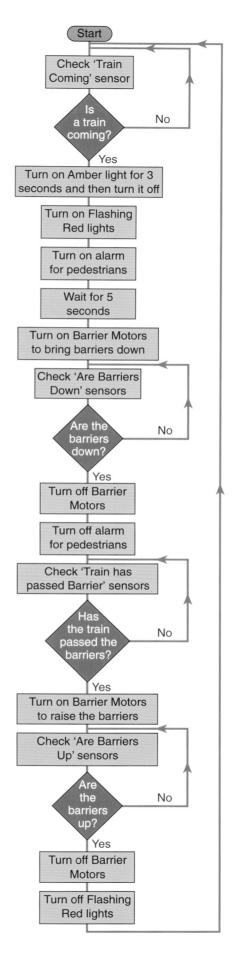

Fig 13.6
A flowchart for an automatic rail-crossing barrier system. Can you see any feedback in this system?

QUESTIONS

1 Explain briefly what a control system consists of.
2 What is the meaning of the term embedded controller? Give its main features.
3 How have control systems made an impact on our lives? Give two examples.

To do control work, you need a control interface connected to your computer and a program to build your solutions. You will need a keyboard, mouse and screen so that you can create the control solution, see what is going on and make changes so that the system does exactly what you want (Fig 13.7).

Fig 13.7 A typical control system used in schools. To write the control program, you need a keyboard and a screen to see that you have not made any mistakes. Once the program is working, you do not need these elements.

There is a wide variety of interfaces and programming methods available. Here, we will talk about approaches to control problems. The specifics of how to write the program will come from your teacher or the manuals with the systems which you have access to.

Designing a control system

You have to analyse the situation. What needs to be done? What outputs are required from the system? You must decide which output devices to use and how many of them. Possibly, you will have to design and make a model which involves mechanical systems to be moved under computer control. You will also need to choose which and how many input sensors to use. What will the system need to know about what is going on (and has happened), so that it can make sensible decisions about what to make the output devices do?

The next step is to plan the sequence of events. Describe what needs to happen and in what order. This will get you to a position where you will be able to create a flow chart. The flow chart will describe in detail all the steps of the sequence that the control system will have to execute – which output device comes on when. It will also describe how the system will react to the signals from the input sensors you select.

When you have completed this, you are ready to build your control model and connect the input sensors and output devices to the interface. Then build your control program. Depending on which program you use, you might have to work out how to create the computer program from your flow chart. This will mean that you have to understand the programming language and be able to write simple computer programs.

Tip If you have not done much programming, don't worry. Keep your program simple and try to break down the problem (and the solution) into small chunks (procedures). Build your solution up with a series of working building blocks rather than have one large and complicated program.

Control program languages

Common control programs for schools use one of two approaches to make programming simple.

Some programs use a visual approach which looks similar to your flow chart. You will build your working answer by constructing the flow chart on screen and filling each step with the appropriate commands. These commands may set the pattern of ons and offs you want on the outputs, and instruct the computer to look at the sensor(s) to see what is happening, or to make some decisions based on what it has just found out about the state of the system.

Other programs use a programming language which you will key into the computer. These often work like Logo programming. They will have particular 'words' or commands which will make the computer do particular things. They will let you build procedures – functional blocks of programming which can then be linked together to create a larger, more complex control program sequence.

Trying it out

When you have a solution – a model connected to the interface and a program to make the model work – it is time to see if it works as expected.

For the test, you will have the initial specification to check the result against. You intended your control system to do a particular job in a certain way. You will need to check that it does everything you designed it to do, that it does it in the right order and that it responds to the input sensors in the right way.

It makes sense to prepare a test plan before you start, which states what you will do to test your system and how you expect it to respond. Alongside this, you should record what your system actually did. The final part of your test is to check that what actually happened was what you expected. If they are not the same, you have to find out why and make some changes to your solution. Finally, try the changed version and do the tests again until your control system works correctly.

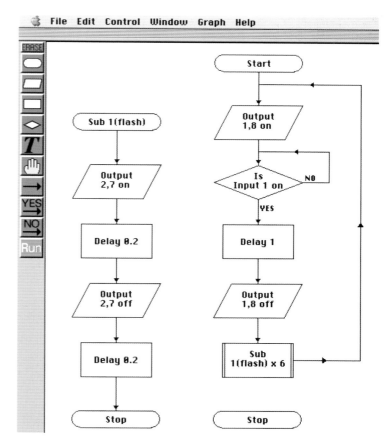

Fig 13.8 A solution to a control problem created with Flowol, which is a flow-chart-based program.

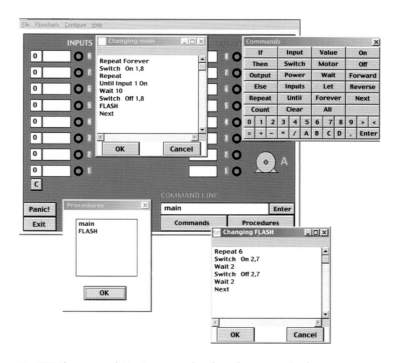

Fig 13.9 The same solution in a procedure-based programming language.

QUESTIONS

1 Your friend wants to design a control system and has asked you to help her. What is the first step you would advise her to take?

2 For what purpose would you use a flow chart when designing a control system?

3 Describe briefly the two approaches to control programming which most students use.

Control systems do not always have to control real objects. It is possible to control imaginary objects on a screen. The most common example of this is to control the movements of a screen turtle using Logo as the programming language. You will probably have come across this in primary school, as well as in secondary school.

How to control a turtle

A turtle responds to commands. To make it move in a certain way, you can put together a sequence of commands, such as FORWARD 100 RIGHT 60 BACKWARD 25 LEFT 135. The commands follow a simple pattern. You tell the turtle what to do together with a number, which tells it how much to do. For example, RIGHT 60 means turn 60° to the right.

This should be familiar to you. By using the whole set of commands available in Logo, you can make the turtle do very complicated things. It is often used in mathematics to help students to understand ideas in geometry. You can also create new words for Logo to understand. This is done by creating procedures.

To draw an equilateral triangle with a side of 150 units, the set of commands would be FORWARD 150 RIGHT 120 FORWARD 150 RIGHT 120 FORWARD 150 RIGHT 120. To save writing this every time you want a triangle, you could write a procedure. The table shows three different procedures which would all create the same triangle.

Type TRIANGLE1 or TRIANGLE2 at the command level and a triangle will be drawn. The procedure TRIANGLE3

is slightly different, as you need to add a number which tells Logo how long to make the sides. TRIANGLE3 150 would make the same triangle as the other two procedures. TRIANGLE3 will let you make any size of triangle you wish by including a variable (here the variable is :LENGTH).

Once you have defined some procedures for simple shapes, you can then write more procedures which use the basic shapes to create regular patterns. For example, using TRIANGLE2 it is possible to produce these patterns.

TRIANGLE2 will produce:

REPEAT 5 [TRIANGLE2 RIGHT 72] will produce:

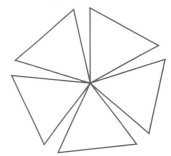

And REPEAT 10 [TRIANGLE2 RIGHT 36] will produce:

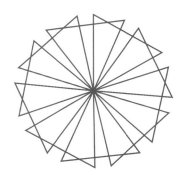

Three procedures to create an equilateral triangle using Logo

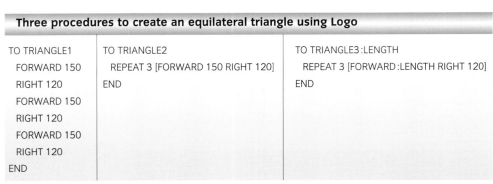

TO TRIANGLE1	TO TRIANGLE2	TO TRIANGLE3 :LENGTH
FORWARD 150	REPEAT 3 [FORWARD 150 RIGHT 120]	REPEAT 3 [FORWARD :LENGTH RIGHT 120]
RIGHT 120	END	END
FORWARD 150		
RIGHT 120		
FORWARD 150		
RIGHT 120		
END		

Programming techniques

As you can see from the examples of Logo commands, there are several ways in which you can program the turtle. If you were going to draw a pattern like the last example, using the procedure TRIANGLE1, it would take you a long time and be very repetitive and tedious. You will save yourself a lot of time by recognising when elements of the program are just repeats of instructions that have gone before. Using repeat commands you will make the procedure elegant and easy to understand.

Creating programs that have variables and letting the computer do some calculations as part of the procedure mean that you can develop very flexible solutions.

If you wanted to be able to draw a range of regular shapes – triangles, squares, pentagons, hexagons – you could build a set of procedures. Your first attempt might be to create a procedure for each shape.

```
TO TRIANGLE :LENGTH
    REPEAT 3 [FORWARD :LENGTH RIGHT 120]
END
TO SQUARE :LENGTH
    REPEAT 4 [FORWARD :LENGTH RIGHT 90]
END
TO PENTAGON :LENGTH
    REPEAT 5 [FORWARD :LENGTH RIGHT 72]
END
TO HEXAGON :LENGTH
    REPEAT 6 [FORWARD :LENGTH RIGHT 60]
END
```

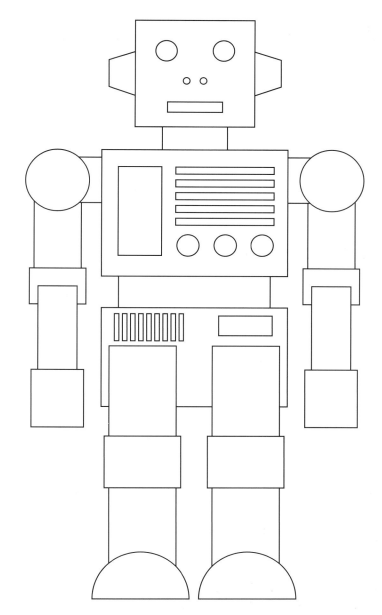

Fig 13.10 It is possible to write a program using Logo which would produce this picture. How many procedures you think would be needed?

It is possible to write just one procedure which uses two variables (instead of the one variable used in the above examples), which will let you draw any regular polygon. You will have to work out the pattern that emerges from these examples. You will need to tell the procedure not just how long the sides are to be but how many sides the shape is to have. The 'super' procedure could be:

```
TO POLYGON :LENGTH :SIDES
    REPEAT :SIDES [FORWARD :LENGTH RIGHT (360 / :SIDES)]
END
```

The command POLYGON 150 6 would draw a regular hexagon with sides of length 150. You have to understand that the turtle must turn 360° ÷ 5 (= 72°) if it is to draw a pentagon, 360° ÷ 6 (= 60°) if it is to draw a hexagon, and so on.

Warning Different versions of Logo might not exactly follow the programming structures in the examples here.

Task 1

In each of the seven scenarios below, you have a diagram of the system to be controlled and a specification of what it has to do. Making a working solution for such systems involves a series of steps which you need to go through to be successful. For each problem you tackle, go through the following steps and document your work so that your teacher can see how you got to your answer.

1. Analyse the situation and select the output devices and sensors to be used in your solution. Then make a sketch of how you will connect them to the interface.

2. Break the problem down into the essential steps of the sequence which are needed for the chosen problem.

3. Create a flow chart which describes all the steps. Include all the details about which outputs will be turned on/off and when, and what the sensors are expected to detect. You need to do this so that you cover every eventuality and make sure that there is no unreliable behaviour in your system.

If you have the resources:

4. Produce a working solution from the flow chart.

5. Then test your solution. Make sure you have a list of what to expect so that you can record what happened.

6. Using the evidence from your tests, evaluate how well your solution works compared with what you expected it to do.

◆ A simple buggy, driven by two independent motors which has to follow the route given in Fig 13.11.

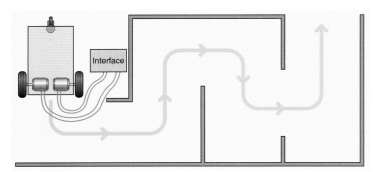

Fig 13.11

◆ A set of lights to be used in a disco. You can choose the pattern(s) and speed of the pattern changes (Fig 13.12).

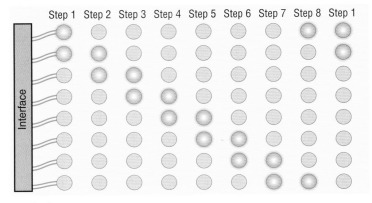

Fig 13.12

◆ A buggy with a single collision sensor mounted on the front, which has to find its own way out of the room shown in Fig 13.13.

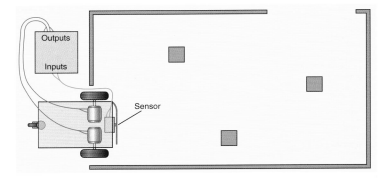

Fig 13.13

◆ An automatic traffic light system for roadworks (Fig 13.14).

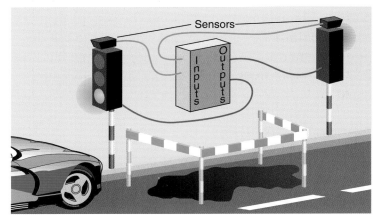

Fig 13.14

♦ A supermarket automatic-door system. It must be able to detect a person coming to the door from either the inside or the outside (Fig 13.15).

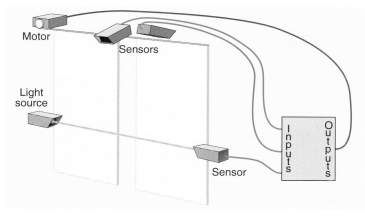

Fig 13.15

♦ An automatic washing machine (Fig 13.16). This should have only one washing programme. How different would the flow chart be if it were a multi-program machine?

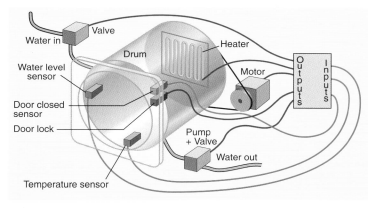

Fig 13.16

♦ A three-floor lift. It needs buttons to call the lift from the outside and buttons inside the lift to tell it which floor to go to.

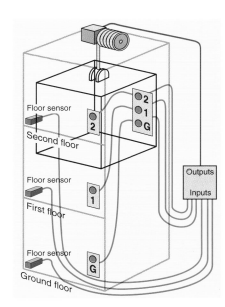

Fig 13.17

Task 2

Controlling a screen turtle with Logo. If your school does not have a Logo program, there is one on the OUP website (**www.oup.com/uk/ictforgcse**). Your teacher or parent may download one from a link on the OUP website.

♦ On pages 132–3, there are some Logo procedures which will draw simple regular shapes. Use these and develop some more. Then write a new procedure, which uses the Logo shape procedures, to draw a simple picture like the one shown in Fig 13.18.

Fig 13.18

♦ Most Logo programs will let you draw lines in different colours and fill shapes with colour. Modify your procedures so that the picture you have drawn becomes a colour picture.

♦ Write programs which will generate the patterns shown in Fig 13.19.

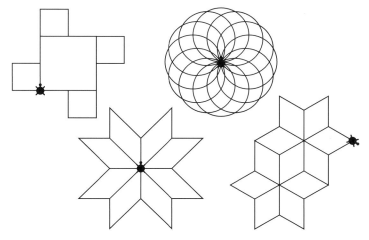

Fig 13.19

♦ Write a program that will create spiral patterns. The spirals do not have to be curved – they could be made up of straight lines.

Computers are used in many areas to collect data from an environment for a variety of purposes (Fig 14.1). The most likely place that you will have come across this is in your science lessons. Here you will have collected data from experiments and processed the data to produce tables or graphs which showed what happened.

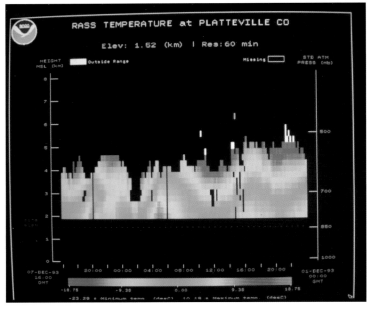

Fig 14.1 A temperature profile formed from data collected at a remote station.

Using automatic data-logging equipment to collect data has three important advantages over manual methods. The first advantage is accuracy. For example, liquid-in-glass thermometers can measure temperature to an accuracy of about 0.5°C. Electronic temperature sensors connected to a computer system are able to measure to an accuracy of at least 0.1°C. (The sensors used in some industries have even higher accuracy.)

The second advantage is the type of data-collecting situations that can be handled. For example, when people are recording information over a long period, their concentration can waver. As a result of this, they forget to take readings when they should. Computer systems, once programmed, will obey instructions and take readings as often as required at any time of day or night. Also, computerised sensing equipment can be placed in situations where it is not safe for humans to

go. An example of this is the constant, real-time monitoring of the performance of a nuclear reactor. This is a highly dangerous environment where measurements must be taken.

The final advantage is speed. No one can measure rapidly occurring events and record them very quickly. Computers can easily take thousands of measurements in a second. This means that events which could not be measured by a person can now be recorded for analysis later.

Computer measuring systems have the capacity to collect large amounts of highly accurate data over very short or long periods of time, which can then be analysed in a wide variety of ways. One such system that you regularly see in action is weather forecasting. The Meteorological Office (and similar organisations in other countries) use automatic remote systems stationed around the world to collect information such as temperature, humidity, rainfall, wind speed and direction, and air pressure (Fig 14.1). They then process this data to help them understand patterns of weather.

The measurement systems mentioned above all rely on the collection of numerical data – the temperature is 21°C or the humidity is 28%. There are also systems which collect visual information. As part of the weather forecasts, you often see images of the weather collected from satellites orbiting the earth (Figs 14.2 and 14.3). These images are not all ordinary photographs. Some of them are taken with cameras which do not respond to light but to heat (infra red), giving meteorologists a different sort of information.

The sensing stations are scattered around the world but they have to feed their collected data to a central computer system to be processed. This is done through a communications network. Since the measurements are not taken directly by the processing computer system, this technique is called **remote sensing** – the sensors are remote from the main system.

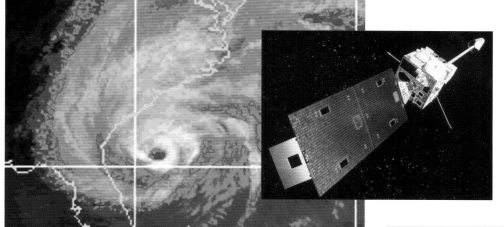

Fig 14.2 Geostationary Operational Environmental Satellites (GOES) provide half-hourly measurements of radiation emitted by, and reflected from, the Earth. From these measurements, atmospheric temperature, winds, moisture and cloud cover are found.

Fig 14.3 A satellite image of Hurricane Floyd taken on 15 September 1999.

Sensors for measuring

All sensors used for measuring with computer systems are electronic. (Computers cannot easily read glass thermometers!) In temperature and humidity sensors, the sensor itself is made of a material whose electrical properties change as a result of changes in the quantity being measured. The sensor, which is built into an electronic circuit, generates varying electrical signals as the quantity changes. These signals are fed to the computer. Like the sensors mentioned in Unit 13, remote sensors need an interface between themselves and the computer.

The continuously varying nature of the quantities being measured produces analogue outputs from the sensors which need to be converted into something that the computer can understand. Computers are digital devices that respond only to ons and offs (binary signals). Temperature, for example, is not an on/off quantity but one which has an infinite number of possible values. To enable the computer to understand these analogue values from the sensors, the interface has to have an analogue-to-digital converter. This turns the analogue values into binary signals (Fig. 14.4).

In Unit 13, many of the sensors had digital outputs. In the railway level-crossing example, the trackside sensor that detects an approaching train needs only to know whether a train is there or not. So, an on/off digital sensor is adequate. A digital temperature sensor would only be able to tell the system that the environment is either hot or cold. It would not be able to tell the system how hot or how cold it is.

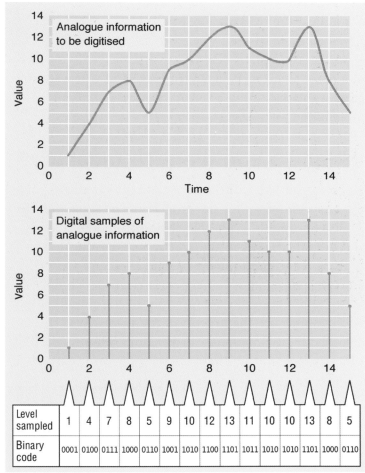

| Level sampled | 1 | 4 | 7 | 8 | 5 | 9 | 10 | 12 | 13 | 11 | 10 | 10 | 13 | 8 | 5 |
| Binary code | 0001 | 0100 | 0111 | 1000 | 0110 | 1001 | 1010 | 1100 | 1101 | 1011 | 1010 | 1010 | 1101 | 1000 | 0110 |

Fig 14.4 The analogue value is sampled regularly and turned into a set of regularly spaced binary numbers that the computer can process.

1. What are the disadvantages of logging data manually compared with automatic data logging?
2. Explain how an electronic temperature sensor works.
3. Explain why the electrical signal from a humidity sensor cannot be fed straight into a computer. Give as much detail as you can.

When you use a data-logging measurement system, you need to analyse the situation and make several decisions as to how to set up the system. What do you need to measure? Which sensors will you need? For how long will the readings need to be recorded? How often will readings need to be taken? If you are not careful about the choices you make at the planning stage, you might not collect the information you want.

Data-logging systems let you store your readings easily in a file which can be analysed later. Will you want to process the data using a spreadsheet or a graphing program?

What do you want to measure?

Suppose you wanted to take measurements to find out the best conditions for growing plants in a greenhouse. Then you might decide that temperatures, light levels and humidity levels in the greenhouse are the appropriate things to measure. The choice of sensors is quite straightforward. A temperature sensor, a light sensor and a humidity sensor would be required. How will you measure the growth of the plants? Will this be recorded by the computer or by some other method?

How to set up the measurement system

This is likely to be a long-term experiment – plants take a long time to grow. The temperature, light levels and humidity are unlikely to change quickly in a greenhouse, so taking readings every few seconds would not be appropriate. You might decide that to take readings every 10 minutes over a period of three weeks is appropriate. This would give over 3000 readings of each quantity. These could then be compared with the growth measurements to see if a pattern can be found.

Another experiment

During the total eclipse of 11 August 1999, some schools set up data-logging equipment to measure temperature and light levels during that morning. If they had set up their experiments in the same way as the one above, then they would have been very disappointed when they came to analyse their results. Taking readings every 10 minutes from 10:00 until midday would have given them 13 measurements, which would have produced the graph shown in Fig 14.5.

Fig 14.5
Taking too few readings can lead to misleading evidence. According to this graph, it does not get very dark during a total eclipse.

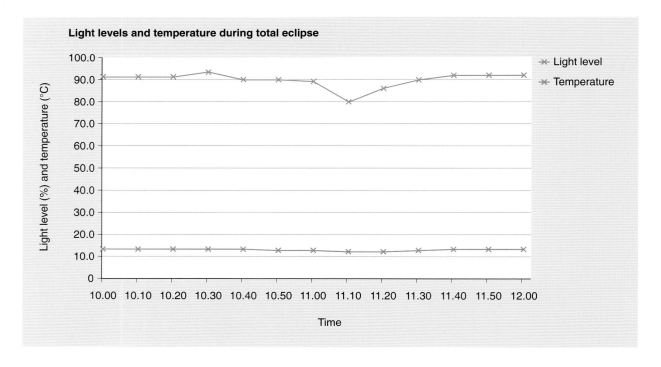

Light levels and temperature during total eclipse

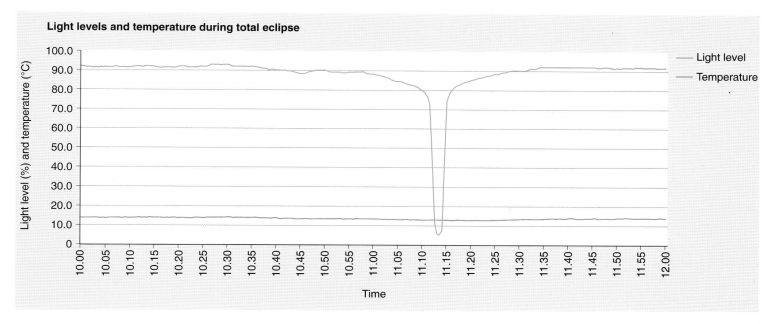

Light levels and temperature during total eclipse

Fig 14.6 *Enough readings were taken here to give a clear picture of what happened. This is how dark it really gets during a total eclipse.*

If they had set the system to take readings every 30 seconds, they would have taken 241 measurements, which would have produced the graph in Fig 14.6.

Choosing the right gap between readings is crucial if you do not want to miss important parts of the data. It would be possible from the first graph to say that it doesn't get very dark during a total eclipse! Totality happened at 11:13 but the readings would have been taken at 11:10 and 11:20. No measurements would have been made during the important moments of the event.

What type of sensors are there?

There is a wide range of quantities that can be measured by data-logging systems. To measure any quantity requires a suitable sensor. There are sensors which can measure, for example, temperature, light level, sound level, air pressure, strength of magnetic fields, voltages and currents in electric circuits, the pH of materials, levels of oxygen present, humidity, and heart rates. A sensor detects changes in the physical quantity it is measuring and, through its electronic circuit, produces a varying electrical signal which the data–logging system can turn into measured values.

An important advantage of such systems is the accuracy with which the sensors can measure. On page 137, the improved accuracy that can result for temperature-measuring systems was mentioned. The accuracy comes from the precise calibration of the sensors.

It is very important that any sensors used in data-logging systems are calibrated correctly. It ensures that as soon as you connect up the system and start taking measurements, you are capturing the real values. If the system were not calibrated, the numbers which the computer receives would be meaningless.

A disadvantage of these systems is usually that you cannot use one maker's sensors with another maker's interface. This would destroy the calibration and distort the values.

QUESTIONS

1   You are designing a data-logging system to monitor the air conditions in a plant making delicate electronic devices. List the decisions you have to make, including your choice of sensors.

2   Why is it important to calibrate sensors? Can a calibrated sensor be used with any interface? Give a reason for your answer.

So far, we have looked at data-logging systems which are put to scientific uses. These systems collect numerical data and then present the information visually. Some scientific systems can capture visual as well as numerical information. Visual systems can capture large amounts of data which over time will show changes in the earth's environment. These are often very remote systems located on orbiting and geo-stationary satellites.

Visual data-logging systems can be used to show the effects of such things as coastal erosion, changes in vegetation, agricultural development, land temperatures (Fig 14.7) and urban growth (Fig 14.8). These systems collect not only the visual data but also other data, so that links can be established between the possible causes and effects.

Infra-red images are also produced by satellite systems. These images show very clearly how heat energy is radiated from, for example, the built environment.

Scientists use systems which are a combination of both imaging and measuring systems. Understanding what is responsible for an observed effect cannot usually be done with pictures alone. Similarly, the numerical values on their own may not always give the full explanation.

Measuring time

Computer systems can measure time intervals of rapidly occurring events extremely accurately. The 'heart' of a computer is a circuit that pulses many million of times every second. The time between the detection of consecutive events at a sensor can be measured by

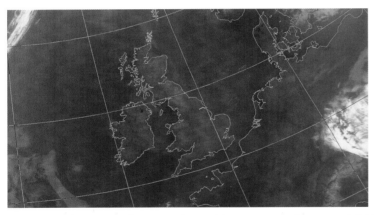

Fig 14.7 Thermal images of Britain and part of the Continent, taken at 02.53 (left) and 12.43 (right) on 27 July 1995. The darker areas have higher temperatures.

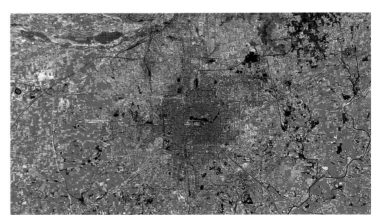

Fig 14.8 False colour satellite images showing the growth of Beijing, China, between 1976 (left) and 1991 (right).

recording how many pulses of the 'heart' occur between them. This is most frequently seen at athletics meetings, where a lap time for each person in a race is recorded to the nearest thousandth of a second.

Fig 14.9 Sensors are used to start and stop the timing systems in a track event, so that each athlete gets his or her own time for the event.

Data logging in control systems

In Unit 13, we looked at control systems but not at the full range of sensors which can be used with such systems. For example, there are many control situations where analogue sensors would be more appropriate to use than digital sensors. Also, many systems need to measure more than one quantity and then decide what to do depending on the measurements taken.

An example of this is the environmental control system in a commercial greenhouse. To get the best growing conditions for a particular plant, the temperature, light and humidity levels need to be carefully controlled. It is not appropriate to crudely monitor the temperature so that the system responds to 'It is hot' or 'It is cold'. The system must make sure that the temperature does not rise above 25 °C or below 16 °C, that the light level does not drop below 2000 lux or rise above 3500 lux (otherwise the leaves may 'burn') and that the humidity is kept between 15% and 60%.

A way of controlling this environment could be as follows. When the sensor tells the system the temperature has fallen to 16 °C or below, heaters would be turned on and all open ventilators would be closed. When the temperature rises to 25 °C or above, the heaters would be turned off and all ventilators would be opened. In a similar way, the light level could be controlled. The blinds would be opened when it

becomes overcast and, when it gets too dark, artificial lighting would be turned on. When it gets too bright, the lighting would be turned off and the blinds drawn to reduce the brightness to an acceptable level. Humidity could be similarly controlled with the measurements being fed back to the system from the humidity sensor.

Feedback

Systems which monitor themselves in this way, by detecting what is going on and adjusting the outputs according to the inputs, are said to have **feedback**. The temperature sensor says it is too cold, so the system turns on the heaters and closes the ventilators. This will raise the temperature and the sensor will tell the system that the temperature is rising. When the temperature reaches the required value, the feedback from the sensor will tell the system to turn off the heaters and open the ventilators.

Feedback is used in many systems but it does not always involve analogue sensors. The examples used in Unit 13 are mostly digital because they work on a simple yes/no answer which is fed back into the system. When the system needs to respond to particular values, then analogue sensors must be used.

Fig 14.10 The humid tropics biome – part of the Eden Project in Cornwall.

QUESTIONS

1 Give two examples of the use of visual data logging.
2 You own a nursery garden in which you have several large greenhouses. Explain how you would ensure that the environment in each greenhouse is right for the plants being grown.
3 What does feedback mean? Give a practical example.

Data logging and display

Each of the following four data-logging scenarios needs to be analysed and a suitable design prepared to show how you intend to go about collecting the required data. For each scenario

◆ analyse the situation and
◆ make some recommendations as to the best way to record and display the essential information.

Remember to document your work so that your teacher can see how you got to your answers.

1 Decide what needs to be measured.
2 Choose suitable sensors to measure the quantities selected in **1**, and decide how they will be set up.
3 Decide how the computer system is to be set up – how many data readings will be taken and how often.
4 How will you make sure that the system will collect all the information you need and not miss essential and important information?
5 In some cases, you will need to think about the best way to store and/or display the findings.

It will not always be possible for you to build these systems in school to try them out. But if you have access to suitable sensors and data-logging equipment, you might like to see if your solution works. You can then make comments on how well the system worked and how effective your solution to the problem was. That is, evaluate your solution.

Task 1

Teachers in a primary school have noticed that sometimes the children find it difficult to concentrate on their work. When they asked the children about the cause, the children blamed the building, saying that sometimes it was not a 'nice' place in which to work. Teachers have noticed that it seems to be worst in the summer and on wet days at any time of year. Design an environmental data collection system that will produce some evidence which will help the teachers to find out what might be the cause.

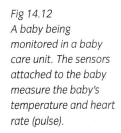

Fig 14.12
A baby being monitored in a baby care unit. The sensors attached to the baby measure the baby's temperature and heart rate (pulse).

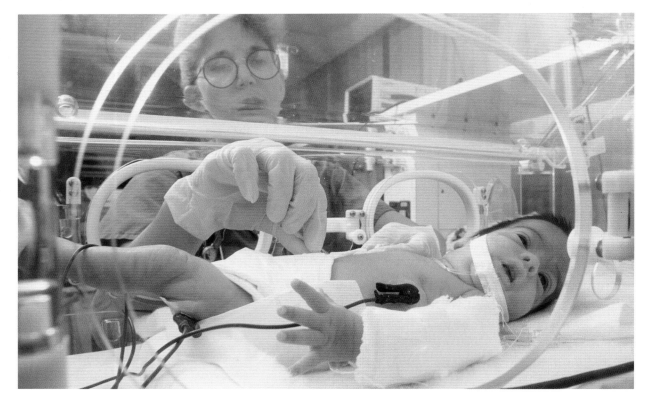

Task 2

A group of environmentalists are monitoring pollution in a stream. Fish and other water-living animals have been found dead on several occasions and the group think it might be due to a lack of oxygen or to some chemicals making the water too acid to sustain life. What evidence will the group need to support these suspicions, and how should it be presented?

Task 3

A baby unit in a hospital needs a system to monitor the welfare of babies in intensive-care incubators. The medical team need to collect data on each baby's heart rate (pulse) and temperature to make sure all is well. This system needs to show the carers what the current position is with the health of each baby. It also needs to store and display the history of the measurements so that the carers can detect any changes (see Fig 14.12).

Task 4

The staff of a supermarket, which sells fresh fruit, vegetables, meats and dairy produce, need a recording system which gives them reliable information about the storage conditions both in the shop and in the warehouse. They need this information to help them to decide whether a particular food is safe to sell even though it has not reached its sell-by date. For example, if a particular food gets too hot or too cold, it can shorten its shelf life and make it unfit to sell before the sell-by date.

Task 5 Measuring the speed of vehicles

Measuring speed is something that computers can do very accurately.

1   Design a sensor/recording system which could be used to time very accurately how long a vehicle takes to go between two sensors a fixed distance apart. The choice of sensors is critical to the accuracy of the system. Explain your choices carefully. Make sure you say why the sensors are the most suitable for the job.

2   How could this system be used measure the speed of vehicles on public roads?

3   What else would need to be built into the system if the police wanted the system to automatically record speeding motorists?

4   How would you make this happen?

5   What evidence would the police need to collect if they were going to prosecute the speeding motorists?

6   Once the police have collected the evidence, how could they use ICT systems to identify the names and addresses of speeding motorists?

7   Is this a reliable method of prosecution? If not, what are the flaws in the system and how could they be avoided?

Measurement with feedback

The next set of 'things to do' are linked with Unit 13. Here, you will need to design, build and test solutions to control situations where feedback is needed to make the control systems work. The things you need to record for each problem you tackle are the same as those listed on page 134. Make sure you plan your solution. Remember to include a flow chart to help you to work out what is needed.

Task 6

In the baby unit of Task 3, each incubator environment needs to be precisely controlled to keep a baby at a particular temperature and to raise an alarm if any measurement reaches a dangerous level.

Task 7

A company wants the environment in its head office to be controlled at all times. During the working day, the temperature is always to be between 20°C and 23°C, the light level should be constant whatever the weather, and the humidity should be capable of being changed to suit the employees' comfort.

Many different industries and businesses use computer-created models to help them to predict the outcomes of ideas. The ability to try something out and see what it 'looks like' has always been used, and computer systems speed up this area of work. Computer systems also have the ability to try many different ideas to see what would happen when one idea replaces another idea.

The most obvious modelling situation that you might have come across in school is modelling something by drawing it. If you have designed something as part of your Design and Technology work, your teachers will have asked you to present, as a drawing, your ideas of what you are going to make. Depending on your chosen subject, your drawing will be either two-dimensional or three-dimensional. If you decide to make changes to the drawing, it can be a messy business.

In Unit 5, we looked at the range of computer programs that let us draw. If you are going to model a situation, you will need to use programs that let you try out different ideas quickly and easily – and let you change your mind and make the changes easily. Since vector drawing programs store each line, box, curve, regular or irregular shape as an independent object, editing the final drawing is very easy. For example, a misplaced line can be easily moved, or a circle that is not wanted can be easily deleted.

When a designer tries to visualise a design, he or she might draw a plan view of it. This is usually to scale so that the person who is to make the real thing knows how large to make it. In this plan view, the designer has the ability to try out several ideas. The designer is asking 'What if …?' questions (Fig 15.1).

For example, a bedroom designer might ask questions such as 'What if we put the bed under the window?' or 'Perhaps it would be better against the long wall?' The designer is modelling the solution by positioning the furniture in the bedroom.

In Unit 5, we mentioned that some of the technical graphics programs use libraries of predrawn objects to place in a room. Using such programs speeds up the modelling process. You don't need to draw each object – it already exists. The job of modelling some solutions is

Fig 15.1 Ground-floor plan of the Faculty of Social Studies, University of Oxford.

simply about moving these predrawn objects around the room to get the best arrangement for the customer. You need to draw the room shape to the same scale as the predrawn objects, but after that it is a simple manipulation task – moving, rotating, adding objects, removing those that don't fit and so on.

How 2-D modelling is used

A railway station has a piece of land that the owners wish to turn into a pay–and–display car park. As they are going to charge rail travellers to park their cars, they want to get as many cars into the car park as possible. They need to look at how much space an average car needs, to make sure that the cars can get into and out of the parking spaces without crashing into other parked cars, and to have some larger spaces for disabled drivers. They also need to position three ticket machines. (See Fig 15.2.)

The first step would be to make a scale drawing of the piece of land. Next, the designer would make a rectangular shape which represents the average car to the same scale. Many copies of this rectangle will be required, so the designer will need to put it into the library if that is possible. If the program chosen doesn't have the library facility, then the designer could use the copy-and-paste facility. The last piece of information required is how wide the lanes between the parking bays need to be to make parking easy and safe. The designer is then ready to build the model.

To work out the best layout to park the largest number of cars, the designer will build a series of different layouts (models) and decide which is the best.

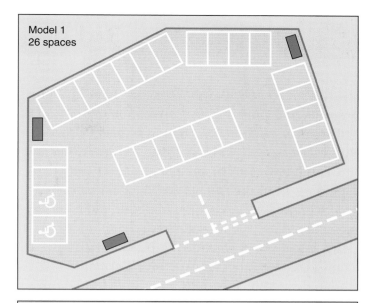
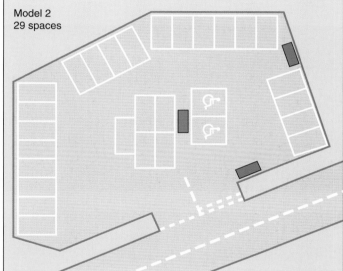
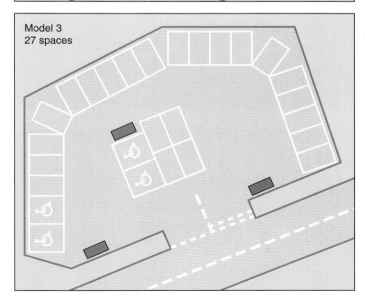

Fig 15.2 A sequence of models to solve the station car park problem. The worst model is Model 1 (26 spaces) and the best is Model 2 (29 spaces).

QUESTIONS

1   You are a designer who has been asked to design a large L-shaped living room, with a door in each part, which is to contain a bookcase, a sideboard, a table and four armchairs. Describe how you would go about it.

2   A supermarket is to enlarge its car park. Explain how a designer would arrive at the best layout for the new part of the car park.

Visual models are usually created to be viewed in three dimensions. Since our world is three-dimensional, designers often use these techniques to help us to see what finished designs will look like. The modelling that occurs here is very similar to the conventional model-making process. In the past, an architect, for example, would get a model maker to build a scale model of the proposed building so that planners and customers could see what the architect intended to build. Trying out different ideas was often an expensive and time-consuming experience because new models might need to be built from scratch to show the changes.

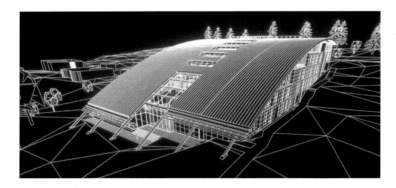

Fig 15.3 Robert Gordon University, Faculty of Management, Aberdeen: wire frame model (top); rendered model (centre); finished building (bottom).

The use of a computer to produce three-dimensional models gives a designer the option to try out many different ideas. Unlike conventional models, the computer can show what the model looks like from the inside as well as the outside. The model can also be placed in a location so that, for example, the environmental impact of a new building can be considered (Fig 15.3).

Product design

Many new products will be modelled using 3-D computer programs which will fully display the proposed products before they are manufactured. Changes can be made and different ideas tried out before a product is made. This can save tens of thousands of pounds, as mistakes are put right before production begins. You may still find that a real model (rather than a computer model) is made sometimes, but this usually will be when the design has reached the final stage. Domestic appliances, such as hairdryers, need to be comfortable in the hand, and such ergonomic aspects of a design cannot be checked using a computer model.

Once a design is finalised, the data held in the modelling system can be transferred to a production system so that computer-controlled machines produce some of the parts that go into the final product.

Reconstructions

Archaeologists use these systems to reconstruct the appearance of ancient sites (Fig 15.4). Also, any fragments of objects they find in a dig can be modelled to help them to see what the objects may have looked like when they were new. If you watch TV programmes like *Time Team*, you will have seen these modelling techniques used.

Archaeologists also use these techniques to create reconstructions of buildings. They may find foundations and parts of walls, which give them the dimensions of a building. They can then create a scale plan of the building and turn this into a three-dimensional model showing what they think the area may have looked like (Fig 15.4).

You may have seen that some of the computer programs used can 'fly' a camera through a site so that you can see what it would have looked like from different viewpoints. This is the same sort of effect that an architect uses to show a client what a new development will look like.

Fig 15.4 Archaeologists used 3-D modelling programs to create this image of the original Roman building from its ruins.

Virtual reality systems

You have probably heard about **virtual reality (VR)** systems. These systems bring together a wide variety of functions covered in this book. The most sophisticated VR systems will create virtual three-dimensional worlds that you view through screens fitted to a headset. As your head turns, you will see a series of new views just as you would if you were really there. These systems use sensors to work out which way your head or eyes are facing, so that they give you the appropriate view. As you move around the environment, the sensors will detect your new position and the VR system will respond by giving you yet another view.

It is also possible to give you some touch feedback about the environment you are in. This relies on your wearing a suit which has devices built in which stimulate your senses into believing you are touching an object. (See also page 153.)

Medical models

Modern medical whole-body scanners can collect a large amount of data about a person's internal systems. The data collected can then be processed to produce a three-dimensional model of the whole body or a part of it. This information is usually collected as a series of 'slices' and the program glues the slices back together to make the three-dimensional model. This model allows doctors to precisely locate, for example, a tumour, and helps them to decide what to do next (Fig 15.5).

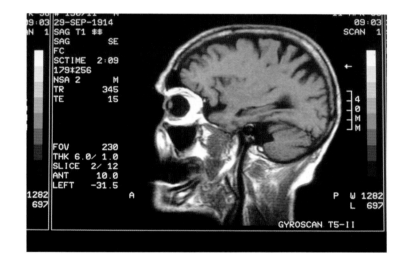

Fig 15.5 A slice image through a brain, obtained by magnetic resonance imaging (MRI).

QUESTIONS

1 What are the advantages of three-dimensional graphical modelling compared with making scale models?
2 Describe how a team of archaeologists would use three-dimensional modelling to investigate the remains of a Roman villa built in AD 300, which contains many buried domestic objects.

In the business world, number-based models are often used. For example, if your parents need a bank loan, their bank will have a model which tells it and your parents how much they may borrow and how much they will have to pay the bank each month over a certain period of time. If the rate of interest changes, the bank will be able to quickly recalculate your parent's monthly repayments. If they want to repay the loan over a different period of time, then again the bank model can work out quickly the new monthly amounts.

Multinational companies use models to predict how successful they should be in any year. Their models look at such factors as how much they expect to sell, the cost of employees' salaries, the cost of running their buildings, and the cost of making and selling their products. Their models also help them to work out how much money they will be able to invest in developing new products and so on. They will then be able to try several different ways of development to see what might be the best way forward.

Fig 15.6 A model that predicts the effects on the Nile delta of a rise in the level of the Meditteranean Sea. Estimates of the rise range from 50cm to over 1m during the next 50 to 100 years. The map below left shows the situation now. The map below right predicts the amount of land lost (shown in pink) by a rise in sea level of 1.5m.

Environmentalists use models to help them to predict the future effect of environmental changes. Global warming is an issue that is frequently in the news. Scientists around the world have studied the historic data and have built models based on this data which, they say, predict rising sea levels in the future (Fig 15.6). How accurate are the models? No one knows.

Modelling with numbers

Number-based models are often used to help to find an optimum value for a given situation. If you were planning a party, you would set a budget. You would decide the maximum amount of money that you could spend on the party. You would book a venue for the party, buy food and drink and have some entertainment. Working out the best party you can get for the money you are prepared to spend is using a number model.

You will find that different venues charge different amounts for the hire of a room but for each room there will be a maximum number of people that it can hold. You can research the cost of different foods and drinks. You could try a range of combinations of foods, drinks and numbers of people to see what each combination would cost. You will find that different forms of entertainment cost different amounts.

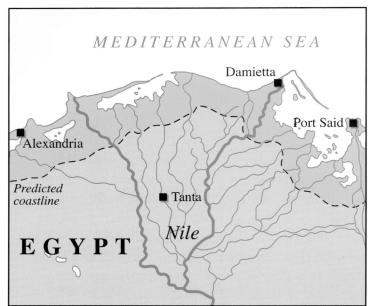

The model you construct will probably be built in a spreadsheet (Fig 15.7). You will design a mathematical model which will calculate the cost of each of the different elements and give you the total cost. You can then alter the amounts for different venues, types of entertainment and a range of different refreshments, and the model will calculate a new total. After trying different combinations, you can decide which is the best party for the amount of money you are prepared to spend.

Party budget

A party planning model

How much do you want to spend?	£ 650.00
How many people are coming?	65

Venue information

Cost of hiring room	Village Hall	£ 300.00	
How many people can the room hold safely?		45	This venue is too small!

Food costs

Type of food	Unit cost	How many?	Total cost
Party bag of crisps	£ 1.75	3	£ 5.25
Pringles	£ 1.00	4	£ 4.00
Twiglets	£ 0.40	10	£ 4.00
Cocktail Sausages	£ 2.99	2	£ 5.98
Sausage rolls	£ 1.75	3	£ 5.25
Chocolate biscuits	£ 0.85	5	£ 4.25
			£ 0.00
			£ 0.00
			£ 0.00
			£ 0.00
			£ 0.00
			£ 0.00
			£ 28.73

Drink costs

Type of drink	Unit cost	How many?	Total cost
Coca Cola	£ 1.29	5	£ 6.45
Lemonade	£ 0.95	3	£ 2.85
Dr Pepper	£ 1.25	4	£ 5.00
Lilt	£ 1.15	2	£ 2.30
Orange Squash	£ 0.99	2	£ 1.98
			£ 0.00
			£ 0.00
			£ 0.00
			£ 0.00
			£ 0.00
			£ 0.00
			£ 0.00
			£ 18.58

Cost of entertainment

ZigaZag Disco	£ 195.00	
Total cost of the party is	£ 542.31	You can afford this party
Cost per person	£ 8.34	

Fig 15.7 'What if we change the cost of the venue?'

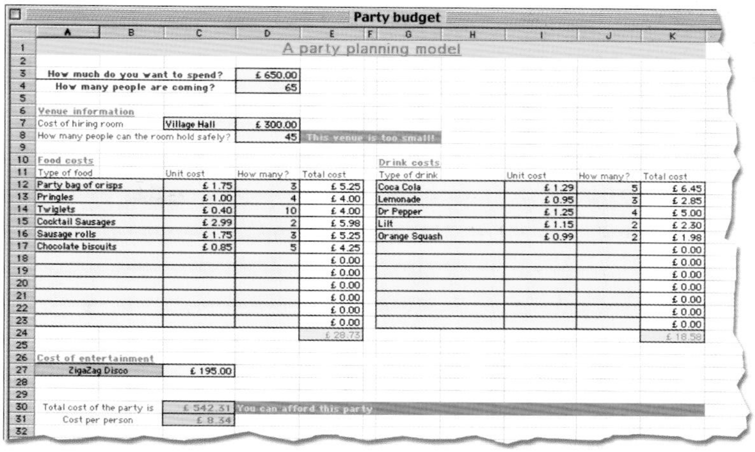

Finding the optimum answer

To find the optimum answer to a problem, you will need to have a strategy. You need to make changes to the variables in the model step by step to see the effect and to help you to find the answer in a planned way.

An example often used in GCSE mathematics course-work is to find the largest rectangular pen a farmer can make for his pigs, given a particular length of fencing. The perimeter of the field – the length of the fencing – is fixed. The farmer can make the perimeter from a variety of combinations of length and width, but he needs to find the largest area. He needs to work this out in a planned way – the strategy.

Suppose the farmer has 200 m of fencing. He could then make a field 99 m by 1 m, 98 m by 2 m or 97 m by 3 m and so on. To find the area, he has to multiply the length by the width. The area of the first pen is 99 m^2, of the second pen is 196 m^2 and of the third pen is 291 m^2 – none the same. Building a spreadsheet model to do this would let him input the perimeter value and the length of one side. He then has to decide how much to change the length each time and the model works out the pen with the largest area.

Farmer's pen

Farmer's pig pen

Perimeter	Change side in steps of	Maximum area
200m	1m	2500 sq m
Length	Width	Area
99m	1m	99
98m	2m	196
97m	3m	291
96m	4m	384
95m	5m	475
94m	6m	564
93m	7m	651
92m	8m	736
91m	9m	819
90m	10m	900
89m	11m	979
88m	12m	1056
87m	13m	1131
86m	14m	1204
85m	15m	1275
84m	16m	1344
83m	17m	1411
82m	18m	1476
81m	19m	1539
80m	20m	1600
79m	21m	1659
78m	22m	1716
77m	23m	1771
76m	24m	1824
75m	25m	1875
74m	26m	1924
73m	27m	1971
72m	28m	2016
71m	29m	2059
70m	30m	2100
69m	31m	2139
68m	32m	2176
67m	33m	2211
2m	98m	196
1m	99m	99

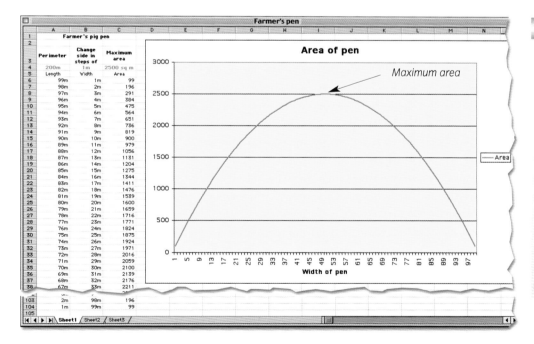

Fig 15.8 The farmer decided the strategy should be to make the sides change by 1 m at a time. Starting with a 99 x 1 field, then 98 x 2 and so on gives these answers.

QUESTIONS

1. How might a large manufacturing company use a number-based model to predict its growth over the next tw years?
2. A charity organisation has asked you to raise money for it by running a fête. The organisation has given you a maximum amount to spend. How would you plan the fête using a computer model – and make a profit?

Another aspect that computers bring to modelling is their ability to simulate something real or imaginary.

Computer games

You probably play computer or console games. Each of these is a model or simulation. The game play is a set of rules (the model) which the computer faithfully follows. These rules define the behaviour of each character – how fast a character can run, how high a character can jump, how strong each character is, and so on. When weapons are involved, the range of fire and the strength of an effect are set in the model, as is the terrain on which the game takes place.

Fig 15.9 Games computers give players increasingly realistic experiences. Here, the skier has to move as though it is the player who is on skis.

Sometimes these simulations are realistic – such as car racing games – but others are fantasy, where the character(s) can do things no human could do.

The simulation responds to inputs to the system. If you are driving a car in a racing game, you control the throttle and gears and you can steer the car. This is almost like driving a real car except for the way in which you operate the controls. On a computer game, you might use the keyboard to control all the functions. In a real car, you have a steering wheel, accelerator and brake pedals and a gear stick. The simulation is not completely real. Visually and through the sound effects it seems real but the other sensations of driving a car are not part of the model. For example, the sensation of accelerating to high speeds is missing.

In arcades, many of the games have been developed to give you a more complete simulation. You sit in front of a steering wheel and pedals, and you drive the simulated car in a way much closer to the real experience.

Simulations in training

Games are not the only simulations. Simulations are used in many walks of life and for many reasons. The most common use of simulators is in training (Fig 15.10). Training a pilot to fly a large aircraft, such as a Boeing 777, is a costly business. If an airline trained its pilots entirely on real aircraft, it would be very costly in terms of the fuel used and the loss of revenue from having to take aircraft out of service. Busy airports would need to be used to give the pilots real in-flight experiences. If the pilot made a mistake on takeoff or landing, it would endanger many lives. Simulation can, therefore, save money and be much safer than training in the real thing.

To minimise the dangers, pilots start their training on a simulator. This is a full-sized replica of the cockpit, which never leaves the ground. It is connected to a unit which makes the simulator behave like a real aircraft. This unit uses a range of computerised systems to create the illusion of flying. The input systems will be the controls in the cockpit. The settings of these will be monitored by a program which will take decisions about what the aircraft should do in response. Through a series of control systems, the cockpit will move and the view seen through the windows will change as well.

This model must be just like the real aircraft to fly. The training would be useless if it were not.

An advantage of training pilots on a simulator is that faults can be introduced into the 'aircraft' that give pilots experience in dealing with emergencies. This produces pilots who, when they are flying real aircraft with passengers, can deal with almost any emergency and land safely. It also means that the airlines can continually train pilots and check their fitness to fly.

Another area where simulators are used is to train workers doing highly dangerous jobs. For example, there is a high risk attached to running a nuclear power station. The problems that occur when reactors fail, as in Chernobyl, are widespread and harm hundreds, if not thousands, of unprotected people. Before anyone is allowed to work in the reactor control room in a nuclear power station, he or she has to train on a simulator and be able to cope safely with a wide range of potential problems – however unlikely their occurrence in a real power station.

Fig 15.10
The trainee pilot sees and feels something which is very real but the outside appearance of the simulator is nothing like a real aircraft.

QUESTIONS

1 What is the meaning of the term game play? Give an example from a computer game that you enjoy.
2 How are simulators used to train airline pilots?
3 List two benefits of computer simulation.
4 What are the limits of computer simulation?

In the primary school

Simulations are often used in schools to help children to learn about new things that are perhaps difficult for them to experience in reality. For example, young children might need to explore a variety of natural habitats as part of their science work, but if they live in a city it could be very difficult to get them to real habitats in the countryside. A computer simulation would let them explore an area as though they were there, and discover the animals that live there (Fig 15.11).

Fig 15.11
A wildlife simulation in which the children have to guide the badger to safely back to its sett. They have to help it find food and drink to keep it alive and out of danger on its journey.

This sort of model will be fairly realistic. The scenes could be photographs of a real environment and could show the children real animals and minibeasts in the right place. Moving through the simulation will probably be done by using the mouse and clicking on parts of the scene. The programmers may have added some realism, such as sound effects which allow the children to hear what it is like to be there. The simulation will not be able to give them a clear idea of how wet the ground is or how hot or cold it is. The simulation might suggest cold by using wind sound effects and by using suitable pictures – for example, rain and a grey sky to suggest a cold day.

In the secondary school

Here a simulation might be used so that students can try out many different variables quickly to ask 'What if…?' questions. A simulation might also be used to do something that is too dangerous for students to do, or that the school does not have the equipment for.

Fig 15.12a shows an electrical circuit diagram similar to one you might have built as part of your GCSE science work. It takes a long time to build such a circuit and to take readings. This picture is taken from a simulation program that lets you build and try out different circuits. In this circuit, there are five $50\,\Omega$ resistors. You can see that the simulation tells you that the current in the main part of the circuit is $330\,mA$ and that the current splits into three different, smaller currents in the three branches of the circuit. Do the three parts add up to the whole?

Your teacher might ask you to investigate what happens if you change the resistor values to $25\,\Omega$ or $100\,\Omega$ (Figs 15.12b and 15.12c). It could take a long time to keep changing the resistors in a real circuit, and if you don't make all the connections properly the circuit might not work reliably. Using this simulation, you can quickly change the values and see what happens (as long as all the wires are joined).

Since the changes are quick and easy to make, you might try many more variations ('What if…?') to understand more clearly what goes on in this sort of circuit. Does the whole still add up to the parts? Do you think this is always so?

If you carry on using this model, you might be able to answer these questions, having investigated a wide range of possibilities. As long as the model accurately copies the real behaviour, you can learn just as much from this as using the real circuits.

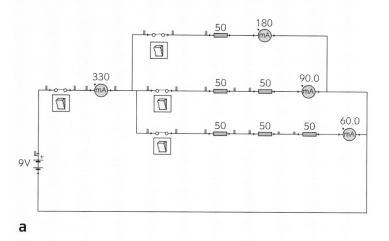

a

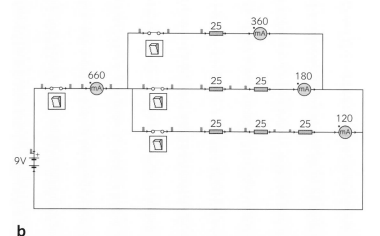

b

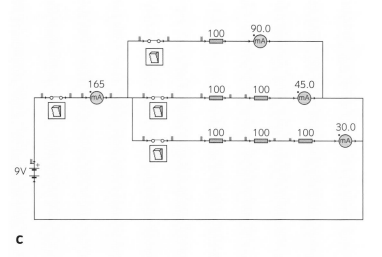

c

Fig 15.12a–c This electrical circuit simulator lets you change values of components to see what happens. Like all models, you can ask 'What happens if I change…?' and get an answer.

Virtual reality simulations

Virtual reality is also used in simulations. For example, surgeons can now be trained to perform new surgical procedures without endangering life. A virtual–reality human model can be created and a trainee surgeon can perform the operation.

The sensor and control systems connected to the operator can give feedback to the surgeon to create an illusion of the real thing. The feedback can be visual through the imaging system, but more important is the feedback which gives the sense of touch. This will help the surgeon to master the safe manipulation of the surgical instruments.

Virtual reality is also used in actual surgery. For example, the 3-D image of a brain tumour can be created from a series of slice images produced by scanning the affected brain, using MRI (Figs 15.5 and 15.13).

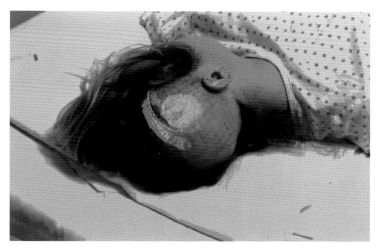

Fig 15.13 Virtual reality image of a brain tumour (green) superimposed on a patient's head before surgery. In this way, the surgeon finds the exact position of the tumour before trying to remove it.

QUESTIONS

1 Describe one use of simulations in the classroom. If you can, write about your own experiences of learning with the help of simulations.
2 What is the meaning of the term virtual reality? Describe why and how virtual reality is used in training surgeons.

Remember to make notes that show your teacher how you built your model and how you used it to give the required answers.

Graphical modelling

Here, you will need to choose a suitable graphics program to create the model. Remember to make notes which give clear reasons for your choice of program. Why is this the right program for the job? What facilities does it offer that you need to do the job?

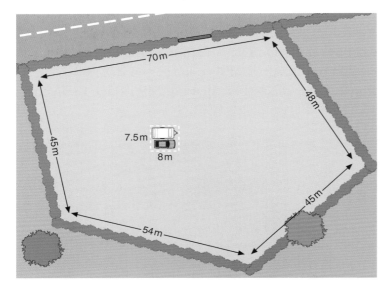

Fig 15.14
A plan of the farmer's field which is to be turned into a caravan site. The photograph shows a typical caravan on a site.

Task 1

A farmer has a field (whose dimensions are shown in Fig 15.14) that he wants to turn into a campsite for caravanners. Regulations state that each pitch has to be at least 7.5m wide (to give enough space for a car, caravan and awning) and 8m deep. For safety, there needs to be a gap between each pitch and the next to prevent the spread of fire.

1 Create a scale drawing of the field.
2 Create a scale drawing of one pitch to the same scale.
3 Create a layout to see how many caravans you can get on the field.
4 This is not the only layout that would be possible. Try some others to see what is the largest number of caravans that can be safely pitched on the field.
5 The farmer wants to put a road around the field so that the caravans don't get stuck in the mud when the field is wet. Draw the best route for this road so that the caravanners have to drive only a short distance across the grass to pitch their caravans. Does this road have an impact on the number of caravans that can be safely pitched?

Another task on graphic modelling, involving table layouts in a fast-food restaurant, can be found on the OUP website (**www.oup.com/uk/ictforgcse**).

Modelling with numbers

Task 2

A group of students are planning a school trip. The coach company can provide 52, 45 or 30-seat coaches. The coach company have quoted £200 for a 52-seat coach, £180 for a 45-seat coach and £150 for a 30-seat coach. The entrance fee for the trip is £4 per child and £6.50 per adult but for every 15 children one adult gets a free trip. The school regulations say that there must be one adult for every 12 students.

1 Set up the mathematics that will help you work out what it will cost for 45 children to go on the trip.
2 Make a plan so that the mathematics can be turned into a spreadsheet model.
3 Build the model and work out the total cost of the trip and what it will cost each person to go on the trip.
4 Use the model to find out the total cost and the cost per person if:
   a 39 children go on the trip

b 60 children go on the trip

c 90 children go on the trip

5 Which is the cheapest and which is the most expensive trip?

Task 3

A packaging manufacturer has been given the brief to make the largest volume open-top box they can from a single sheet of A4 card (297 mm × 210 mm). The manufacturer needs to know how to cut and fold the card to do this (Fig 15.15). A worker suggests that they build a spreadsheet model to find the best answer to this.

1 If you take an x mm square out of each corner to allow the sides to be folded up to make the box, how long will the sides of the box be?

2 How tall will the box be?

3 Plan a spreadsheet model which will calculate the volume of the box.

4 To find the largest volume box that can be made from this piece of card, the manufacturer needs to try different 'What if x is...?' questions. Can you put a value for x into a cell in the model so that the model will automatically work out the volume of the box? If not, can you modify the model so that you can?

5 Now work out a strategy that you can use with the model so that you can find the largest volume box that can be made.

6 What are the dimensions of this box?

Using a simulation

Task 4

Crocodile Clips Elementary is an electrical circuit simulator program that your school may already have. If not, it can be downloaded from the website. Fig 15.16 shows a simple circuit using a battery, a bulb, a switch and a fuse.

When you operate the switch in the circuit, the bulb comes on. But if you were to design a circuit that used more bulbs or batteries, it would be possible to blow the fuse.

1 Create some circuits that use more bulbs. See how many bulbs are needed in a circuit to overload it and blow the fuse.

2 Is this the only arrangement that you could build which blows the fuse? If not, try some others. What is the minimum number of bulbs that you need in your circuit to blow the fuse?

3 Instead of changing the number of bulbs, change the number of batteries to see whether it is possible to blow the fuse this way.

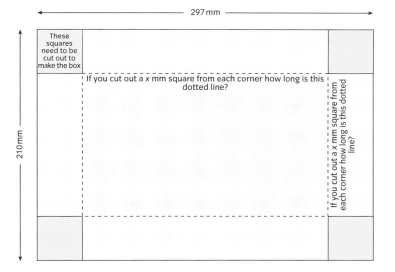

Fig 15.15 The card, with cut and fold lines, whose maximum possible volume you have to find.

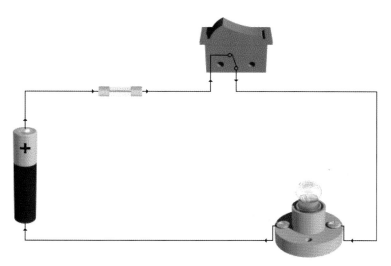

Fig 15.16 A simple circuit from the simulation program Crocodile Clips Elementary.

Application software is the name given to software that instructs a computer to carry out a specific task. It is application software (for example, a spreadsheet) that people choose to help them with a task when they use a computer. Computer programmers use what is called **language software**, such as C++ or Visual Basic, to create both system and application software (see pages 8–9).

Application software has been specifically developed to help you perform a task – whether writing a letter using a word processor or sketching a picture with a draw program. Application software is easy to set up (install) on a computer. Many new computers are sold with the application software and system software already installed.

When application software is installed, it is set up in the way that the software company thinks most people will want. This is known as being installed with the **default settings**. For example, in a word processor, the default settings would include what the font will be when a new document is created, what menus will be shown, what format a file will automatically be saved in, and so on.

It is important that you realise that you do not have to keep to these default settings. The application software has been deliberately set up to allow users to change (customise) the settings to their specific requirements (Fig 16.1). In Microsoft Word, for example, it is possible to change the position of toolbars on a screen, what toolbars to show (for example, Drawing, Word Art, Web etc) and even what icons should be shown on a toolbar.

An application such as Word allows users to set up **templates**. A template is a predesigned file that sets up a structure for a document. A template contains all the settings for a document, such as fonts, menus, page layout, any special formatting and styles (Fig 16.2). Templates can be created for many different tasks – for example, letters, faxes, birthday invitations and GCSE coursework. It is also possible to change the Normal template (on which every new document is based) so that each time the application starts, your personalised settings are loaded.

Whilst application software is sufficient to meet the needs of many users, some organisations and businesses require applications to be modified (customised) to their needs. Programmers altering coding or writing new coding can do this.

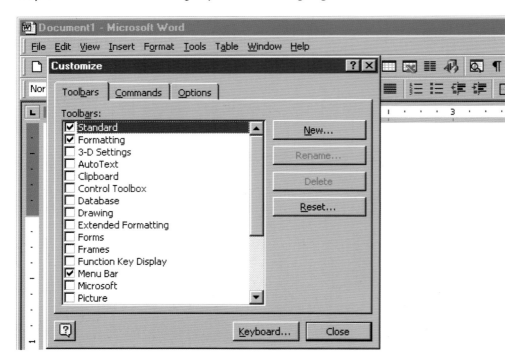

Fig 16.1 It is easy to customise (change) the settings for most programs to suit your needs. This is a screenshot of the customise menu from the popular word-processing application Microsoft Word.

For example, it is likely that the database of students in your school or college was created using a database application but modified to meet the specific requirements of a school/college student database.

There are also specialist applications known as expert or knowledge-based systems. An **expert system** is an application that performs a task that would otherwise be performed by a human expert. The facts and rules for an expert system are provided by human experts and, once programmed, the expert system can *very quickly* help a user make a decision or solve a problem.

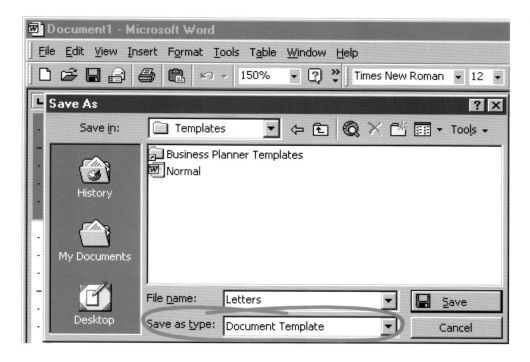

Fig 16.2 By saving a document as a template, you can set up (configure) future documents exactly how you want them to be.

Expert systems are widely used. Examples include:

◆ Medicine – to diagnose illnesses.
◆ House buying – to choose the best mortgage.
◆ Buying and selling of company shares – to choose the best shares to invest in.
◆ Gas industry – to find faults in the gas supply.
◆ Building industry – to help quantity surveyors in the construction of new buildings.

QUESTIONS

1 What is meant by the following terms: default settings, template, expert system, artificial intelligence?
2 Give three ways in which expert systems are used.

Expert systems are created using a special computer language such as **PROLOG** (**Pro**gramming **Log**ic). They are part of a category of computer applications known as artificial intelligence. **Artificial intelligence** is that part of computer science concerned with getting computers to behave like humans. Apart from expert systems, artificial intelligence includes programming computers to understand human languages, and programming robots to see, touch, hear and smell and to play games such as chess. Such has been the advances in artificial intelligence that a world champion chess player has been beaten by a chess program run on a super-computer (Fig 16.3).

Fig 16.3 In 1997, the Big-Blue super-computer – programmed using artificial intelligence chess software – beat the world champion chess player Gary Kasparov.

You have already seen (pages 8–9) that language software is the name given to a list of instructions to a computer. Programmers use language software to create system software and application software. There are **low-level languages** (machine language and assembly language) and **high-level languages**.

Most of the programs in use today are written in a high-level language, such as C++, Pascal, Visual Basic and Java. These languages are called high-level because they use keywords similar to English and are easier to write than low-level languages. Importantly, unlike low-level languages, high-level languages enable programs to run on most types of computer. In schools, high-level languages such as BASIC, Visual Basic and Logo are often used.

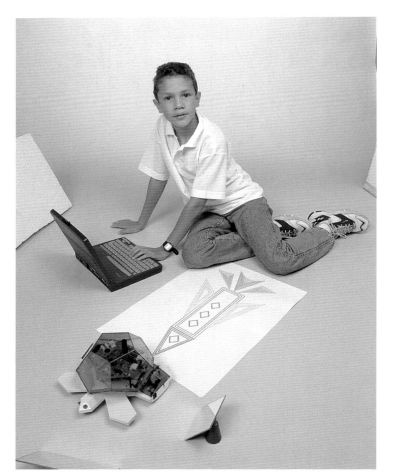

Fig 16.4 A floor turtle can be programmed using Logo.

COBOL (**Co**mmon **B**usiness-**O**riented **L**anguage) is a high-level language used in business programs. These programs are mainly used on mainframe computers.

Logo is a language that is often used to teach programming to students. You might have used Logo to control an on-screen turtle to draw graphics, or to control a floor turtle (robot). To program the turtle to draw a square, you enter the following instructions:

```
FORWARD 200
RIGHT 90
FORWARD 200
RIGHT 90
FORWARD 200
RIGHT 90
FORWARD 200
RIGHT 90
```

In these instructions, RIGHT 90 means turn right through 90° and FORWARD 200 means go forward 200 units. One of the secrets to all good programming is not to type in more than you have to. A **procedure** is a sequence of instructions that can be called on to run at anytime within the program. In the example above, the instructions FORWARD 200 and RIGHT 90 had to be given four times. It is possible to simplify this by writing a procedure called SQUARE:

```
TO SQUARE
    REPEAT 4 [FD 200 RT 90]
END
```

It would be possible also to add a variable – a number which could be changed easily – called LENGTH. This would allow you to enter the size you wanted, rather than its always being 200 x 200. Using procedures and variables are some of the most basic steps in programming. Other examples of using Logo are shown on pages 132–3.

Another popular high-level programming language is **BASIC** (**B**eginner's **A**ll-purpose **S**ymbolic Instruction

Code). BASIC has been used for many years because it is relatively easy to learn, and is still used today to program business and scientific applications. The following example of BASIC asks a user to enter a number and then multiplies the number by 100, and prints (or shows) the answer:

```
10 PRINT 'Enter a number'
20 INPUT NUM
30 PRINT 'Your number * 100 is';NUM*100
```

Microsoft has developed BASIC into an object-orientated and visual programming language (using icons, menus, buttons etc) called **Visual Basic**. Visual Basic is used to create applications for the Windows operating system. Visual Basic is a highly popular programming language, particularly as programmers can use predefined libraries of code that can be adapted for their application.

Visual Basic can be difficult to learn, but there is an easy way to use it. A version of Visual Basic, called Visual Basic for Applications, is included in several Microsoft programs such as Excel and is used whenever a **macro** is recorded or run. A macro is a series of commands that a program can perform automatically (Fig 16.5). You record macros in a similar way to using a tape recorder to record music – there are no difficult words or commands to remember. For example, if you had a list of students and their classes in Excel, you could record two macros, one to sort by surname and the other to sort by class. These macros could be assigned to on-screen buttons that could be created with the draw tools. Then every time you wanted to sort by either category, you would just click the on-screen button.

The actual code to sort by surname is shown in Fig 16.6.

```
Sub Sortbyname( )
    Range("A2:B13").Select
    Selection.Sort Key1:=Range("A2"), Order1:=xlAscending, Header:=xlGuess, _
    OrderCustom:=1, MatchCase:=False, Orientation:=xlTopToBottom
    Range("A1").Select
End Sub
```

Fig 16.6 The code for sorting by surname.

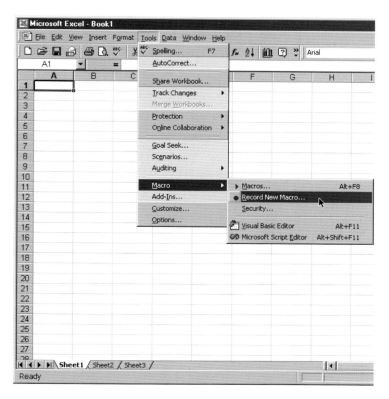

Fig 16.5 Macros are very easy to record and run.

The best bit is that you don't have to type, or remember, any of this – it is all done for you! To see these examples in action, download the Excel file **Example functions in Excel.xls** from the OUP website, **www.oup.com/uk/ictforgcse**.

QUESTIONS

1 What high-level language is often used to write business programs?
2 Give one reason why Visual Basic is a popular programming language.
3 What is a macro? Give two reasons why you might want to record and run a macro.

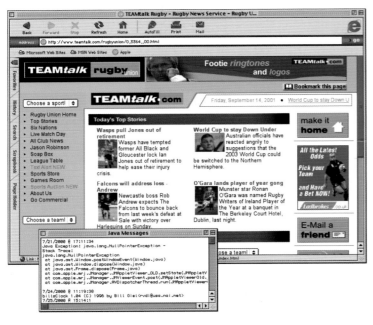

Fig 16.7 Java applets such as this enable web content to be viewed by all users – regardless of which operating systems are being used.

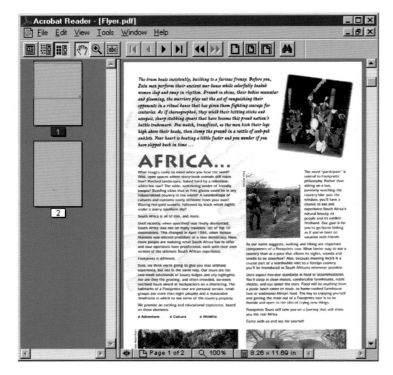

Fig 16.8 Portable Document Format files allow all computer users to see the content and layout of a document.

The development of the Internet and the World Wide Web has seen the development of 'mark-up' and programming languages specifically aimed at web authoring.

Java is an object-oriented programming language developed by Sun Microsystems to run on different types (platforms) of computers. Examples are computers running Windows 98, Windows NT, Macintosh and UNIX operating systems. All users, regardless of which operating system they are using, need to access the content of web pages. As Java runs on all of the major operating systems, small Java applications, known as **applets**, ensure that everyone can access web content (Fig 16.7).

Java applets can be downloaded and run by most web browsers such as Internet Explorer and Netscape Navigator. Java applets are often used to make web pages more interactive and to play music, animations and videos. In some cases, games are also programmed as Java applets.

Another company, Macromedia, has developed Flash and Shockwave for the World Wide Web. **Flash** is a vector graphics file format for adding animation and interactivity to multimedia web pages. Flash files can be played back with downloadable Shockwave software or a Java program. **Shockwave** software is a format for multimedia audio and video files within HTML documents, and is known as a **plug-in**. A plug-in is a small piece of software that plugs into a larger application to add more features.

Other popular plug-ins include **Acrobat** from Adobe Systems and **RealPlayer** from Real Networks. Acrobat allows documents to be saved in the **Portable Document Format (PDF)**. The advantage of PDF files is that the content and layout of a document is preserved (Fig 16.8), yet can be viewed on any computer using the free downloadable software Acrobat Reader. RealPlayer enables audio and video to be played from web browsers in real time.

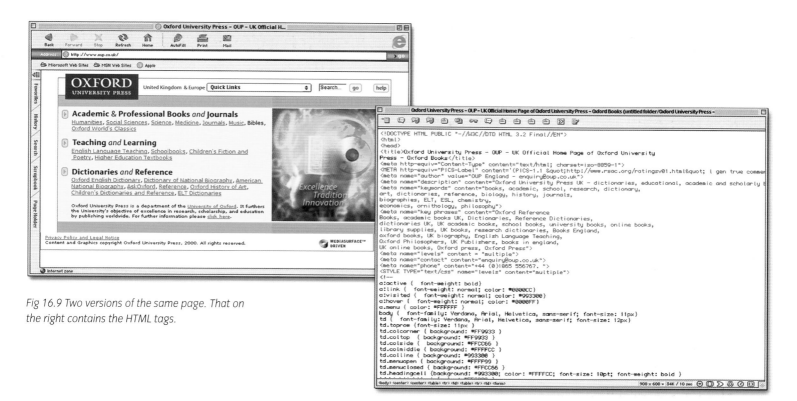

Fig 16.9 Two versions of the same page. That on the right contains the HTML tags.

HTML (**H**yper**T**ext **M**arkup **L**anguage) is used for documents on the World Wide Web. HTML uses tags to mark elements, such as text and graphics, in a document (Fig 16.9). By using tags in this way, web browsers are instructed how display these elements on a web page and how to respond to user actions, such as clicking with a mouse on a hyperlink that connects the users to information in other web pages.

Web publishing

There are specific application programs, such as Microsoft Front Page, that provide the tools for you to design and create your own web pages and to edit existing HTML documents. It is possible though to create and change web pages in other applications such as Microsoft Word, as well. In fact, you can save a document as a web page from any Microsoft Office 2000 program. This allows others on the Internet, or on an intranet, to view or edit the document. The advantage of this is that, by choosing Save As Web Page, you can save a document as an HTML file. A folder is also created that contains supporting files, such as a file for each graphic (GIF or JPEG), spreadsheet etc.

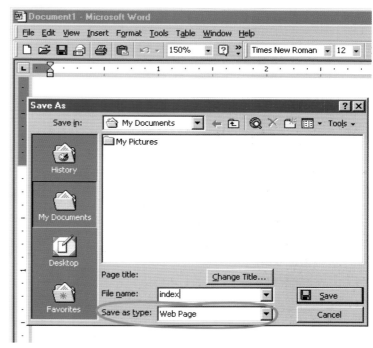

Fig 16.10 Web Page dialogue box in Word 2000.

QUESTIONS

1. Explain why Java is a good computer language to use for Internet applications.
2. What is an applet?
3. What are the advantages of saving a file in PDF format?

As part of your GCSE ICT coursework, you will undertake projects and assignments that involve the **information system's life cycle**. The same information system's life cycle is used for real–life ICT projects that can involve hundreds of people and cost millions of pounds. It is therefore very important that everybody knows what they are doing and when. So what is the information system's life cycle?

The information system's life cycle has a number of key stages. These are shown in Fig 16.11.

Each stage of the life cycle is very important and must be completed before the next one is started. The system life cycle applies to all your GCSE coursework, regardless of whether you are working with individual applications (DTP, spreadsheets etc) or as part of an integrated project.

Fig 16.11 The system life cycle.

 START

SYSTEM INVESTIGATION

How does present system work?
What can be done to improve things?

FEASIBILITY STUDY

More detailed study to find out if and how improvements can be made and the cost.

MAINTENANCE

Correcting any errors in software and/or hardware.

MONITORING AND EVALUATION

How is the system working?
Is it doing the job it was designed for?

SYSTEMS ANALYSIS AND DESIGN

In-depth analysis of requirements. Detailed design of final system in terms of input, output and processing.

IMPLEMENTATION, INCLUDING USER TRAINING, SYSTEMS TESTING AND DOCUMENTATION

Hardware, software installed, whole system tested. Technical documentation for other sofware engineers and user documentation produced.

SOFTWARE PACKAGES MODIFIED AND/OR PROGRAMS DESIGNED, CONSTRUCTED AND TESTED

Statement of the problem and analysis

You need to explain what goes on at present and to state the problems with the present system. Remember that there is often more than one way to tackle a problem. For example, it is not just a case of designing a leaflet, as leaflets come in different sizes, with different numbers of pages, in/not in colour, with/without graphics, and so on. You should always identify, and evaluate, more than one way of tackling a problem.

How can this be done? A feasibility study could be undertaken to find out if your suggested solution would work and be viable. Can the software do the task? Is the proposed system cost effective? Another way would be to interview people who might use the system, or to look at any existing documentation and output. Questionnaires – as long as they ask the right questions – are another valuable tool to find out exactly what is required.

The analysis should also include what data is to be input, processed and output, as well as set performance criteria. Performance criteria list the desired outcomes. In other words, what has to happen to show that you have completed your task properly. For example, the leaflet to be produced will be A5 size, in colour, with a picture etc.

Design

The design stage involves your choosing a particular design and giving clear reasons why you have chosen that as the best solution. It is good practice to have at least three potential designs (hand-drawn or computer-generated) that clearly demonstrate your thinking and that outline the tools and techniques you will use to solve the problem.

Included in the design section should be a detailed testing plan showing what is to be tested and how the testing will be carried out. You should also include a dataflow diagram. Sometimes a user guide – explaining how to use the system – would also need to be designed.

Implementation

The fun bit! The implementation stage involves carrying out your final design using your chosen software. It is good practice to keep a record of what you do stage by stage, as well as detailing any changes that you make (in the light of using the software) to your initial design. You may also have to make changes as a result of testing, and these changes need to be recorded.

In GCSE coursework/projects, examiners do not see your software solution in operation. Examiners will therefore expect to see written or printed *evidence* of what you have done. It is vital that there are printouts, stage by stage, of your solution to the problem. If you have created a spreadsheet, for example, don't just print out the final spreadsheet. Print out the development of the spreadsheet stage by stage, together with any graphs and tables, as well as the formulas or macros used. Write on (annotate) each print out to explain what happened on screen.

Testing

Whether your solution works is obviously important! Your testing should follow what you planned in the design section. Does the formula in the spreadsheet actually work? Were answers checked against expected results or checked manually using a calculator? Again, evidence will need to be produced which shows that testing has taken place. Write on (annotate) each print out to explain what happened on screen.

Evaluation

The evaluation section allows you to give a brief overview of the situation, as well as to comment on whether you have achieved all of the performance criteria. In other words, have you achieved what you set out to do? What do other people think? For example, if you produced a leaflet for a school play, did it attract more people to a performance? Remember things can often be improved, and good evaluations often involve thoughts on how a solution could be improved with, say, more time and money.

These days we often take telecommunications for granted. Millions of people use mobile telephones, send e-mails, browse the World Wide Web, listen to music on the radio, and watch on television the latest news stories from around the world. Distance is no longer a barrier to communicating with other people. A telephone call to a relative in Australia or an e-mail to a pen friend in the United States no longer arouses great excitement or awe – as it once would have – it is just treated as part of everyday life. This is a sign of how important telecommunications is in our lives.

Telecommunications is the name given to the sending and receiving of any type of data by means of wires, optical fibres or radiowaves. This means that telecommunications includes the sending and receiving of computer data, television pictures, images, voice, sound and faxes. Telecommunications also involves communication over great distances (Fig 17.1). Here are some examples of telecommunication systems:

◆ Computer networks and the Internet
◆ Radio
◆ Telephones – including mobile (cellular) telephones, and facsimiles (faxes)
◆ Television – including satellite television, cable television and terrestrial television (BBC 1, BBC 2, ITV 1 and Channels 4 and 5).

Many telecommunication systems use **satellites** to send and receive data using microwaves. There are thousands of satellites in orbit around the earth. Some satellites are used for sending and receiving telephone calls, television pictures and computer data, while others are dedicated

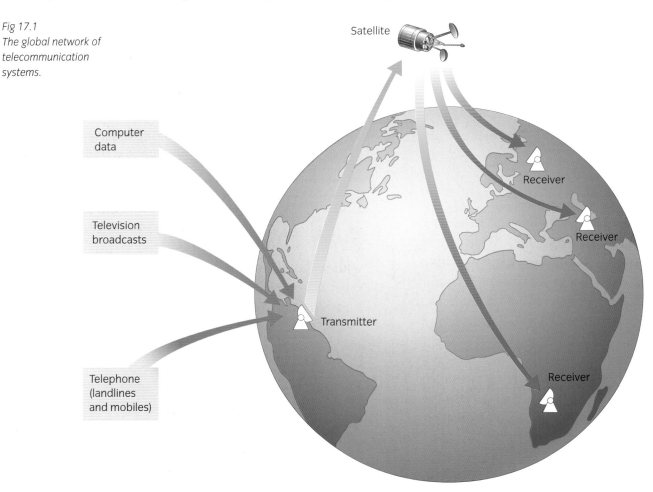

Fig 17.1
The global network of telecommunication systems.

to certain tasks such as helping with weather forecasting and scientific research. A communications satellite receives signals sent from a ground-based station, amplifies them, and then retransmits them on a different frequency to another ground-based station.

How a telecommunications system works

A telecommunication system consists essentially of a transmitter, a transmission channel and a receiver. The transmitter first converts the data to a form which can be sent over wires or optical fibres or by radiowaves to the receiver. The receiver converts the data to a form that can be understood by either a person or a machine (Fig 17.2).

All voice, radio and television communication starts off as continuously changing analogue signals. For the purpose of telecommunication, these analogue signals are converted into digital signals. This process is known as **analogue-to-digital conversion**. Signals are converted from analogue to digital mainly because many more digital signals can be squeezed into the transmission channel than analogue signals. Also, digital signals give higher quality and more reliable transmission than analogue signals. The equipment is also cheaper.

Analogue-to-digital conversion is the *opposite* process to that described on pages 20–1, where you saw how a modem works. A modem enables a computer to send data to, and receive data from, another computer over a telephone line. A computer is a digital device using binary code to switch off (0) and on (1) millions of transistors. The telephone system is an analogue device designed to transmit the human voice. A modem converts digital information to analogue information, and then back to digital information.

In the last 20 years, the development and use of computer networks, including the Internet, has led to the further development of telecommunication systems. Television, telephone and radio systems have traditionally been based on analogue coding. The advantage of computer-based telecommunication systems is that they are digital not analogue (see pages 12–13). Digital coding results in better sound and image quality compared with analogue. Digital coding also has the advantage of better security and, because of the reduction in the size of data (compression), more data can be sent in a shorter time compared with analogue.

A recent development is the Bluetooth short-range radio system. Bluetooth is a new 'wireless' technology for handheld devices, such as mobile telephones and palmtop computers, to communicate with each other without having to use any wires. It is expected that eventually many devices, such as computers, televisions, stereos, refrigerators, mobile telephones and cookers, will be connected together using Bluetooth technology.

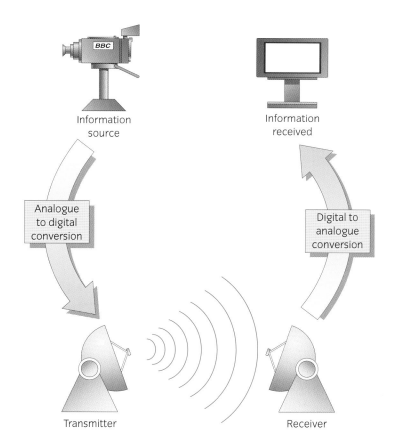

Fig 17.2 How a telecommunication system works

QUESTIONS

1 What is meant by the term telecommunications?
2 Write a paragraph explaining the importance of telecommunications in the world today.
3 How do telecommunication systems work?
4 What can you see are the advantages of devices being linked together by Bluetooth technology?

Connecting to the Internet

There are different ways that computers can be connected to the Internet. Most personal computers are connected to the Internet through a modem (Fig 17.3), which is connected to a telephone line. This form of connection is known as **dial-up networking**. On many PCs, you can actually hear the computer dialling up and connecting to the **Internet Service Provider (ISP).**

The speed at which a modem sends and receives data is measured in kilobits per second (kbps) or megabits per second (Mbps). Basically, the greater the speed of the modem or Internet connection, the faster you can browse the Web and send or receive information. Dial-up connections are the cheapest, and slowest, way to connect to the Internet. The standard speed at present for modems using dial-up networking is 56.6 kbps.

Telephone companies have been keen to increase the speed of Internet connections. This has led to two major developments: ISDN and ADSL. **ISDN** (**I**ntegrated **S**ervices **D**igital **N**etwork) is a high-speed digital alternative to using the existing telephone network. ISDN can send/receive data at 128 kbps (or faster when parallel lines are installed). **ADSL** (**A**symmetric **D**igital **S**ubscriber **L**ine) transforms the existing telephone wires into high-speed digital data lines. With ADSL, data can be sent and received much faster than with traditional modems or ISDN, with speeds up to 8 Mbps. ADSL does not require a dial-up connection, as users are permanently connected to the Internet. For more information on ISDN and ADSL, see page 20.

Many cable television customers can connect to the Internet using a **cable modem** which sends and receives digital data through a connection to a fibre-optic cable television system. Cable television is a broadband service – a single cable can carry several channels at once – which results in data being sent and received at very high speeds (1.5 to 3 Mbps). Other recent developments by digital television companies, such as ITV Digital, include accessing the Internet at home on a television set rather than a PC.

Fig 17.3 A modem (shown above) enables a computer to send data to, and receive data from, another computer via a telephone line, as illustrated below.

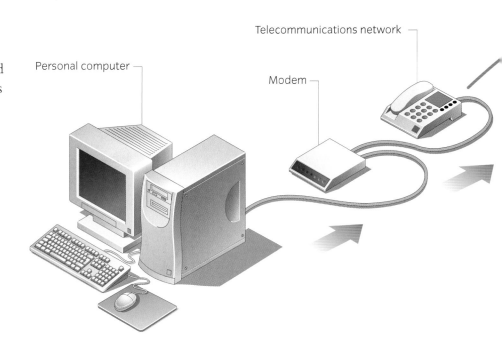

Telecommunications network

Personal computer

Modem

With so many different computer networks linked together on the Internet, there has had to be a standard way in which different networks are linked together. The set of rules, sometimes known as a **protocol**, for sending and receiving data over the Internet is known as **TCP/IP** (**T**ransmission **C**ontrol **P**rotocol/**I**nternet **P**rotocol). TCP/IP breaks down the data into little chunks, or packets, which are sent to other computers on the Internet. TCP/IP then ensures that the data is reassembled into its original form.

Getting data sent to the right computer on the Internet is very important, particularly when there are so many. When you address a letter to be sent through the post, you have to be specific about where you want it to go, giving house number and post code. The same principles have to be applied when using the Internet.

A **host (server)** computer on the Internet is one that provides services such as e-mail, news or data to other computers. Each host computer has its own unique address to identify it. This address is known as an **IP address** (**I**nternet **P**rotocol address). This IP address is usually four numbers separated by full stops: for

example, 194.238.196.100. The first two or three numbers identify the computer network, with the rest identifying the individual computer.

It is much easier to type in and remember a **domain name**, such as www.oup.com/uk, than having to remember the IP address. But as far as the computer is concerned, the IP address is crucial. Every time you send an e-mail, or browse a web page, your IP address is sent behind the scenes. This way your Internet usage can be tracked!

Internet cache

When you are using the Internet, your web browser stores pages and files on your hard disk as you view them. These pages and files are stored in a Temporary Internet Files folder. This is known as **caching**.

The caching of 'temporary' pages and files is important, as it speeds up the display of pages of sites that you have already been to. This is because a computer can access files more quickly from hard disk than from the Web.

QUESTIONS

1   Explain what is meant by dial-up networking.
2   What advantages are there in connecting to the Internet via cable rather than a normal telephone line?
3   Why is TCP/IP so important to the Internet?
4   What is an IP address? Why is this so important for computers on the Internet?

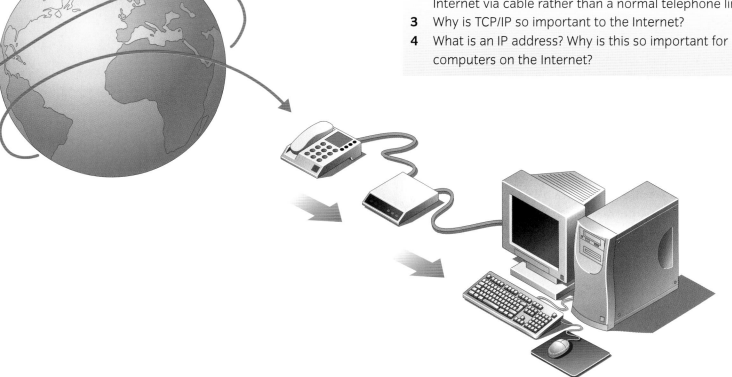

Advantages of the Internet

The Internet is increasing in size day-by-day as more and more people take advantage of what the Internet has to offer. The advantages of the Internet are:

◆ You can find information on the Web on virtually any topic you like. There is enormous education potential, particularly:
   ◆ Collaboration between students (and teachers) on projects of interest
   ◆ Simulations, e.g. dangerous experiments can be shown on the Web
   ◆ Research and finding out more information
   ◆ Gathering of data, e.g. weather data
   ◆ Access to online experts
   ◆ Just to explore and to have fun!
   ◆ Information on the Web can be multimedia: that is, text, graphics, video, animation and sound.

◆ Cultural differences between people all over the world can be broken down as they communicate and find out more about each other, using e-mail, the World Wide Web, newsgroups and Internet Relay Chat. E-mail is particularly popular because it is quicker than postal mail, messages can be sent at the same time to more than one person, and text messages can be sent to mobile phones.

◆ Computer files can be uploaded and downloaded using FTP (File Transfer Protocol).

◆ With faster access to the Internet, it is possible to have interactive games and TV on demand.

◆ Some people can now work from home rather than in an office.

◆ Many commercial organisations advertise, sell goods or provide services on the net: for example, shopping and banking.

◆ You have online access to doctors and medical advice.

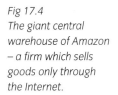

Fig 17.4
The giant central warehouse of Amazon – a firm which sells goods only through the Internet.

Disadvantages of the Internet

There are disadvantages and genuine areas of concern about the Internet. These are:

◆ The cost of computer equipment, connections, of telephone charges can be high.

◆ There is no control on the quality of information available on the Internet, therefore some information may not be accurate or may be highly offensive, such as racist propaganda. Also, some material is illegal and obscene, e.g. child pornography.

◆ Security – many schools, colleges, businesses and other organisations access the Internet via a computer network. It is possible for hackers to gain access, via the Internet, to the network. To prevent this, a security system called a **firewall** is used, which stops the computers on a network communicating directly with computers on the Internet. Instead, all communication is through a **proxy server** that is outside the network. The proxy server acts a gatekeeper, filtering Internet sites and deciding what files or messages should come in to, or go out from, a computer network.

◆ Searching for information can be difficult unless the user knows how to narrow down searches in a search engine.

◆ The protection of copyright material: for example, downloading copyright music without paying for it.

◆ The possibility of downloading computer viruses that can harm data held on a computer or on a network.

Using the Internet in business: a case study

There has been a rapid increase in businesses setting up websites to sell goods and provide services. These businesses are known as **dot com companies** because their Web address ends with '.com'. An example of a dot com company is the online bookseller Amazon, which sells millions of books via the Internet.

The advantage of selling books in this way is that there is no need to have bookshops in towns and cities.

Fig 17.5 Buying goods and services on the Web means that websites must be protected from prying eyes and thieves. Data is encrypted on secure sites that display this icon. Never give personal or financial information to websites that are not secure.

Shops, as we know, open and close at certain times. A website, however, is open 24 hours a day. By not having bookshops, Amazon saves hundreds of thousands of pounds in staffing, rents and other running costs.

Would-be purchasers view the Amazon website for the books they want. The website has a large online database allowing users easily to search thousands of books by author, title, category etc. Once the decision has been made to purchase a book, credit card details are taken online. To stop anyone else on the Internet getting the credit card number and stealing the owner's money, the credit card number is **encrypted** (scrambled). (See also page 171.)

An e-mail is sent by Amazon confirming that an order has been received. The book is packed and sent by first class post – often within 24 hours – from a large central warehouse (Fig 17.4). To let you know when you can expect the book, another e-mail is sent confirming that the book has been dispatched.

The growth of dot com companies has led to an important debate about the future of shopping. Will, for example, the online buying of books mean the end of bookshops? Walking around bookshops, touching and reading books, is an enjoyable experience for many people which online buying cannot provide.

QUESTIONS

1 Give seven reasons why the Internet is so popular.
2 Give two advantages of e-mail.
3 What is encryption? Why is encryption used for some data on the Internet? Give four other reasons why people need to be careful when using the Internet
4 Explain what is meant by the following terms: firewall, proxy server.
5 What do you think about the future of shopping using the Internet?

The success of the Internet has led businesses and other organisations to use the same standards of the Internet (TCP/IP, HyperText Transfer Protocol, HTML), along with Internet web-server software, to set up an **intranet**. Many schools now have their own intranet (Fig 17.6).

An intranet is a private network based on Internet standards but only available *within* a business or other organisation. Nobody else outside of the business or organisation is allowed access to the intranet. An intranet is *not* directly connected to the Internet, but some intranets do allow access, via so-called gateway computers, to the Internet. For users of an intranet, it looks and functions just like a website.

Intranets may, depending on how they are set up, consist of local area networks (LANs) and wide area networks (WANs). A **firewall** is used to stop computers on other networks, including the Internet, accessing an intranet. Intranets are used by many businesses and other organisations to:
◆ Distribute documents
◆ Share information
◆ Distribute software
◆ Access databases
◆ Help with staff training
◆ Facilitate group work
◆ Enable teleconferencing

Intranets are becoming increasingly popular, as they are less expensive to build and manage than other types of private network. Also, users of intranets are familiar with how to use them because they look and behave like websites on the Internet. This saves time and money on staff training.

More and more schools are setting up their own intranets. This is because whole-school information, such as examination timetables, room changes, sports teams and results, can be readily shared with staff and students. Each department in the school can have its own intranet page(s) along with relevant information for

students, such as revision guides and homework tasks. Students also have the opportunity to share their work with others. Because of this, many schools' intranet home page, from which so much information can be shared and distributed, has become an important 'one-stop shop' for network users.

Once intranets were developed, it became clear that businesses and other organisations sometimes wanted to allow others, such as suppliers and customers, to have limited access to their intranet. This would lead to a closer relationship with customers, a better exchange of information and improved efficiency. Therefore, **extranets** were developed. Extranets allow authorised outsiders limited access to an intranet. Not everyone is allowed access to an extranet. Only authorised users are allowed. They must have valid user names and passwords and an identity that establishes which part of the extranet they can access.

Extranets enable businesses to work closely together. A car manufacturer, for example, might develop an extranet to allow all of its various suppliers (of tyres, lights, windscreens, seats etc) and car showrooms to keep in very close contact regarding orders and deliveries. An

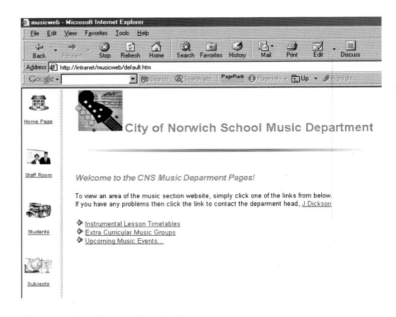

Fig 17.6 A school intranet in action.

extranet could be used to share information not available to the public, as well as to exchange data and to develop joint training programmes. Data can be exchanged using **electronic data interchange (EDI)**. Electronic data interchange is a special way to transfer business documents, such as orders and invoices, between computers. The aim of EDI is to speed up communication between businesses and other organisations, and eventually to do away with paper transactions. EDI often involves putting the data into special computer code to stop other people looking at the data. This is known as **encryption**.

EDI is one aspect of electronic commerce, known as **e-commerce**. E-commerce is the term used for the buying and selling of goods and services on the Internet and, in particular, the World Wide Web. E-commerce is worth tens of millions of pounds as companies, such as Amazon and the giant computer company Dell, sell their goods directly to people via the Web. Many observers and entrepreneurs see e-commerce as bringing about a revolution in business and commercial practices (Fig 17.7).

QUESTIONS

1 What is an intranet? How is an intranet *different* from the Internet? If your school has an intranet, what sort of things is it used for?

2 What is the difference between an Intranet and an extranet?

3 Explain what is meant by: EDI, encryption and e-commerce.

Fig 17.7 E-commerce is bringing about a revolution in the way goods are bought and sold.

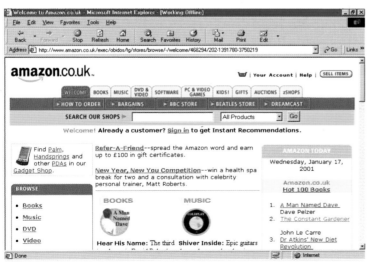

A computer **virus** is a program that infects computer files and makes them do something unexpected or damaging. A copy of the virus program is inserted into a computer file, and when the file is used and loaded into memory, other files become infected. All of this goes on behind the scenes, with computer users unaware that a program or a file has become infected. If one of the infected files is sent by e-mail, or given to other users on floppy disk, then other computers are infected and the virus spreads.

Viruses are an increasing threat to computer systems. In 1986, there was only one known computer virus. Today, between ten and fifteen new viruses appear every day. Unfortunately, the situation is made even worse with some people pretending there is a new virus when there isn't. A hoax virus is an e-mail that is intended to scare people about a non-existent virus threat. Computer users often forward these alerts, thinking they are helping others, but they only cause panic and stop other users from working on their computers.

Viruses often have damaging effects on computer systems. For example, some viruses can destroy a computer's hard disk or take up memory space that could otherwise be used by programs. In 1999, the so-called Melissa virus resulted in many of the world's largest companies having to shut down their e-mail systems completely.

In the year 2000, millions of people opened an attachment to an e-mail headed 'I love you' (Fig 18.2), and thus infected their computers and spread this virus. The virus sent itself to everyone in each computer's e-mail address book and then started damaging files on the recipient's computer. Again, only by shutting down e-mail systems throughout the world was the virus contained – but at a price. Millions of pounds worth of business was lost as e-mail systems were shut down. It also illustrated how quickly a computer virus can spread throughout the world, causing chaos among the world's governments and major businesses.

These viruses were transmitted by e-mail, but viruses can also be spread by downloading programs and files from the Internet. Another way in which viruses can be spread is by using programs or files on floppy disks or CD-ROMs that have been infected.

There are three main types of virus:

- Those that infect program files. The virus code is attached to program files and when the program is loaded, the virus is loaded as well.

- Those that infect system/boot files. The boot file is a small program that tells the computer how to load

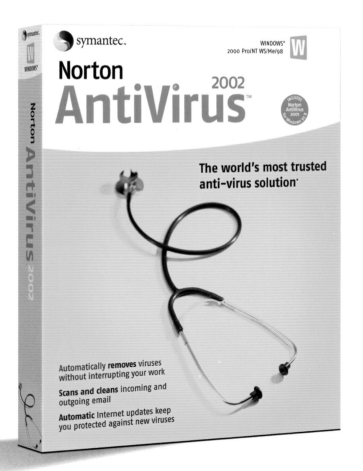

Fig 18.1 The best protection against computer viruses is to install anti-virus software

the rest of the operating system. By infecting this boot (start-up) file, the virus is loaded into memory and is able to run whenever the computer is on.

- Macro viruses. These are written in a macro language associated with an application such as Microsoft Word. The macro virus is carried by a document file and is executed when the document is opened. Over half of the known viruses are macro viruses spread by e-mail attachments.

Preventing viruses

The best way to protect a computer against viruses is to:

- **Install anti-virus software**. Anti-virus software protects the operating system, programs and files against viruses. Anti-virus software regularly scans a computer for viruses and then removes any viruses that are found. Anti-virus software can be set up to automatically check floppy disks, Internet downloads and e-mails for any viruses. Because new viruses are being discovered on a daily basis, leading anti-virus software products, such as Norton Anti-Virus, McAfee Virus Scan and Dr Solomon's, allow subscribers to download anti-virus updates from their websites to keep protection up-to-date.

- **Turn on program virus protection**. Some programs – for example, Microsoft applications – have built-in macro virus protection. When this is the case, make sure that it is turned on (enabled).

- **Try to know the origin of each program or file you use**. In the age of the Internet, this is very difficult – hence the need for anti-virus software. As a rule, beware of free software and software downloaded from the Internet. In contrast, have greater trust in commercial software purchased on CD-ROM, as this will have been checked for viruses before being sold.

- **Never double-click on an e-mail attachment that contains an executable file with an extension EXE, COM or VBS**. This is how the 'I love you' virus was spread.

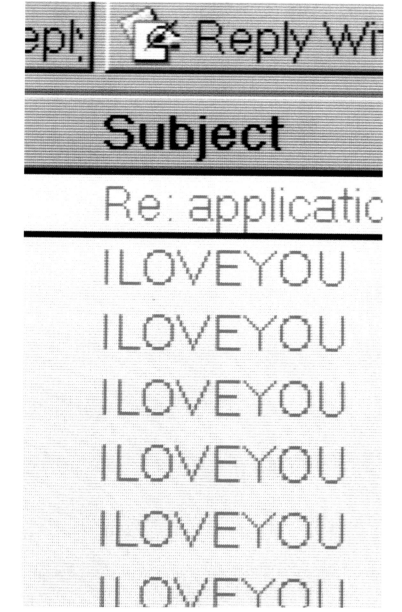

Fig 18.2 This screenshot was taken from a computer in Frankfurt, on 5 May 2000. It shows an e-mail inbox with subject names reading 'I LOVE YOU'. This powerful computer virus crippled computer networks around the world.

QUESTIONS

1 What is a computer virus?
2 List three ways in which a virus can damage or corrupt software.
3 List four steps that could be taken to stop a computer being infected by viruses.

Copyright

Copyright is the name given to the protection in law of the rights of the person(s) responsible for creating such things as text, a piece of music, a painting or a computer program. The best way to understand why copyright is important is to take the case of a popular word processing program such as Microsoft Word. Over many years hundreds of computer programmers have been paid by Microsoft to improve Word. The cost of this runs into millions of pounds. If someone else were to copy the program, or steal it, it would be both unfair and illegal. The illegal copying and stealing of software costs the software industry millions of pounds a year. The **Copyright, Designs and Patents Act, 1989** makes it a criminal offence to be caught copying or stealing software. The Act also makes it an offence to:

◆ copy or distribute software without permission

◆ run copyright software that has been bought on two or more computers at the same time unless the software agreement (licence) allows it

The Federation Against Software Theft (FAST) is an organisation that fights against those breaking the law on copyright. In particular, this organisation is campaigning against software piracy (Fig 18.3). Software piracy is the theft of computer programs and the unauthorised distribution and use of these programs.

The main types of piracy are:

◆ The copying of software (and its packaging) to try to make it look like a genuine product.

◆ The copying and selling of recordable CD-ROMs than contain pirated software.

◆ Downloading copyright software from the Internet. Because software can be downloaded from certain sites does not mean that it is free or legal for you to download.

◆ The use of software on more computers in a network than the number of computers for which there are software licenses.

For more information, contact the FAST website: www.fast.org.uk.

Hackers

Hackers are people who gain access to computer systems without permission and who then may mess about with the programs and data. While some hackers do not do any damage, others do – for example, by leaving a computer virus. In the past, student hackers have broken into people's e-mail accounts and got into hospital, business and atomic energy computer systems.

Fig 18.3 Software piracy is against the law in many countries, but is not outlawed worldwide.

MICROTHEFT
THE MIRROR PAGE 9

The Mirror

NEWS

Hacker strikes at heart of Microsoft

The Guardian

Hackers tap into Microsoft secrets

Daily Mail

FBI called in as hackers leak Microsoft secrets to Russia

Independent

Microsoft humiliated as hackers crack Windows

The Daily Telegraph

Fig 18.4
How five British newspapers reported, in October 2000, that hackers had gained access to Microsoft's source code for Windows and Office applications.

Some criminals have got into people's bank accounts and stolen money. Because of this, the **Computer Misuse Act, 1990** was passed. This Act states that it is against the law to gain unauthorised access to computer material. In particular, it is illegal to do any of the following.

◆ Deliberately plant computer viruses that damage program files and data.

◆ Copy computer programs illegally (computer piracy).

◆ Hack into a computer with the intention of seeing or altering information.

◆ Use a computer to commit crimes (frauds): for example, to create a fictitious worker and get money paid into this non-existent person's bank account.

◆ Use your employer's computer to carry out unauthorised work.

People found guilty under the Computer Misuse Act can expect to receive a large fine or a prison sentence.

Some people regard hacking as posing a major threat to the world's governments and major companies. In October 2000, the giant software company Microsoft – whose Windows operating system is used on 95% of the world's computers – admitted that hackers had gained access to its top-secret source code for Windows and Microsoft Office applications (Fig 18.4). Getting access to this source code has been described as the equivalent of finding the secret ingredients and recipe for Coca-Cola. What the hackers will do with the stolen source code is unclear, but this case highlights the damage a few people can do to one of the world's top companies, which, up until then, was regarded as having an excellent security system against hackers. This case also raises the question that if hackers can gain access to Microsoft source code, is any computerised data safe?

QUESTIONS

1 Explain what is meant by **a)** copyright and **b)** hacking.

2 What are the main points of the Copyright, Designs and Patents Act, 1989 and the Computer Misuse Act, 1990?

Data protection can mean two things. One is to do with the ways in which computer users can protect their data against loss or damage. The other is the Data Protection Act, which sets down rules about what information can be kept by others about you.

Protecting data on computers

There are some important steps that all computer users should take to protect their data against damage, loss or even attack by computer viruses. These are:

- **Backing up** Making copies of your files is important, as files can be lost, deleted or in some cases corrupted, so that they do not work at all. By regularly saving different versions of a file, or by saving a file onto a floppy or removable disk, you will always have a recent copy of what you have done. Most computer networks automatically back up data on to tape each night.

- **Computer viruses** Virus protection programs not only scan a computer for harmful viruses but also protect and intercept viruses attempting to infect system or application software.

- **Locking disks** Floppy and removable disks can be locked by covering the write-protection hole. This prevents the changing, deletion or infection of files.

- **Network security** Each individual user on a network is given a user name with an individual password. This prevents other users accessing an individual's file, changing program settings, or installing, copying or deleting software.

Fig 18.5 The 1998 Data Protection Act has strict rules for processing personal information.

Data Protection Act, 1998

Many people and organisations have their details held on other people's computer files. For example, your school has details about you and your family, as does your doctor. Most people recognise that having computerised records helps schools and doctors in their work. However, this growth in personal information in other areas has many problems and dangers.

First, information about people held on one computer can easily be transferred to another computer. In fact,

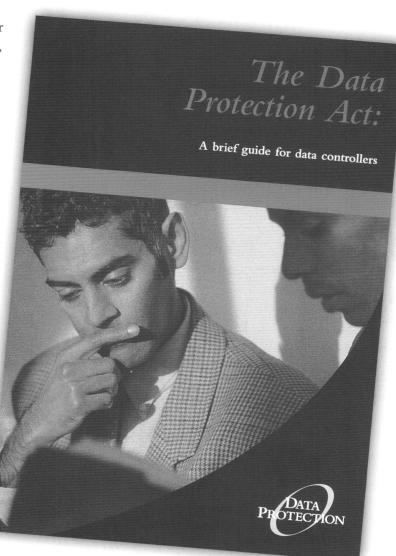

some companies make money out of selling personal information. For example, if you subscribe to a computer magazine you may receive a letter from another company trying to sell you software. You may not mind this, but you should have a choice as to whether your personal information is passed on.

The information held on you might also be wrong. It could have been entered incorrectly, it could be out of date or you could have been confused with someone else! Whichever way, this information could be damaging. Just think of the damage that could be caused if the information held on you stated that you had been in trouble with the police when you hadn't, or that you owed money when you didn't. These examples emphasise the importance of information being handled properly.

This is where the 1998 Data Protection Act comes in. This Act sets out in law the rules for processing personal information (Fig 18.5). A Data Protection Commissioner is responsible for enforcing the Act. The Act applies to some paper records, as well as those held on computer. According to the Act, people who have data held about them are called **data subjects**. The organisations and people who have the data are called **data controllers**. The Act works in two ways:

◆ It gives people rights about the way in which their personal information is used.

◆ It ensures that data controllers are open about how the information is used, and that they follow the eight rules set out in the table (on the left).

You have a legal right to find out what information is held about you on computer and in some paper records. You can do this by writing to the person or organisation you believe holds the information (Fig 18.6). You are not, though, allowed to check information held on you concerning such things as national security, crime prevention/detection, salaries and income tax.

For more information about your rights, see the data protection website www.dataprotection.gov.uk.

Data Protection Act, 1998: The eight rules of 'good information handling'

Anyone in the UK processing personal data must comply with the eight principles of good practice. They say that data must be:

1 Fairly and lawfully processed
2 Processed for limited purposes
3 Adequate, relevant and not excessive
4 Accurate
5 Not kept longer than necessary
6 Processed in line with data subjects' rights
7 Secure
8 Not transferred to countries without adequate protection

Be open...

Fig 18.6
This symbol alerts people to the fact that their information is being collected, and directs them to sources which explain how their information is to be used.

QUESTIONS

1 List four ways that people can protect their data against damage, loss or attack by computer viruses.
2 Give the two ways in which the Data Protection Act of 1998 works.
3 What rights do individuals have regarding the information that is held about them?

Throughout this book, there are numerous examples of how information systems play an increasingly important part in your life – from programmable video recorders to e-commerce on the Internet. The changes in information and communication technology (ICT) have been so great that we talk about an 'ICT revolution'.

Changes in the workplace

The ICT revolution has brought about widespread changes in the workplace. Most offices now use computer systems, often connected by a LAN or WAN. Applications such as word processors, databases and e-mail, as well as mobile telephones, are used by millions of people every day. Although the aim of having a paperless office has been a long time coming, major companies such as IBM are spending millions of pounds in writing software to ensure that all paper-based transactions will in future be completed electronically with no paper involved. Videoconferencing via WAN and the Internet enables meetings to take place without the participants having to leave their offices.

Fig 18.7 Information systems are now an essential part of office work.

Millions of people, known as **teleworkers**, now work – on a full or part-time basis – at home or move about the country using a PC and a modem to communicate with their employers and/or clients. The benefits of teleworking are: time and money is saved by not having to travel to and from a main office; hours can be flexible; people can work together over a very large area and employers save money not having to run large offices. However, teleworking is isolating, as one of the enjoyable aspects of a job in an office is socialising with other people.

In retailing, you still might know of small shops where computers are not used. Here, goods will be priced individually by hand. When prices change, so do the pricing labels. The prices of the goods that are sold have to be manually entered into a till. Itemised receipts sometimes have to be hand written. Checking the stock levels in the shop and re-ordering have to be done by individually counting the different product lines.

Compare this with how a large supermarket uses computer systems. Goods do not need to be individually priced. This is because each item has a barcode that is swiped through a barcode reader at the **point of sale (POS)** computer terminal at the checkout. The price for each item is held centrally on a database and the price for each item is sent back to the POS terminal. All of the items bought by a customer are automatically listed and added up and any discounts, due to loyalty cards, given. Payment can be made using credit/debit cards that are swiped through a reader. The money is automatically transferred to the supermarket's account. A bill, listing each item that has been bought, is then printed off and given to the customer.

Each supermarket's computer is linked to a warehouse and main computer system through a wide area network. As the items are swiped through the barcode readers at the checkouts, the stock levels of each product line are automatically updated. When the stock of a product gets too low, the product can be automatically re-ordered from the warehouse and delivered the next

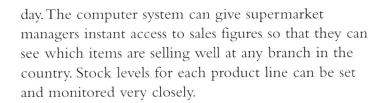

Fig 18.8 A barcode reader being used to 'swipe' goods at a point of sale (POS) terminal at a supermarket checkout.

Fig 18.9 Millions of cheques are processed every day using magnetic-ink character recognition (MICR).

day. The computer system can give supermarket managers instant access to sales figures so that they can see which items are selling well at any branch in the country. Stock levels for each product line can be set and monitored very closely.

Using the Internet for **e-commerce** and selling goods and services direct to customers is a growing business worth millions of pounds. New businesses and e-banks have been created, but such is the importance of e-commerce that all major retailers also have e-commerce operations.

Banks now depend on computer systems to run their business. Funds are instantly credited and debited from customers' accounts. Networked **automated teller machines (ATMs)** throughout the world allow customers to withdraw cash and check their account details. Salaries can be automatically paid into accounts and bills paid using direct debits. Credit and debit cards enable customers to buy goods and services at most retail outlets, with the purchase cost automatically debited to the customers' accounts. Each day, banks process millions of cheques using **magnetic-ink character recognition (MICR)**.

In the manufacturing industries, computer-aided design and manufacturing (CAD/CAM) is in widespread use as computer systems are used to design and make products. Robots are used in the electronics and vehicles industries. Unlike humans, robots do not need a break. They can save on labour costs and can work in dangerous conditions.

QUESTIONS

1 What are the advantages of using an information system in a supermarket? Can you think of any disadvantages?
2 Explain what is meant by teleworking.

Education

ICT is also having a major effect on education, with extra government money providing more Internet-enabled computer systems for schools. ICT supports and enhances learning in every subject. Special needs students have benefited greatly from ICT by, for example, using voice input systems.

Economic effects

The economic effects of information systems have been described on pages 178–9. One area of concern has been that the introduction of information systems has led to unemployment, particularly in manufacturing (for example, the replacement of workers by robots) and in office work. However, it is also true to say that information systems have led to an *increase* in other types of job, such as teleworking. In some factories where there is widespread use of the latest computer technology, some of the 'new' jobs involve packing boxes and sweeping up. Jobs such as these have led to the accusation that the introduction of information systems is leading to the deskilling of some of the workforce. Government evidence would suggest, however, that the use of information systems has created more jobs than have been lost by its introduction.

Social effects

The widespread use of information systems has led to more efficient ways of working and to a decrease in the hours that many people have to work. This allows more time for people to spend on leisure pursuits. Without a second thought, millions of people use personal computers at home, mobile telephones and information system devices such as video recorders. The growth of telecommunications, including the Internet, has led to a situation where people can share information in a 'global village'. Distance is no longer an issue, with people communicating as if they were living closely together in a small village.

There is disagreement about the effects on young people of spending a long time on computers and playing computer games. Some people argue that prolonged use makes youngsters withdrawn and less likely to socialise with others, whereas others argue that playing games can develop problem-solving skills and encourage collaboration and teamwork.

Fig 18.10 Millions of people now use personal computers at home.

Environmental effects

The widespread adoption of information systems has also had environmental effects. On the one hand, the need to power millions of computers has increased the electricity consumption, while on the other hand, the consumption of electricity and other forms of energy has been reduced as computers carefully control air-conditioning and heating systems. Information systems have enabled teleworking from home. This can mean less travel to and from work and therefore a reduction in traffic pollution. Although the age of the true paperless office is some years away, there has already been some saving on the use of paper (and therefore trees) as data is communicated and stored digitally.

Fig 18.11 In this car manufacturing plant, robots now do the jobs previously done by people.

Legal, ethical and moral effects

There continue to be genuine concerns about the legal, ethical and moral effects of information systems. You have seen that a great deal of personal information is held on computers and that the Data Protection Act has been passed to try to ensure that personal information is held and processed responsibly. Laws have also been passed to try to stop hacking and the pirating (stealing) of software. All of this raises some important ethical and moral issues such as the following:

- How far should the law go in giving the police access to everyone's personal data, or e-mails, in order to fight crime or to defend national security?

- How far should established and new technologies, such as closed-circuit television (CCTV) and microchip smart cards, be used to monitor people's activities?

- Should there be government control of the Internet? Some people argue that a major strength of the Internet is that everyone has the freedom to express what they think, and that this is what democracy is all about. Others argue that racist propaganda and pornography should be banned.

- What will happen to people who cannot afford to buy a computer system and who therefore are not part of the ICT revolution? Will they lose out financially and socially, and become in effect second-class citizens?

- In the year 2000, the UK government admitted that thousands of people who owe income tax would not have to pay, as their tax details had been lost in the change over to a new computer system. Is this fair?

QUESTIONS

You are going to give a short talk to your class about the important ethical and moral issues raised by information systems. Read carefully the five points given here about these issues. Then write a short answer to each of the questions, clearly explaining your views on the subject.

Millions of people use computers regularly for work, education and leisure. As with any other equipment, computers should be used safely and in a way that doesn't harm users' health. This is important, as there is evidence that using a computer for a long time can affect your health.

Health problems

Using a computer for long periods of time, and not properly using computer equipment or furniture, can result in serious injury. Some examples of this are given below.

Repetitive Strain Injury

Aches and pains, swelling and difficulty of movement are all symptoms of disorders affecting fingers, wrists, arms and neck that can be caused by lengthy or improper use of computers. The common name for these disorders is **repetitive strain injury (RSI)**. RSI is caused by long and regular periods of typing or using the mouse. It can also be caused by poor workstation set-up. RSI, also known as 'mouse arm', can be extremely painful. Tens of thousands of people suffer from it.

What can be done to stop RSI?
- Take regular breaks or changes in activity. Short breaks of 5-10 minutes every hour are recommended.
- Place the mouse immediately to the left or right of the keyboard.
- Hold the mouse loosely and don't use the mouse continuously for long periods.
- Use wrist and/or arm rests.
- Keyboards should be easy to use, tilted and separate from the screen.
- There should be sufficient space in front of the keyboard to rest hands or arms.
- Sit in a comfortable position, and regularly change the way you sit (posture).
- During regular breaks, stretch and move your hands, wrist and neck as a form of exercise.
- Be relaxed. RSI can be caused by tension.

Back problems

Back problems can be caused by poor or incorrectly set furniture or equipment.

What can be done to stop back problems?
- Chairs should be adjustable in height, able to swivel and have a tilting backrest.
- Chairs should be at the correct height to use the keyboard and screen.
- Sit in a comfortable position, and regularly change the way you sit (posture).
- Desks should be large enough to take all the computer equipment.
- Take frequent short breaks, and stand up or walk around.

Eye problems

Eyestrain is the most common health problem linked to using computer screens for long periods. Eye problems are also linked to poor lighting, glare and being too close to, or too far from, the screen. The size of fonts and colours used in software can all affect the eyes. Think about this when designing software solutions for your GCSE coursework.

What can be done to stop eye problems?
Computer screens should:
- Not flicker
- Allow the brightness and contrast settings to be easily changed
- Tilt and swivel
- Be positioned to avoid glare and reflections from lights or windows, and be fitted with glare-reduction filters.

Stress

Using computers, or having your work monitored by computers, can be stressful. Also, modern communication technologies, such as e-mail, portable notebook computers and mobile phones, mean that some people cannot take proper breaks as they can always be contacted immediately. This, too, can be stressful.

Pregnancy

There are concerns that pregnant women's unborn babies may be affected by electromagnetic radiation from the computer screens used by these women. Computer manufacturers now produce low-emission screens to combat this.

Safety

A safe working environment is very important. Computers are powered by electricity, so the following measures must be taken in all workplaces.

- Electric sockets are not to be overloaded with lots of plugs or long extension leads.
- No cables are to be left on the floor (or benching) for anyone to trip over or damage.
- Cables are not to be coiled – the heat generated may be sufficient to start a fire.
- Computer equipment is to be regularly tested for safety.
- CO_2 fire extinguishers are to be available in case of fire.
- Food and drink are not to be consumed around a computer in case of spillage.

The law

The **Health and Safety at Work Act, 1974** sets out the law on general health and safety issues. More specific legal standards for computer safety are contained in the **Health and Safety (Display Screen Equipment) Regulations, 1992**. These regulations apply only to people who use computer screens continuously as part of their work. They do not apply to students at school or college.

The computer manufacturer Compaq has an excellent website dealing with health and safety issues and computers. Check it out at

http://www5.compaq.com/comfortguide

Also, check out the Health and Safety Executive at

http://www.hse.gov.uk

QUESTIONS

1. List the potential health problems linked to using ICT equipment for long periods.
2. Design an A5 leaflet alerting people to safety issues related to computer use in offices.

D **c**oursework

19.1 **i**ntroduction

Coursework is a very important part of GCSE examinations in ICT. Your final grade will be made up from marks for your coursework and marks for the written examination. The coursework part is worth 60% of the maximum mark. Coursework can therefore make a big difference to your final mark. If you do well in your coursework, you can achieve a grade C before you answer a single question in the written examination.

This unit will give you step-by-step ideas of what you need to do to get the best possible mark.

Choosing a project to work with

The size and scope of a piece of coursework varies, depending on the examination board that you are doing your GCSE with. Normally, you will submit between two and four pieces of work for a full-course GCSE,

and one or two pieces for a short-course GCSE. A piece of coursework may have a fairly narrow focus into a particular area of ICT – such as desktop publishing or databases. Or you may have to produce an extended piece of work – possibly a system which solves a series of problems for an organisation.

Before you start your coursework, you will need to be familiar with the requirements of your examination board. Your teacher may be able to give you the examination specification or you may be able to visit the examination board's website to get a copy of it.

What works best?

If you have a choice of the area to work in, choose an area that you already know something about. This means that you do not have to spend as much time finding out

Fig 19.1
Talking to the leader of a student drama group revealed that the tasks involved in putting on a play are many and varied. Some of these could be made easier by using ICT systems.

184

what to do. You can use your experience to find a really good way of using ICT – and you may already have an idea of how ICT could be used to improve something.

Make your project manageable. Don't try to build systems for large and complex scenarios. If you do, you may not understand how all the different elements work, and find yourself in all sorts of difficulties. You could end up losing valuable marks because the solutions you create do not work. You need to do something that does work so that you can show your ability.

What do you have to produce?

You are not producing this work just for yourself. It is for the examination board. You are going to produce a report on what you did, how you did it, and why you did it in this particular way. The examiners are not in the room with you, so they will not know what programs you had available. They will not have watched and helped you like your teachers do. You need to tell them everything. This might seem unnecessary but it isn't!

Remember – a printout from a piece of work only shows the answer. It does not show how you got to the answer and what you did to get to the answer. The examiners are more interested in seeing how well you understand the tools that you used and how well you have used them. You can't gain marks for things you have not written down.

Identifying an area to work on

It makes sense to do some background research into your chosen scenario to help you to make it real. There is a tension between what the scenario needs and what your GCSE board needs. Make sure you select something that will give you the scope to get the best grade you can.

You need to find out what goes on in your chosen scenario. What are the information requirements? How does data flow through the system? What might be the advantages of using computer-based information systems in this scenario? Set the scene so that the examiners know what it is all about.

Your research should highlight what goes on at the moment and identify problem areas that need investigation and possibly need a solution. At this stage, an outline is all that you need. You will develop this as you progress through the work.

Once you have selected the area and done some background research into the aspects that need a solution, it is time for you to do an in-depth analysis of the problem(s). If it is a piece of coursework that requires you to focus on just one aspect (such as producing a DTP booklet or poster), you may not need to do the first step. If it is a wider ranging problem where the solution will consist of several related elements, you need to break down the problem into manageable tasks. These tasks will need to make a functioning whole.

Breaking down the problem

The first job that you need to do is to break down the problem into tasks that you can solve. The drama group, for example, might want you to build a system to run the group (see page 185). This is not clear enough and doesn't tell you what needs to be created. An interview with the group's leaders might reveal that they want a system to perform four main tasks. The system must provide a group database which can store information about members of the group. It should produce tickets, posters and programmes for the next production. It should deal with the costs of running the group and its productions. Finally, it should produce a rehearsal schedule both as a list and as a set of individual letters to all members of the cast and stage crew.

These tasks may still be too big and need breaking down further. The publicity for the next production is at least three sub-tasks but they will be related. It makes sense to develop the poster separately from the tickets even though each will contain some of the same information. Similarly, the programme will need to be done separately, but again will contain some of the common information.

What data will be input?

Once the tasks have been identified, the next stage is to decide what data will be supplied to your solution. The database of group members would need information from all the members of the group. How will this be collected? The posters, tickets and programmes may all need the group logo on them, along with the details of the production. How will these be generated? The method of inputting this data needs to be thought through. Is it direct keyboard entry or will it be imported from another program?

For each task, you need to decide what data needs to be collected, assembled and prepared for input. This will help you to decide at the design stage what you need to build to accept this data.

What information will be output?

As part of your analysis, you need to look at the flow of information. What is going to happen to the data and what will be expected from the system? This will help you to decide on the links between different parts of the system. The group logo will need to be used in a range of places. A list of members from the database might need to be incorporated into the programme (the cast list).

You need to state what you expect to produce from your solution, and to make sure that you have collected the correct data to be able to produce these outputs. You need to talk about the processes that will be needed to produce the required output.

The reason for having a group database will probably be to produce lists of different sub-groups of members in the group. This means that the information that is collected in the first place must allow the user of the system to extract the correct information from the system.

How will you know when you have succeeded?

When you think you have finished your piece of work, you will need to evaluate it and to state how well your solution solves the problem. To help you to do this, you

What needs to be done to put on a play?
From the interview I found out that the following areas are involved.

MUST have:
Group name,
Play title,
Performance date,
Seat number,
Seat cost

TICKETS

BOOKING SYSTEM FOR PERFORMANCES

INCOME

AUDITIONS FOR PARTS

EXPENDITURE - SETS, COSTUMES, REFRESHMENTS

COSTINGS → WILL WE MAKE A PROFIT?

INCOME FROM ADVERTISING + TICKET SALES + INTERVAL REFRESHMENTS

REHEARSAL SCHEDULE

LISTS OF PEOPLE INVOLVED IN PARTICULAR REHEARSALS

LIGHTING + SOUND + EFFECTS

PUTTING ON A PLAY

POSTERS

NEWSPAPER ADVERT

ADVERTISING PLAY

LOCAL RADIO

Needs: Group name, Date, Time, Venue, Play title, Ticket costs...

ADVERTISING FROM SPONSORS?   ABOUT THE PLAY

PROGRAMMES

STAGE CREW   → CAST

INFORMATION NEEDS TO BE IN PROGRAMME

CAST LIST

TO NOTIFY PEOPLE OF THE PARTS THEY HAVE

SETS + COSTUMES

?

THESE COULD BE INCLUDED IN A DATABASE OF MEMBERS OF THE GROUP

Cast list could be searched for and exported from the database and inserted into the programme and lists made!

This needs to hold personal information – name, address, telephone numbers, role in production (cast or crew or none?). If cast which part, which scenes are they in?

— Areas where ICT could be used
— No scope for using ICT

need to set some criteria (performance criteria) that the system can be evaluated against. What is it supposed to do?

For the logo, one criterion might be that it can be used at different sizes and still clearly identify the group. On the tickets, the logo will need to be small, and on posters it will need to be large.

A sensible set of criteria for each element needs to be established.

Summary of analysis

◆ Choose the area and research what is needed.

◆ Identify the problems or tasks that need a solution.

◆ For each task, decide on data to be input, the processing that is needed and the outputs that are required to solve the task.

◆ What links exist between the tasks?

◆ Set the performance criteria that help you to evaluate how successful your solution is.

Fig 19.3
Ways in which you could solve this problem.

Ways that I could design the ticket sales system for the play.

MANUAL SYSTEM

I could have a paper seating plan and cross off each seat as a ticket is sold.

+ Cheap and easy to produce.
− If mistakes are made on the seating plan, messy to correct it.
− Might be easy to make mistakes when adding up the money.

SEATING PLAN

TUESDAY — A B C D ...
1, 2, 3, 4, 5, 6

WEDNESDAY — A B C D ...
1, 2, 3, 4, 5, 6

This would need a book to record the money taken from the sales.

MONEY TAKEN BOOK

TUESDAY		WEDNESDAY	
TICKET	COST	TICKET	COST
A3	£4.00	B2, B3, B4	£12.00
B1, B2, B3	£12.00	C3	£4.00
...	...	A4, A5	£8.00
		A1	£4.00
	TOTAL ...		TOTAL ...

USING A CALCULATOR

This would help to make the money side of things more accurate BUT would still need the manual paper recording system.

+ Adding up the money should be more accurate.
− Still uses lots of paper.

USING A COMPUTER

This could be done using a) a spreadsheet or b) a purpose-built computer ticket system.

a) Spreadsheet

TUESDAY

	A	B	C	D	E	F
1						
2	A					
3	A					
4	A	C				
5						
6						

NUMBER OF TICKETS SOLD: A = 3 C = 1 TOTAL INCOME = £14.00

Formula counting As
Formula counting Cs
Formula which calculates the income ((3 × £4) + (1 × £2) = £14)

Put code letters into cells - A = Adult C = Child. Formulas could count the number of 'As' in cells and the number of 'Cs'. Then a formula could work out the total automatically by multiplying the number of 'As' by £4.00 and the number of 'Cs' by £2.00 and working out the total.

+ Automatically calculates the income from selling tickets.
+ Mistakes can easily be put right.
+ As long as no data entry errors, it would be accurate - could build data validation into it and make it as accurate as possible.
− People using the system will need more training with this system than the paper system.

b) A computer ticket system

+ Best tool for job.
− Very expensive.
− Would need specialist training to use.

Once you have analysed your problem, you will have a task or range of tasks which need to be solved. Don't just go straight to the computer and try to start building a solution. Designing your solution is worth quite a lot of marks, so don't throw them away.

Some students try to cover up this omission and write the design after they have built their solution. However, usually this shows up because they write about what they did and not about what they intended to do.

In what ways could you do this task?

Look at each task and make comments about the ways in which you could go about solving the task. It might be that there are manual ways that do not involve the use of a computer, or that there are several ways of using a computer. There is no rule as to how many ways you should consider – just look at realistic methods.

The programmes for the play could be produced on a typewriter, by a word processor, or using a desktop publishing program. The choice of the most suitable method depends on how complex the finished programme needs to be but you are not making a choice now (that comes later). At this stage, you are showing the examiners how much you know. You are showing them how many different methods there are which might help you to solve the problem.

You can now see how important it is not to miss out the design process. Show the examiners what you know and gain the marks.

What tools could you use for the task?

Here, you need to show how much you know about different computer programs which could perform the tasks needed to solve the problem. It is not usually good enough to mention only one program. Also, you may need to decide on hardware requirements. Will you need any other devices such as a scanner or control interface?

If the task is about writing a letter to a customer of a particular business, there are several programs that you could use. For a Windows-based PC, you will find programs called Notepad and Wordpad and you may also have Microsoft Word. Ask yourself what facilities you need. What needs to go into the letter and how should it be formatted? Which of these three programs will do what you want?

For this part of the design stage, you need to make an informed choice from the tools that are suitable for the task. What are the differences between Notepad, Wordpad and Microsoft Word? But this is not really the first question you have to answer. First, you should establish what needs to be in the letter.

For example, if the letter needs to have the company logo inserted in the top-right corner and to have the text typed below the logo – justified and including bold, italic and underlined typefaces – then you have identified the facilities you require.

If you know these programs, then you will know that you cannot put a picture into Notepad. So this program is unsuitable. Notepad is also not very versatile with text styles.

Wordpad can handle pictures but only if you copy and paste them from the program that created the pictures. There is no import facility. The formatting of the text is no problem here. This means that Wordpad does have the required facilities and so would be suitable.

Microsoft Word will let you import pictures without needing to use the program that created them. It can also do all the required formatting of the text. So, in terms of facilities, there are two programs which are capable of doing the job.

This stage does not need to be large, but it does need to cover the ways which you know of that could be used to solve the problem. You are not expected to do an in-depth study of each piece of software, but you do need to show how much you know about computer programs and associated pieces of hardware.

Which program is the best one to use?

Now that you have found which programs can do the job, it is time to choose just one and to give some clear reasons why it is the best. These reasons should focus on the suitability of the facilities for the task. If there are several programs that would do the job, do not automatically choose the most advanced or the most expensive. It might be the very best for the job, but it also might be quite hard to achieve the desired output. Remember that you have to be able to use it. If you are going to have to spend time learning how to use this program, then it might not be the most sensible one to choose.

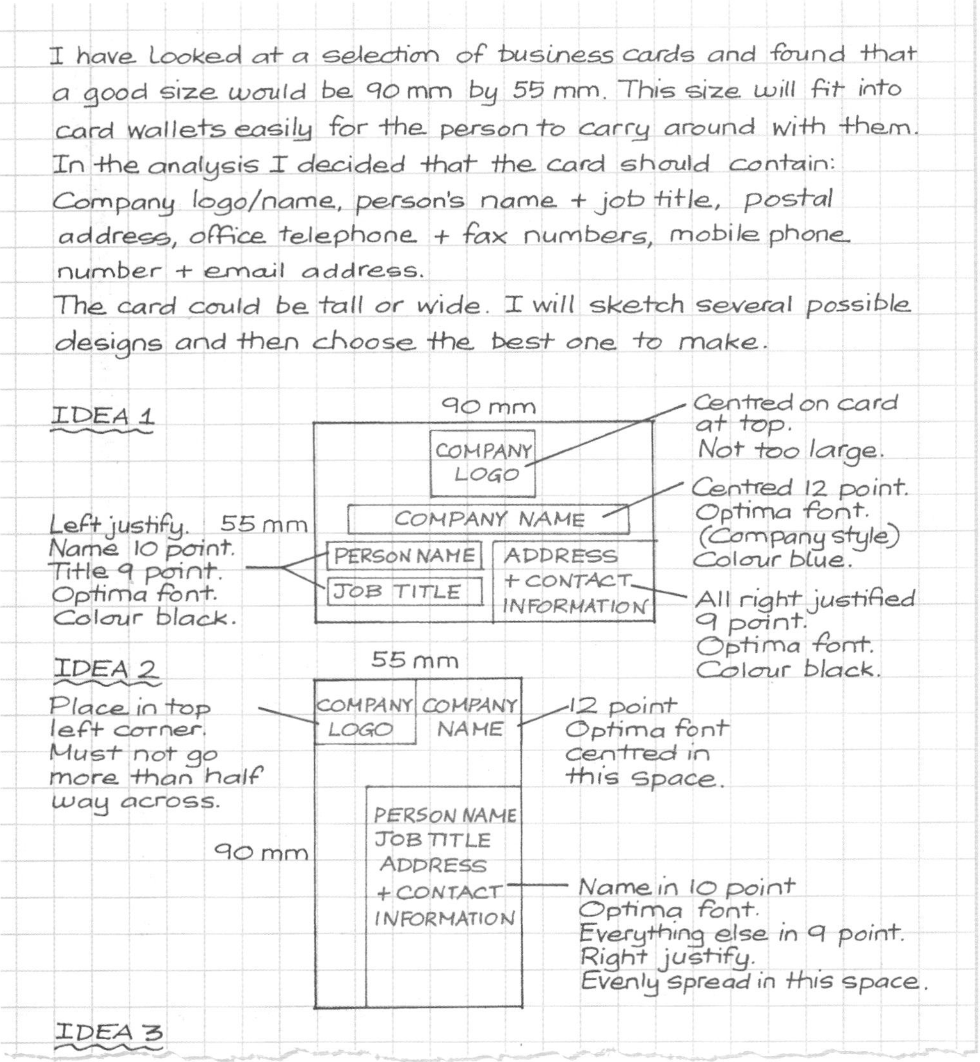

What do you intend to create?

Now you have made the choice of software, you are ready to create your design. The examiners need to see what you intend to build. If they do not see your intentions, how are they going to know whether you were successful in building what you intended? Again, it is about convincing the examiners that you know what you want to build and how to go about it. The examiners will usually look at this section to see how much of your original design you managed to build. It provides them with useful evidence about how well you understood what you were doing. They need the evidence to give you the marks.

Your design intentions can take a variety of forms. Where the output is visual, as in a graphics problem, a data-capture form or a booklet, sketches of what you intend to create are a good starting point. How will the elements of the presentation be laid out? What sort of fonts will you use and at what size? You may need to say how you intend to bring all the elements together. Will graphic elements need to be resized?

A database design will need to show clearly the intended data structure (fig 18.5). What fields will be needed and what data types will the fields be? Will a data-capture form be needed and does this need to be designed? How will you ensure that, as you transfer the data from the form into the database, mistakes are minimised? Are you going to use any data validation? Again, some

I have looked at a selection of business cards and found that a good size would be 90 mm by 55 mm. This size will fit into card wallets easily for the person to carry around with them. In the analysis I decided that the card should contain: Company logo/name, person's name + job title, postal address, office telephone + fax numbers, mobile phone number + email address.
The card could be tall or wide. I will sketch several possible designs and then choose the best one to make.

IDEA 1

90 mm

COMPANY LOGO — Centred on card at top. Not too large.

COMPANY NAME — Centred 12 point. Optima font. (Company style) Colour blue.

Left justify. Name 10 point. Title 9 point. Optima font. Colour black. — 55 mm

PERSON NAME
JOB TITLE
ADDRESS + CONTACT INFORMATION — All right justified 9 point. Optima font. Colour black.

IDEA 2

55 mm

Place in top left corner. Must not go more than half way across. — COMPANY LOGO | COMPANY NAME — 12 point Optima font centred in this space.

90 mm

PERSON NAME
JOB TITLE
ADDRESS + CONTACT INFORMATION — Name in 10 point Optima font. Everything else in 9 point. Right justify. Evenly spread in this space.

IDEA 3

Fig 19.4 Design layout for a business card, showing where everything will go and in what styles the text will be.

elements of this would benefit from a sketch of the desired output, but the definitions of the fields and the structure of the database will need to be clearly explained. The techniques you wish to employ to ensure that the data is accurate will need to be clearly described.

When a spreadsheet is required, the mathematics needed will have to be worked out. Once you have understood the mathematics, you will have to think about how you will lay out the spreadsheet so that data entry is straightforward and the answers from the formulas will be logically related to the input data. Again, a sketch layout is useful, but how the cells will relate to one another will need some written description. This might take the form of some annotation on the sketch layout.

Control and measuring systems need to show what you are going to control or measure. Here, you will need to select appropriate sensors or devices to control. For a control system, the sequences will need to be designed, which you may present as a flow chart.

Fig 19.5 Design sketches for a database system.

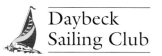

Daybeck Sailing Club

Data structure for the members database

Field name	Type	Size and notes
MEMBERSHIP NUMBER	AUTONUMBER	UNIQUE VALUE
TITLE	VALUE LIST	Value to select from: Mr, Mrs, Miss, Ms, Dr
FIRSTNAME	TEXT	20 characters maximum
SURNAME	TEXT	30 characters maximum
ADDRESS: HOUSE NUMBER/NAME	TEXT	20 characters maximum
STREET/ROAD	TEXT	20 characters maximum
TOWN	TEXT	20 characters maximum
AREA	TEXT	20 characters maximum
COUNTY	TEXT	20 characters maximum
POSTCODE	TEXT	7 characters maximum
TELEPHONE NUMBER	TEXT	11 characters
TYPE OF MEMBER	VALUE LIST	Values: Adult, Child, Senior Citizen
GENDER	VALUE LIST	Values: M or F
PAID SUBSCRIPTION?	VALUE LIST	Values: Y or N
DATE SUBSCRIPTION PAID	DATE FIELD	

Cannot be a number field because all telephone numbers start with a zero, and number fields will not register a zero at the beginning of the number.

I will use value lists for some of these fields to make sure the data in the database is accurate and consistent. For example – all the member type field can only contain ADULT, CHILD or SENIOR CITIZEN and nothing else.

To collect this information from new members I will need a data capture form. This will need to have all the information laid out so that it is easy to fill in and reflects the size of the fields in my database.

For example, the person's title will be a series of tick boxes and the person puts in one tick. The same will happen for the TYPE OF MEMBER, GENDER and PAID SUBSCRIPTION? fields.

Fields that have a maximum size should have a row of boxes. The number of boxes should be the same as the field size – e.g. postcode should be seven boxes (seven characters).

NEW MEMBERSHIP FORM

What is your title? (Tick one box)
Mr ☐   Mrs ☐   Miss ☐   Ms ☐   Dr ☐

What is your...
FIRST NAME ☐☐☐☐☐☐☐☐☐☐☐☐☐☐☐☐☐☐☐☐
SURNAME ☐☐☐☐☐☐☐☐☐☐☐☐☐☐☐☐☐☐☐☐☐☐☐☐☐☐

Address
HOUSE NUMBER/NAME ☐☐☐☐☐☐☐☐☐☐☐☐☐☐☐☐☐☐☐☐
STREET ☐☐☐☐☐☐☐☐☐☐☐☐☐☐☐☐☐☐☐☐
TOWN ☐☐☐☐☐☐☐☐☐☐☐☐☐☐☐☐☐☐☐☐
COUNTY ☐☐☐☐☐☐☐☐☐☐☐☐☐☐☐☐☐☐☐☐
POSTCODE ☐☐☐☐☐☐☐

TELEPHONE NUMBER
☐☐☐☐☐ ☐☐☐☐☐☐

Type of Member (Tick one box)
Adult ☐   Child ☐   Senior Citizen ☐

Gender (Tick one box)
M ☐   F ☐

This form does not need a membership number because the database will automatically create this and the new member will not know this information.

Paid subscription and date subscription paid will not be needed here. The membership secretary will put this into the database when they have paid.

My database will need to be laid out to match the data capture form. The order of the data entry needs to be the same as the form to make it easy for the membership secretary to put this information into the database.

Coursework that has several sub-tasks

If your design problems involve several aspects, and therefore several different programs, you may need to use information from one part to help with another part. Your design needs to take this into account. For example, when you need a list of customers which is to be used to send a mail-merged letter, you will have to design the database so that you can extract this list (Fig 19.6). You might need to export this list to a file, which can then be imported into the chosen word processor, and which can then be used to produce the mail-merged letters. The links between the parts need to be made clear during the design of each part.

Why are you doing it this way?

All the way through this section, you are making choices – which program to use, how to get the chosen program to do what is needed, how to let one piece of information be used by another part of the system. All the way through the design, make sure you always give clear reasons for any action you intend to take. The examiners will then know exactly what to expect when you build your solution.

Testing plans

At some point, you will need to show that your solution works. While you are designing your solution, it makes sense to think about how you will test it. Draw up some plans to show what you will do to demonstrate how well your system works.

How you test a solution to a task will depend very much on what the solution has to do. For example, a poster is meant to be highly visual to convey its information or message in a way that cannot be misunderstood. Testing might be confined to checking the performance criteria. What information did the poster need to contain? Does it contain this and show it clearly, or do some parts not stand out as well as they

could? To do such a test, you might sample the reaction from some 'users' – your friends or teachers – by asking them some questions about the poster.

Testing a data-capture form can be more structured. Give the form to a sample group of people and ask them to fill it in. When you designed the form, you would have had a clear idea of the sort of answers you wanted. Your test could focus on the sort of responses you got and whether they were what you expected.

Databases need clear, structured testing plans. You will have set up the database to accept certain types of data in fields which were defined to accept only those types of data. You might also have set up fields to have a maximum data size. Initially, tests can focus on how the database responds to data entry. For example, if a surnames field is set up to take a maximum of 20 characters, what will happen if you enter the surname Featherstonehaugh-Smythe? A field designed to contain only Mr, Mrs, Miss, Ms and Dr and reject anything else, could be tested by trying to enter other titles. Where numbers are being entered, there may be a range of numbers the field will accept. When you input a number outside this range, what does the system do?

With both databases and spreadsheets, you will want to test the performance of the processing. You will want to test their ability to extract the right information or to give the right answers. The best way to test how well they work is to have some test data that you can input, which will give answers which are easy to work out. This will test whether the formulas in a spreadsheet work to give the right answers, or whether a particular search on a database gives the correct list.

The test plan should detail what you are going to test and how you intend to test it. You should show what data you will enter and what answers you expect the system to give you. When you do the tests, you will obtain valuable information which will help you to evaluate your work.

The drama group needs to send a letter to all the people who came to the auditions and have been given a part in the next production.

The letter needs to be addressed personally, tell them which part they have and when the first rehearsal is.

The information on who has which part and their addresses will be in the members database. I need to get a list of these people so that I can set up a mail-merge letter to send them a personal letter with their details on it.

This is how I intend to do this:

DATABASE

FIRSTNAME	Jane
SURNAME	Palmer
ADDRESS 1	Treetops
ADDRESS 2	1 Ridgeway
ADDRESS 3	East Barlow
ADDRESS 4	Essex
POSTCODE	CM15 0PR
HAVE A PART	Y [X] N [ ]
WHICH PART	Lucy

SEARCH FOR 'HAVE A PART = Y'
AND PRODUCE A LIST.

FIRSTNAME	SURNAME	ADDRESS 1	ADDRESS 2	ADDRESS 3	ADDRESS 4	POSTCODE	WHICH PART
Steve	Bull	Flat C	Mark Hatch	Carbury	Middlesex	RM14 8PU	Mr Tumnus
Jane	Palmer	Treetops	1 Ridgeway	East Barlow	Essex	CM15 0PR	Lucy
Veronica	Stracy	29 AshHill	Walsington	Essex		CM9 14PX	The Witch
Carl	Zambeno	Red House	1 High Road	Barrow	Essex	CM99 3RJ	Aslan (Lion)

SET UP A MAIL-MERGE LETTER   RUN THE MERGE

<<FIRSTNAME>> <<SURNAME>>
<<ADDRESS 1>>
<<ADDRESS 2>>
<<ADDRESS 3>>
<<ADDRESS 4>>
<<POSTCODE>>
Dear <<FIRSTNAME>>
Congratulations, you have got the part of <<WHICH PART>> in our next play 'The Lion, the Witch, and the Wardrobe' by C.S. Lewis...

Jane Palmer
Treetops
1 Ridgeway
East Barlow
Essex
CM15 0PR
Dear Jane
Congratulations, you have got the part of Lucy in our next play 'The Lion, the Witch, and the Wardrobe' by C.S. Lewis...

Summary of design

◆ How could the task be done and with what programs? Choose the best way forward and give reasons for your choice.

◆ Design the structure of your solution, including annotated sketch diagrams that show clearly what you intend to build. State why you are doing things this way.

◆ Create testing plans to show how you will demonstrate that your solution works.

The design is finished if you can answer Yes to this question: If I give this part of my report to one of my friends, would he or she be able to build my solutions?

Now you know what you are going to make and how you are going to do it, the time has come to build it. Here, the examiners want you to tell them what you actually did. It is not good enough just to have built it and printed it out. A printout shows only that your solution exists. It does not show how well you used the programs to get to that printout. Remember that the examiners are not in the room while you create your coursework. Therefore, your report should tell them what you did at all stages.

Developing your solution

You need to show how the solution was developed, and that what you have built works and really is a solution to the problem that you set out to solve. A good way to do this is to break down the solution into the key stages of building the solution and then to write the report in this step-by-step approach. This makes sure that you don't miss out any vital stages of the development of the solution.

To implement a database, you will need to define the fields, possibly to create the screen layouts and then input the data. The first stage of your report should show how you created the database and set up the field structure. You could do this in several ways.

You might just write about what you did. This will certainly show the examiners how well you understood the basics of setting up a database. However, it might not show them how well you knew the facilities of the database program you were using. Some databases let you print out the database structure when it has been completed. This will be very useful evidence to include in your report. It will show what you asked the program to do. How your set-up made data entry easy and accurate could be shown here. The data validation and verification techniques you used show how well you knew the program. If your database doesn't let you print this out, you might like to produce a screenshot of the set-up procedure to show what you did. Including this in your report will show which facilities you actually used.

There is a potential problem here. There are many database programs that you might have used and it could be that the one you chose is one which the examiners are not familiar with. (Examiners cannot know in detail every possible program.) So, you need to show exactly how you used the available features. You might find that using the printouts of the database structure is not sufficiently clear, so you would be wise to add some more information. One way of doing this would be to annotate the printouts with some further notes, which will give a better idea of how well you used the program.

Creating the layout for the data entry comes next. Your design should have given clear ideas of what you were going to produce. What you do here should closely follow what you said you were going to do. Showing the stages you went through to get to the finished data entry form is important. For example, screenshots or printouts taken as you progressed show clearly and readily the development, which helps the examiners to assess your understanding. Annotating the printouts is also a good idea. These visual techniques will save you from writing a large amount. You need a balance of words, pictures and notes that tell the story of what you did.

The last stage will be to put the data into the database. You could talk about how easy this was to do from the data collection forms, and suggest how it could have been made easier. When you have finished this you should have a functioning database, which you can print out to show the finished system. This may also need some annotation to reinforce some important things you need to tell the examiners about this piece of work.

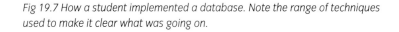

Fig 19.7 How a student implemented a database. Note the range of techniques used to make it clear what was going on.

Setting up the members database

The first step to setting up the database is to open a new file and define the fields. As I said earlier I have already decided on the information that needs to be held on each member and decided on the type of field I will need. Below is a screenshot from Filemaker Pro showing how I defined my fields. Membership number and County fields automatically enter data as the record is created. Membership number puts a unique number into the field and County puts Suffolk as the county since the club is based in Suffolk. The user of the system cannot alter the Membership number but if the person does not live in Suffolk this can be deleted from the County field and the correct county inserted.

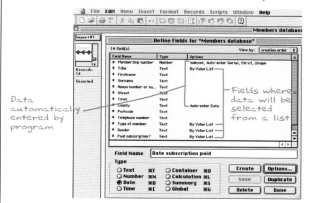

Data automatically entered by program

Fields where data will be selected from a list

The complete field definition is shown here.

Field Name	Field Type	Formula/Entry Option
Membership number	Number	Serial Number with Current Value: "16" Increment: "1" Prevent data that is automatically entered from being changed Do not allow users override validation Unique values only Indexed
Title	Text	Value List (Custom Values): Mr Mrs Miss Ms Dr
Firstname	Text	
Surname	Text	
House number/name	Text	
Street	Text	
Town	Text	
County	Text	Auto-enter: "Suffolk"
Postcode	Text	
Telephone number	Text	
Type of member	Text	Value List (Custom Values): Adult Child Senior Citizen
Gender	Text	Value List (Custom Values): F M
Paid Subscription?	Text	Value List (Custom Values): Y N
Date subscription paid	Date	

Auto-enter setting

Cannot be changed

Auto-enter setting: can be changed

The four value lists used: only these values can be entered into these fields

Once the fields had been created I then produced the input form layout for the screen. I decided on a simple list that closely followed the order on the data capture form that I designed earlier. In my design I identified some fields (those where I put tick boxes on the data capture form) which it would make sense to make data entry simple and accurate if I used the idea of check boxes or radio buttons. This is how I set up the Title field so that it had radio buttons. I chose radio buttons because they only allow one value to be selected. If I had used check boxes the user could put in more than one value from the list and this would not be as accurate. It would be possible for a person's title to be **Mr Mrs**.

Radio buttons chosen as input method for this field

This is how a record looks when it is filled in.

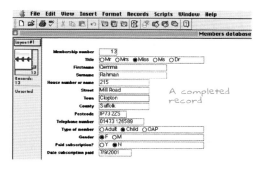

A completed record

The next screenshot shows a new record that has the Membership number automatically inserted (14 in this case) and the County of Suffolk automatically put in as well. When I tried to change a Membership number the program would not let me do this but I could change Suffolk to another county.

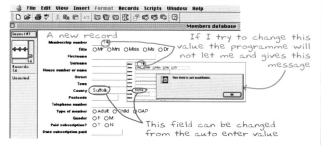

A new record

If I try to change this value the programme will not let me and gives this message

This field can be changed from the auto enter value

I have now set up my database and can now enter the data on the members.

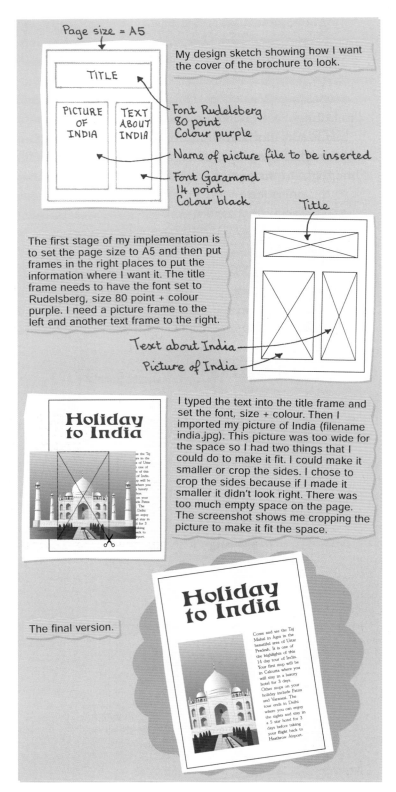

Fig 19.8 The building of a DTP holiday brochure.

Implementing your designs for other types of program need to be just as well documented as the example on pages 194–5.

When creating a poster, you need to show which tools from the graphics or DTP program you used. How did you set up the area for the poster title? How did you import or create any pictures you included on the poster? How did you use any special effects that the program might have to make one element stand out? Again, there are stages you went through in developing the final solution and you should take the examiners through these stages. If you were using a frame-based DTP program, the first thing you should have done was to create a template page with empty frames on it. If this can be printed out, and the frames seen and the printout annotated, the examiners can see the relationship between your design and the first steps of implementation. As you input the data on to the layout, there were some key stages that would be worth printing out to show the order you did things in.

If a picture had to be resized, show the picture as it was when you imported it, and then talk about how you resized it. (Perhaps you only need to make an annotation on the printout.) Finally, show the effect of resizing by including another printout. You might apply some effects to the main text. Once you have the text on the page in the right place, you may want to use the special effects that are available in your DTP program to give it the right impact.

You may want to make some changes to your original design ideas. A colour combination that you thought would make something stand out might not work when you see it printed. Tell the examiner what is wrong with the first complete version, describe the changes you made and include a printout of the changed version (Fig 19.9).

It is important that the formulas and functions you used to make the spreadsheet work are clearly shown. Too often, students only include the final printout and the

I thought it would be a good idea to make everything red but the background being the same colour makes the writing very difficult to read so I changed the background colour to blue.

ORIGINAL VERSION

Red Sea Holiday

NEW VERSION

Red Sea Holiday

Fig 19.9 A point in the development of the solution where the student was not happy with the result

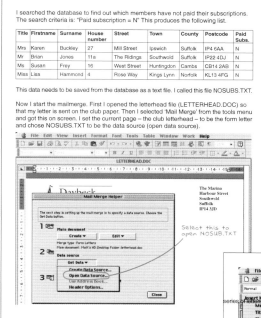

I searched the database to find out which members have not paid their subscriptions. The search criteria is: "Paid subscription = N" This produces the following list.

Title	Firstname	Surname	House number	Street	Town	County	Postcode	Paid Subs.
Mrs	Karen	Buckley	27	Mill Street	Ipswich	Suffolk	IP4 6AA	N
Mr	Brian	Jones	11a	The Ridings	Southwold	Suffolk	IP22 4DJ	N
Ms	Susan	Frey	16	West Street	Huntingdon	Cambs	CB14 2AB	N
Miss	Lisa	Hammond	4	Rose Way	Kings Lynn	Norfolk	KL13 4FG	N

This data needs to be saved from the database as a text file. I called this file NOSUBS.TXT.

Now I start the mailmerge. First I opened the letterhead file (LETTERHEAD.DOC) so that my letter is sent on the club paper. Then I selected 'Mail Merge' from the tools menu and got this on screen. I set the current page – the club letterhead – to be the form letter and chose NOSUBS.TXT to be the data source (open data source).

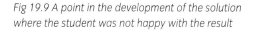

Fig 19.10 Transferring data from a database into a mail-merged letter.

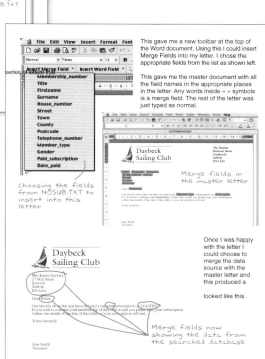

This gave me a new toolbar at the top of the Word document. Using this I could insert Merge Fields into my letter. I chose the appropriate fields from the list as shown left.

This gave me the master document with all the field names in the appropriate places in the letter. Any words inside « » symbols is a merge field. The rest of the letter was just typed as normal.

Once I was happy with the letter I could choose to merge the data source with the master letter and this produced a ... looked like this.

examiners cannot see very much from this. In the design, you would have set out where different formulas were going to be used. The examiners need to see that you really did use them. Most spreadsheets allow you to print out a formula view. This shows all the workings of the spreadsheet – not just the numbers. You need to include in your report the formula and data views, and the stages of development – not just the final answer.

If you built a control system, you would have built the things that need to be controlled and then incorporated any sensors that were required. Photographs of these are very helpful in showing what it is that you were controlling and how you thought about the use of devices and sensors. Along with this, there was also the development of the control program, which needs documentation with printouts and annotations.

Implementing coursework with linked tasks

Some examination boards expect that the coursework developed will be in response to a broad need and so involve several areas of information technology coming together. Information produced in one part may be needed for another part to do its job. When you implement these tasks, you must not forget about this requirement.

Making changes to your design

It is normal for things not to go exactly according to plan. Don't worry – examiners expect to see changes. The important point is to tell them *why* you needed to make any changes to your original plans. It could have been that you found a better way to do things, which gave a better solution. It could have been be as simple as the need to change colours so that certain things stood out.

Whatever your reasons, you must make sure that you tell the examiners. The examiners will look at your design and expect to see it built. If you haven't explained why it is different, you will not get the highest marks.

Does it work?

Once you have a solution to your problem(s), you need to make sure that it works and that it is indeed a solution to the problem. This could be part of testing your solution, but it could be quite separate. Earlier, we talked about testing plans. These are a series of tests to which you will subject your solution to make sure it performs as it should. This is not necessarily the same as showing that the solution performs the required jobs in an ongoing way for the scenario.

For example, you may have set up a test for a spreadsheet using simple numbers to check that the mathematics in the formulas works. (Simple numbers allow you to check the answers on a calculator or by doing the sums in your head.) The job the spreadsheet has to do for the organisation it is designed to help will not use simple numbers. But once you have checked that the spreadsheet works, you will feel confident that it will give the right answers for actual working numbers.

Again, just producing a printout to show that your solution works will reduce your final marks. If you are searching a database, for example, the examiners will need to have a printout of the whole database. A simple list view will save paper and be the most useful format here. Then you have to establish what you needed to search for. This will probably have been established in the analysis. The next step is to tell the examiners how you set up this search in your database. Make it clear exactly what goes into searching and include, if you can, a printout to show what the search criteria look like.

Once you have executed the search, you can then print out the results so that you and the examiners can see how successful it was. You may want to check that this is correct by referring back to the full database. Here, comments, notes or annotations on printouts are very informative and helpful.

What do you do if it doesn't work?

First, state in your report that your solution doesn't work. Then go on to say exactly what doesn't work. You might have clear ideas as to what the problem is, in which case you can go on to redesign your solution and correct the problem. This will need to be put into your report. You do not need to go back to your design section – this is the next stage of development and so goes into the implementation section.

If you can't immediately work out the cause of the problem, you will have to carry out a full investigation to find it. Once you have discovered what the problem is, then you can put it right.

A problem that might occur here is time. You may not have enough time to correct the problem(s). Is this going to affect the final mark for your piece of work? It depends on how serious the problem is. If the solution works but is not perfect, you probably will not be penalised. However, if the problem goes back to an inappropriate design containing flaws which you did not spot until you built your solution, then your marks will almost certainly be affected.

Advice Try to avoid choosing a task that is too difficult!

To show that my video shop database works I will input some data that I can use to test the system. It will have about 15 to 20 records and have information in it which will test that it performs as I expect it to under a range of situations. Will it take long names? Will it find particular customers? I will put two customers with the same name into it to see if I can find the right one.

This test will be done on 12/5/2002.

First name	Surname	Title	Address	Postcode	Telephone	Mobile	Video title	Date taken	Return due	Overdue?
Kirsty	Argall	Miss	11 Fir Close, Witney	OX14 7DG	01923 116568	–	Die Hard 101 Dalmations	4/2/2002 8/4/2002	6/2/2002 10/4/2002	Yes Yes
Wendy	Banstead	Mrs	88 Dean Court, Oxford	OX7 5LL	01321 651118	07774 11287	Battle of the Roses	22/3/2002	24/3/2002	Yes
Frederick	Bloggs	Mr	12 High Street, Oxford	OX4 1AA	01321 654824	07721 97512	Titanic Blair Witch Project	1/4/2002 12/5/2002	3/4/2002 14/5/2002	Yes No
Frederick	Bloggs	Mr	4 Lime Close, Thame	OX22 4FG	01252 664152	07779 17746	Brassed Off	11/5/2002	13/5/2002	No
James	Featherstonehaugh-Smythe	Dr	The Gables, Thame	OX22 5BW	01252 884166	07954 15636	Babe	8/1/2002	10/1/2002	Yes
Ian	Greasby	Rev	The Vicarage, Thame	OX22 4QQ	01252 755498	–	Angel Heart	11/5/2002	13/5/2002	No
Sarah	James	Ms	14 Canal Street, Oxford	OX8 2QZ	01321 186483	07746 18765	–	–	–	–
Karen	Lancaster	Ms	6 Ward Street, Oxford	OX8 4FF	01321 664588	07954 33548	–	–	–	–
Gillian	Morrison	Mrs	2 Hill Rise, Woodstock	OX18 7DW	01844 621136	17744 11668	Gladiator Das Boat	18/3/2002 10/5/2002	20/3/2002 12/5/2002	Yes No
Daniel	Newton	Mr	64 Beech Drive, Oxford	OX9 2GH	01321 112648	–	–	–	–	–
Gifford	Olney	Mr	2 Broad Street, Oxford	OX5 8XX	01321 222486	07984 11544	Batman Returns The Great Escape When Harry met Sally	3/5/2002 11/5/2002 11/5/2002	5/5/2002 13/5/2002 13/5/2002	Yes No No
David	Spencer	Mr	22 Bridle Way, Oxford	OX7 6JJ	01321 115666	07926 15666	–	–	–	–
Mark	Towsend	Mr	13 Kings Road, Oxford	OX6 2DW	01321 995477	–	Saving Private Ryan	14/1/2002	16/1/2002	Yes
Gale	White	Ms	8 The Ridings, Witney	OX14 6HJ	01923 944477	07996 11654	Heat	10/5/2002	12/5/2002	No
David	Zane	Mr	1 Rayes Lane, Oxford	OX1 4FG	01321 112776	07845 16639	Unforgiven	3/3/2002	5/3/2002	Yes

I can then use this data to see if it works as I can look at this and predict what results I should get from searches that I do.

Fig 19.11 A way to show that your solution works. The whole database needs only about 15 to 20 records for this.

Summary of implementation

◆ Show all stages of development.

◆ Make sure your report tells everything that you did.

◆ Remember to use annotation on printouts.

◆ Show that your solution works – it does what is needed for the organisation.

◆ If you need to make any changes to the design, make sure you say why the changes have to be made.

Testing what you have built is very important. It is something all examination boards expect you to do. Some boards require comprehensive testing plans. Testing plans were mentioned on pages 192–3, and you might think about testing while you are designing. This is where you specify what your solution will do. If you get it wrong at the design stage, any testing you do might well fail.

Testing plans fall into one of two groups. In one group are tests which try to break the system that you have built. In the other group are tests which show that your system performs the desired jobs. You might think it odd that you would try to break your system. What you are doing here is finding out what might happen if an untrained person tried to use the system and did something silly.

Testing a system to breaking point is often referred to as seeing what happens when the system comes across extreme, erroneous or extraneous data. What will the system do if a user puts in a very large number, a long name, the wrong sort of data for that field, and so on? What you should be doing here is testing the functionality of the system. Does it accept relevant data as you would expect and reject inappropriate data?

The second type of testing is to make sure that the system processes the data correctly and produces the information you require. Does it carry out searches correctly? Does it produce the right figures? Are the mail-merged letters addressed to the right people? Does the control system do the right things in the right order?

Fig 19.12
A record from the
video shop database

This is what a record in my video shop database looks like.

G&T Video Shop

	Today's date
	12/5/2002

Title ◉Mr ○Mrs ○Miss ○Ms ○Dr ○Rev

First name Frederick

Surname Bloggs

Address 12, High Street
Oxford

Postcode OX4 1AA

Telephone No. 01321 654824   Mobile No. 07721 97512

Video title	Date taken	Return due	Overdue?
Titanic	1/4/2002	3/4/2002	Yes
Blair Witch Project	12/5/2002	14/5/2002	No

I am now going to test it to make sure that it inputs data accurately and lets me find the information that the shop owner needs to find. He needs to make sure that he can find a particular customer to book out a video, delete a video when the customer returns it and will produce lists of overdue videos so that the owner can contact the persons and ask them to return the video.

What should a testing plan look like?

A plan needs to state clearly what you are going to test and how you are going to perform the test. As you have designed the system, you ought to have a clear idea of how it will behave. You need to state what the test is, what you will do to carry out the test, and what you expect the result of the test to be. If the test involves inputting data to the system, you need to say what this data is. If it involves a search of a database, you need to state the search criteria – how you will set up the search – and then what you expect the result of the search to be.

You may need to set up some test data from which it will be easy to see and check that the system works correctly. If this is the case, your test plan needs to show what the test data is and what results you expect to get when you use it.

The example that follows is an outline of part of a test plan for a video–club customer database (Fig 19.12), which tests some aspects of functionality as well as processing.

Aspect under test	What I will do to test it	Data I will test with (if needed)	What I expect to happen
Entering a new customer into the database	1 Try radio buttons to make sure that I can select only one title for a person.	None	Only one title will be selected.
	2 Try to put a silly title into the title field.	Try to enter SSSSS into the title field.	It should not let me type text into this field. I should only be able to select a title by clicking on a button next to the text.
	3 Enter a long surname into the 'Surname' field to see if it will deal with long names.	Try to enter 'Featherstonehaugh-Smythe'.	It should accept this surname. This database should make the field as long as it needs to be to accept the data.
Renting a video to a customer	4 Can it find a particular customer?	Find 'Frederick Bloggs' by selecting Search from the menu and fill in First name = Frederick and Surname = Bloggs and then make it perform the search.	It should find all customers called Frederick Bloggs. There are two such people in the database.
	5 Try the 'Date taken' field to see what happens when a user enters an incorrect date.	Try to enter 1/13/2001	The database should report an error. The field is set up as a date field and since this is not a proper date (there are only 12 possible months), it should not accept it.
Finding information for the business	6 Find all customers who have overdue videos.	Set up and perform a search for 'Overdue?' field = Yes	It should find all customers who have an overdue video. There should be 9 overdue videos in the test data.

The testing plan will now need to be carried out. For each element on the plan, you will need to show the outcome of the test. This might be a printout or just a description of what happened. If it is a printout, you might need to annotate it so that the examiners see the important part of the test. You will need to comment on how successful or otherwise the test was. If it was not successful, you will need to comment on what didn't work as you had anticipated. Then you need to try to find out why the plan went wrong and see if you can put things right.

If there is time, you might want to correct the problems and try the tests again. There may be a problem which you cannot correct because it is a feature of the program you have used. Whatever the reason for a problem, you need at least to try to understand it and to have some ideas as to how you might correct it. Then write about it and show the examiners that you do understand why things are not quite as you had hoped they would be.

In the example test plan on page 201, the results of the tests were as follows.

1   Database performed as expected. Only one title could be selected using the radio buttons.

2   Database performed as expected. Since the data entry to this field is done by clicking with a mouse, it was impossible to enter SSSSS. This field did not respond to any keyboard inputs. One thing that came to mind was that I might not have all the possible titles in my list. What if a Sir or Lady or other titled person wished to become a member? I could extend the list to cover these possible titles if it were really needed.

3   Database performed as expected. The field was large enough to take Featherstonehaugh-Smythe as a surname. There are no limits as to how much text is entered into a field with this database as far as I can tell.

The space on the data entry layout will take Featherstonehaugh-Cholmondely-Smythe, which is 36 characters long. I think it is extremely unlikely that it will need to take longer names than this.

4   Database performed as expected. The search did produce all the customers who are called Frederick Bloggs but there were two in the database. If I were using this system to record video loans and returns, I would want to get to the correct person in one go. I can see that, when there are lots of customers in the database, there is a strong possibility that there will be identical names – several John Smiths, for example, and I will need to get the right John Smith very quickly if I don't want queues forming in the shop. The best way to overcome this would be to put a unique key field into the database. This could be the customer's membership number, and there would be no duplicate numbers issued. If I did a search on this number, it should take me straight to the customer's record.

5   Database performed as expected. The database program told me that 1/13/2001 was not a valid date and would not let me carry on until I had put a date that it understood into the field.

6   Database performed as expected. It produced all the records that had an overdue video. I was not completely happy, because when a customer had more than one video on loan it gave me those videos as well. However, at least I got a list of people whom I needed to contact about returning videos.

The example shown here gives you some idea of how to tackle this particular aspect. It is not complete and will vary depending on what aspects of your solutions you are testing. You can see that it gave this person some ideas to think about. Some of the things can easily be put right but others might not be possible to correct in the time available. This should not affect your marks as long as most of your solution works well.

Test 3.

The surname field will take very long names as shown in the printout here. It will take at least 36 characters.

Test 4.

I set up a search for: FIRSTNAME = FREDERICK AND SURNAME = BLOGGS and the system found two results as shown here.

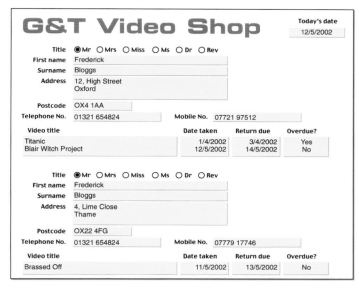

If I wanted to find the Frederick Bloggs who had an overdue video, I would not want a list to look through. Perhaps I need to redesign the database so that it has a key field. Perhaps give every member a unique membership number.

Test 5.

When I tried to put 1/13/2002 into the 'Date taken' field, the database returned the following message.

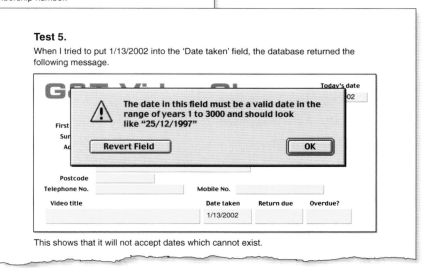

This shows that it will not accept dates which cannot exist.

Fig 19.13 Output from the database which confirms that the system gives the expected answers.

Summary of testing

◆ Create a testing plan which will test the ability of your solution to enter data accurately and to process data.

◆ Devise some test data that will show how well the solution works.

◆ Make sure the plan describes what you expect to happen.

◆ Run the tests and record what actually happens.

◆ Comment on the results of the test.

At the end of your project, you need to summarise how successful you have been in designing and producing solutions to the problems you identified. Don't just say how much you enjoyed doing this work but tell the examiners how well you think the solution performed.

All through your report, you should have evidence showing how well your work has gone. At the start, you should have established some performance criteria. Check your solutions against these criteria. Have you managed to build solutions which covered all of these? If you haven't incorporated all these features, why didn't you manage this? It could be that you changed your mind and came up with something better, or perhaps it was just not possible to do this with your programs, or the way in which you used them.

The testing section will have a great deal of evidence showing how well the solution(s) worked out. Some things will have gone well and done just what they were supposed to do, but there may well be things that weren't entirely satisfactory. You need to discuss all this in your evaluation. Your results will suggest things that need to be improved and you may have ideas about how to make these improvements.

If you were building a system for someone else to use, did that person try to use it? That user would have told you whether your system was easy to use and would have suggested things that needed to be improved. If you tested your system in this way, you need to include the user's reactions. What was easy to use and what was not so easy? What did the user suggest could be improved? Were you told how the user would like it improved? Include answers to these questions in your evaluation. You might have interviewed the person after he or she had used the system, in much the same way as you might have interviewed that person at the outset. The result of this interview could be included here.

If your solution was a complete success, say so. If it worked but you feel there are some parts that could be improved, again say so, but do fill your report out with

detailed information about these improvements. It could be that your solution works well but you have now learned some more about a particular program, so that if you were to do this sort of work again, you would go about it in a different way.

Remember that you do need to refer back to what you set out to do and discuss how well your solution meets your original aims.

They way in which you evaluate of your work will depend on the sort of coursework you are doing. The simplest coursework will probably revolve around single tasks, such as producing a database and extracting certain information from it, or producing a booklet using a DTP program. The type of evaluation discussed above will satisfy this type of work.

If you are attempting something more complicated which requires the use of several different pieces of software to solve a series of tasks around a common theme, you will not be just solving tasks. With this type of coursework you will be building a system which consists of a range of linked elements. Your evaluation of such work will need to be in two parts. First, you will evaluate each task in the way outlined above, and then you will evaluate the whole system.

It is important that the whole system (as well as each part) also functions. It might be that the database worked well, the logo created in the graphics program was a success, and so on. But when you imported the logo into a word processor to make a letterhead, the quality of the image was poor. You might have searched the database for a list of people to whom you wanted to send a personalised letter. The list could have been correctly produced, but when you tried to transfer it to the word processor to produce the letters, it wouldn't work.

If you evaluated just the tasks, your solution would appear to be successful, but the whole system would be less successful. Remember to evaluate the whole as well as the parts.

Fig 19.14
The evaluation shows
that the solution can
be used again when
new members of staff
join the company.

Evaluation of my business card

The business card for Technology Umbrella was successful. At the beginning of this piece of work I stated some criteria which the card had to meet. Below is a list of the criteria and comments on how well my solution met those criteria.

Criteria	Comments on how well criteria were met
It should be 90 mm tall and 55 mm wide – a tall card (not a wide one).	The card was 90 mm by 55 mm.
It should contain the company logo at the top left corner and the company name next to it. The logo should not go more than half way across the card. The name should be in Optima font, size 12 point.	The company logo was inserted and made smaller to fit into the top left-hand corner of the card and the company name was placed next to it in the correct font and size. I checked that the logo did not go more than half way across the card and it was a tiny bit wider than half way. I could go back and make it smaller. The logo was still clear after I made it smaller.
The person's name should be clear and easy to read and be in Optima font, size 10 point and right justified.	This was the case. I felt that if the person had a very long name I might not be able to fit it onto one line with this font size.
All other details should be right justified and in Optima font, size 9 point. It should fill the space evenly top to bottom.	This was the case and it was clear to read. I felt that if any person had a longer email address then it might not fit on. The email address on this card does not have much space left so it might cause problems. This part might need to be changed.

Overall the design has met the criteria and is a very effective solution to the problem. The business card file could be re-used by Technology Umbrella to produce cards for other workers by simply making changes to the text – the person's name, job, mobile telephone number and email address would need to be changed. The rest of the information would stay the same.

Summary of evaluation

◆ Refer back to what you set out to do. Have you achieved this?

◆ Do the individual tasks work?

◆ If it is a system, does the whole system work?

◆ Make sure you state how well the system performs and discuss areas for improvement.

Why do you need a user guide?

For some pieces of coursework you might be building a system for someone else to use – an organisation, a small business or an individual. If your examination board requires you to develop such a system, an essential part will be to provide a user guide.

The point of a user guide is to show the users how to operate the system you have developed for them.

What should it contain?

The user guide should only explain how to use what you have built. It should not explain how to construct the working solution. For example, if you have built a spreadsheet which shows the state of an organisation's finances as part of the solution, the guide should not tell the user how you set about building the solution. (You should already have done this for the examiners in the implementation section.) The user doesn't need to know this. The user needs to know how to use the solution. Don't tell the user how to put formulas into cells and how to set up the layout. The user needs to know how to open the spreadsheet file, how to put data into the spreadsheet to get the answers needed about the organisation's financial situation, and how to save and print the answers.

Is any part of the system re-usable? You may have built a system which is intended to be used in an ongoing way. A spreadsheet accounts system will need to be started afresh every financial year. You will need to tell the user not only how to put data into it, but also how to re-use it and start again next year. If you have produced a poster template, you will need to tell the user how to create a poster for the current event from this template and how to re-use the template to create a poster for the next event.

A user guide should be a document that takes the users step-by-step, through the use of each part that has been created for them. There are some parts that you have built that might not need to be included. For example, if you have designed a logo for an organisation, the users will not need to know how to create a logo. They will need to know how to use it. There might be occasions when they will need to import the logo into a document. This would not be needed if you have already created template documents (like headed notepaper), which have the logo in place.

Think carefully about what needs to be included and what doesn't. The guide will probably not contain everything you have built.

The best users guides are well illustrated. If you can capture screen images of the various stages in using a solution and include these with the written description, users will see at once what they have to do. Annotation of these screenshots will focus the users' attention on, for example, exactly where they need to enter data, how to set up a search, how to create new records and how to delete data that is no longer needed.

It is important that you don't spend an enormous amount of time on this (most marks are gained in the design and implementation sections). At most, a user guide will be worth about 10% of the available marks for the piece of coursework. It does not need to be a large document. It needs to be brief but clear and cover all the essential steps that the users need to go through to make effective use of what you have built for them. You can usually assume that they know how to load programs and have a basic knowledge of computers. It needs to tell them what they don't know – how to use the systems that are new which you have built to help them with their problems.

Summary of a user guide

◆ Tell the users how to use the system to do what they need. (Do not tell them how to build it for themselves.)

◆ Make sure the guide takes the users through all the steps and doesn't omit important parts.

Remember Annotated pictures will be very helpful and save a lot of writing.

Fig 19.15
An example of a clear user guide for a club accounts system.

A user guide for the accounts system for the club

To use this spreadsheet you need to open the file Accounts.xls. This should open a blank spreadsheet ready to input your figures. The spreadsheet is organised to automatically calculate the finances of the club – all you have to do is put the starting balance into cell B3 (the yellow cell).

Type your starting balance here

Accounts.xls

	A	B (Jan)	C (Feb)	D (Mar)	E (Apr)	F (May)	G (Jun)	H (Jul)	I (Aug)	J (Sep)	K (Oct)	L (Nov)	M (Dec)	N (Totals)
1					Statement of the club's 2001 Accounts									
2	Item	Jan	Feb	Mar	Apr	May	Jun	Jul	Aug	Sep	Oct	Nov	Dec	Totals
3	Balance b/f		£0.00	£0.00	£0.00	£0.00	£0.00	£0.00	£0.00	£0.00	£0.00	£0.00	£0.00	
4														
5	Income													
6	Subscriptions													£0.00
7	Refreshments													£0.00
8	Rent from parties													£0.00
9	Grants													£0.00
10					Put income into these cells									£0.00
11														£0.00
12														£0.00
13														£0.00
14	Total in	£0.00	£0.00	£0.00	£0.00	£0.00	£0.00	£0.00	£0.00	£0.00	£0.00	£0.00	£0.00	£0.00
15														
16	Expenditure													
17	Electricity bills													£0.00
18	Gas bills													£0.00
19	Water bills													£0.00
20	Maintaining building				Put spending into these cells									£0.00
21	Cleaning bills													£0.00
22	Buying refreshments													£0.00
23	Petty cash													£0.00
24														£0.00
25	Total out	£0.00	£0.00	£0.00	£0.00	£0.00	£0.00	£0.00	£0.00	£0.00	£0.00	£0.00	£0.00	£0.00
26														
27	Balance c/f	£0.00	£0.00	£0.00	£0.00	£0.00	£0.00	£0.00	£0.00	£0.00	£0.00	£0.00	£0.00	
28														
29														

Sheet1 / Sheet2 / Sheet3

This cell shows the current state of the finances

You will see all the zeros on row 3 and 27 change to the value you type in here (B3).

Then enter your income and expenditure into the appropriate cells. For example, if you receive a grant of £1000 in February, then click on cell C9 and type in 1000. Income should go into an orange cell and expenditure into a green cell.

The system will automatically calculate the finances for you and the pink cell (M25) will always tell you the current state of the accounts. When you update the accounts with new data, don't forget to save the file. You can print the accounts out in the usual way at any time – choose PRINT from the FILE menu.

How do you re-use the spreadsheet for next year's accounts? Again open the file, but to start a new one choose SAVE AS from the FILE menu and give the file a new name – *do not save it with the current name*, this will destroy the present accounts. Now delete all the data in the orange and green cells and put the new starting balance into the yellow cell (B3). This figure should be the figure that was in the pink cell (M25) at the end of the current year.

If you need a new category of income or spending, you will notice there are some blank cells in column A next to the coloured cells. Simply type in the new category name and then enter the numbers in the correct cells and the system will do the rest for you.

Foundation Tier

1 a Tick four boxes to show which of the following are **output** devices.

Tick four boxes only

Dot-matrix printer	☐	Keyboard	☐
Plotter	☐	VDU	☐
Mouse	☐	ROM	☐
CD-ROM	☐	DTP package	☐
Speaker	☐		

b Name **one** other output device, **not given** in the list.

c Name **two** input devices, **given** in the list above.

d Name **one** other input device, **not given** in the list above.

(AQA/NEAB)

2 You have a friend who wants to buy a word–processing package. He has asked for your advice. Assume that all word-processing packages will allow you to enter, save and print text and change margins. Give **four** other features your friend might need in his new word-processing package. Explain why he might need each of the features.

(AQA/NEAB)

3 A Mexican restaurant uses a spreadsheet to estimate sales. This is part of the spreadsheet.

	A	B	C	D
1	**Dish**	**Price (£)**	**Quantity sold**	**Takings (£)**
2	Burrito	6.00	6	36.00
3	Topopo	5.00	3	
4	Pescado	6.50	8	52.00
5	Hongos	7.00	4	28.00
6	Fajitas	8.00	5	40.00
7				
8			Total takings =	171.00

a i Write down the **value** that should be displayed in cell D3.

ii Write down the **formula** that should be entered in cell D3.

iii Tick **one** box to show the formula in cell D8.

Tick one box

sum(C2:C6)	☐
D2+D4+D5+D1+D6	☐
B8*C8	☐
sum(D2:D6)	☐
sum(B8*C8)	☐

b Tick **two** boxes to show other forms of information contained in a cell.

Tick two boxes

Calculators	☐
Text	☐
Menus	☐
Files	☐
Numbers	☐

c The price of Hongos is raised to £7.50.
i Describe how the restaurant should alter the spreadsheet.
ii Describe the automatic changes that the spreadsheet will make.

d This graph was generated from the spreadsheet the Mexican restaurant used to estimate sales.

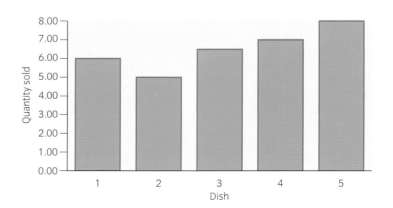

Tick **three** boxes to show which of these statements is most likely to be true.

e A spreadsheet can be used to generate different types of graph.

Using words from the following list, name the types of graph shown.

Pie chart	Scatter diagram
Line graph	Field experiment
Flow chart	Bar chart
Plate diagram	

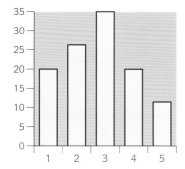

Type of graph is a

Type of graph is a

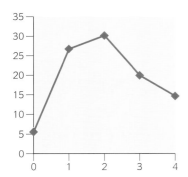

Type of graph is a

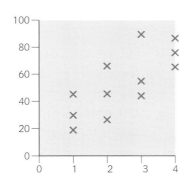

Type of graph is a

(AQA/SEG)

4 Ian and Anne are keen bird watchers. When they go bird watching they write down notes about the birds they have seen. Below is an example from Anne's notes.

> Saturday 5th April, 1997.
> Llandudno, North Wales.
> Jackdaw nest.
> Eggs bluish, dark brown spots.
> Nest made of grass and wool with sticks on outside.
> Nest found bottom of cliff face.

a i Anne and Ian decide to use a computer to store their bird information. Give **two** reasons why they decide to use a computer.

ii Give the name of the type of software Anne and Ian should use for their bird information.

b They store the notes about each bird they see as a record in a computer file called **BIRDWATCH**.

When Anne enters the notes into the computer file she encodes the data when possible. Explain the meaning of 'encodes the data'.

c Ian had to set up some data fields for the file **BIRDWATCH**. Each data field has a field name of no more than eight characters. For each field Ian has to give a maximum length.

Fill in the table below by choosing six fields.
For each field:
    give the field a sensible name
    describe the contents of the field
    give a suitable length

Field name	Description	Length

d The data is validated as it is input to the computer. The maximum length is used to validate the data. Explain what is meant by 'data validation'.

e Ian takes photographs of the birds and their nests. He wants to store these photographs as computer files in his computer. State the steps needed to do this.

f Anne buys Ian a CD-ROM about British birds. Give **two** advantages of CD-ROMS over floppy disks for storing information about birds.

(EDEXCEL)

5

The diagram above shows a LAN (Local Area Network) which is used in an office.

a Fill in the table to show **two** differences between this network and a WAN (Wide Area Network).

	LAN	WAN
Difference 1		
Difference 2		

b Give **two** advantages to the **office staff** of having the network rather than the same number of separate computers.

c Give **one** disadvantage to the **office staff** of having the network.

(AQA/NEAB)

6 Rashid has a home computer system. The computer system has a CD-ROM drive. Rashid uses his computer to play games, to prepare school work and to access the Internet.

a CD-ROMs can store text information. Give **three** other types of information that can be stored on CD-ROM.

b Rashid's father has a bookshelf with a number of encyclopaedias on it. Rashid has the same information stored on CD-ROM. Give **two** reasons why Rashid prefers to use his CD-ROM rather than his father's encyclopaedias.

c Rashid uses the Internet for his history project. Before he could use the Internet he had to buy an extra piece of hardware to connect his computer to the Internet.
   i Name the piece of hardware that Rashid had to buy to use the Internet.
   ii Name the type of software that Rashid must have if he is to use the Internet.

d Rashid stores his schoolwork on floppy disks. He then takes the floppy disks into school and uses them on the school network system.

   Rashid's teacher does **not** like pupils bringing in their own floppy disks to use on the network system. Give **one** reason for this.

e After checking with his teacher, Rashid puts his disk into a floppy disk drive on a network workstation. Describe **two** important differences between a floppy disk drive and the hard disk drive which is part of the network system server.

f On the school network system there is only one printer connected to the network server. Rashid is the only student trying to use the printer, although several other students are using the network at the same time.

   Rashid sees that the printer is sometimes very fast but sometimes is very slow. Explain why the speed of the printing may vary.

g State **three** reasons why Rashid's school has chosen to install a network rather than stand-alone computers.

(EDEXCEL)

7 A class is collecting information about weather. They need to collect information about the temperature.

They will use a temperature sensor and store the data in a file on disk.

a i What do we call this method of collecting and storing data?

ii Why is this better than a manual method?

b Data is collected every 5 minutes for 24 hours. The data is transferred to a spreadsheet for processing

i Why is five minutes a suitable time interval?

ii The diagram shows part of the spreadsheet.

	A	B	C
1	Time	Temperature (0C)	
2	00.05	11	
3	00.10	11	
4	00.15	10	
5	00.20	10	
6	00.25	10	
7	00.30	10	
8	00.35	10	
9	00.40	10	
10	00.45	11	
11	00.50	10	
12	00.55	10	
13	01.00	10	
14	01.05	10	
15	01.10	10	

286	23.45	12	
287	23.50	12	
288	23.55	11	
289	24.00	11	
290	Average temperature (0C) over 24 hours)	11.5	

The spreadsheet contains 288 sensor readings.

What formula must be in cell B290 to work out the average temperature?

B 290 =

c The pupils want to produce a bar chart showing how the average temperature changes each hour during the day.

Choose the **three** tasks they must carry out and put them in the correct order.

A Construct the chart from the data

B Clear all the readings from column B

C Collect data by taking one reading every hour

D Add new formulae to calculate the average temperature for each one hour period.

E Collect data for just one hour

F Select the data for the bar chart

(AQA/NEAB)

8 The ValueSave warehouse will use robots to move stock in the warehouse following deliveries. The robots will follow instructions based on a grid system, and using Forward, Backward, Left, Right, Load and Unload. From D1 to D4 would be **Forward 3**.

E4	D4	C4	B4	A4
E3	D3	C3	B3	A3
E2	D2	C2	B2	A2
E1	D1	C1	B1	A1

a **Write** instructions to get the robot to pick up a box and take it from A1 to D3 and then go back to A1.

b i **Name one** sensor the robot could use to avoid contact with any obstacles.

ii **Describe** how this sensor would be used.

c i **Name one** sensor the robot could use to help it to pick up a box.

ii **Describe** how this sensor would be used.

d **Give two** reasons why ValueSave would want to use robots in their warehouse.

(OCR)

9 Rashid enjoys playing computer games. He often downloads demonstration versions of games from the World Wide Web. One day he discovers his computer system is producing lots of error messages. Several important data files have disappeared. His computer has a virus.

a What is a computer virus?

b Suggest how the virus may have got into Rashid's computer system.

c How can Rashid remove the virus from his computer system?

d What precaution can Rashid take to help prevent more viruses getting into his computer system?

(AQA/NEAB)

10 Information technology is being used in a variety of places such as industry, commerce and the community.

a **Give two** ways in which IT can help school students in the following tasks.
   i Writing an essay for GCSE English coursework.
   ii Carrying out research for a project.

b **Give two** ways that the Police use IT to help them in their work.

c **Describe two** effects the increased use of IT has had on the car manufacturing industry.

d **Give two** concerns that people might have about organisations keeping data about them on computer.

Higher Tier

1 A secretary uses this computer.

a The secretary needs to know what each part of the computer can do. Write the label of the part next to the task it can do.

Task	Label
Save work	
Select from a menu	
Connect to the Internet	
Contain the processor, memory and network card	

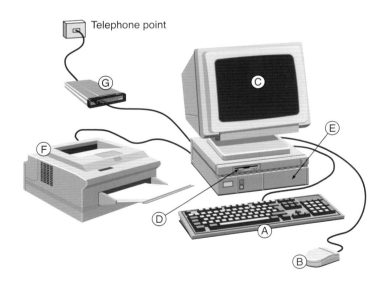

Telephone point

b The secretary has this software:

graphics	web browser
data logging	word processing
spreadsheet	

From the list, write the name of the software the secretary would use to:
   i work out the budget
   ii find out the latest business news.

c The secretary uses desktop publishing (DTP) software. The secretary wants to put an article that was written using a word processor into a DTP document. Describe how this could be done.

d The secretary wants a very high quality printout of a DTP document that includes pictures.

   i State **one** type of printer that could be used.

   ii Tick **one** box to show the print resolution of a printer the secretary should use.

Print resolution in dots per inch (dpi)	Tick one box
12 000 x 12 000	☐
1200 x 1200	☐
300 x 300	☐
100 x 100	☐
10 x 50	☐

   iii Describe how the secretary's computer could be upgraded to make it more suitable for professional DTP.

(AQA/SEG 2000)

2 An architect is buying a computer system which he will use to produce designs for houses. He decides to buy a system with the following specification.

   128 megabytes of RAM
   High–resolution 19–inch colour monitor
   9 gigabyte hard disk drive
   Fast processor

a Explain why each of these is necessary for this application.

   i 128 megabytes of RAM

   ii High–resolution 19–inch colour monitor

   iii 9 gigabyte hard disk drive

   iv Fast processor

b What type of printer would you recommend for this application? Why would this printer be suitable?

(AQA/NEAB)

3 John wants to use desktop publishing (DTP) software to produce his birthday invitations. His first attempt is shown in Figure 1.

Figure 1

> Come to my party
> at
> 12 Bridge Street
> on the
> 12th of June
> Time: 7 pm

He uses some of the facilities of his DTP software to improve the invitation and his final design is shown in Figure 2.

Figure 2

Come to my birthday party

at
12 Bridge Street
on the
12th of June
Time: 7 p.m.

a Give **two** facilities of his DTP software used to produce the invitation in Figure 2.

b John wishes to use the mailmerging facility of his DTP software to create personalised party invitations. What is meant by mailmerging?

c John wishes to use email (electronic mail) to send invitations to his friends. What is email?

d In addition to his computer system (which includes a CPU, keyboard, monitor, mouse and disc drives) what **extra** hardware would John need to send email?

e Why would he need this **extra** hardware?

f Email could be used to help with his schoolwork. Give **three other** examples of ways the Internet could be used to help with schoolwork.

(WJEC)

4 A teacher uses a spreadsheet to compare pupils' test scores.

	A	B	C	D	E	F
1		**English**	**Science**	**Maths**	**Total**	**Average**
2	Khan67	45	34	146	48.66667	
3	Singh	45	56	56	157	52.33333
4	Turner	97	38	89	224	74.66667
5	Needham	34	45	39	118	39.33333
6	Jones	56	50	45	151	50.33333
7	**Average**	59.8	46.8	52.6		
8						
9						
10						

a i Write down the cell reference of a cell that contains text.
  ii Write down the cell reference of a cell that contains a number.

b i Write down a formula that could be in cell E5.
  ii Tick **three** boxes to show the different formulae that could be in cell F5.

Tick three boxes

= E5/3	☐
= Average(B5:E5)	☐
= (B5+C5+D5)/3	☐
= Sum(B5:D5)	☐
= B5+C5+D5/3	☐
= Average(B5:D5)	☐

c Describe **two** ways in which the display of numbers in column F could be improved. For each way, give **one** reason why this improves the display in column F.

d The teacher uses the spreadsheet to produce **one** graph showing the English, science and maths marks for each pupil.

    i Circle the letter of the graph the teacher should use.

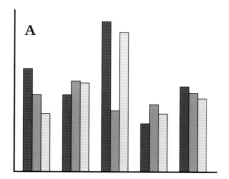
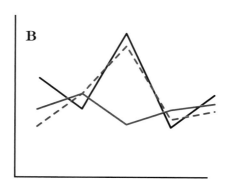
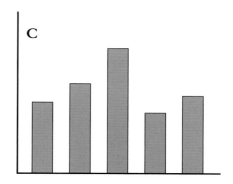

    ii On the chosen graph, write other information that would help the teacher understand the graph.

(AQA/SEG 2000)

5 Complete Bedroom Design is a firm which makes, designs and installs bedroom furniture. The firm uses information technology methods to:
- produce a catalogue of equipment and prices
- design the best arrangement of bedroom furniture
- help with financial matters and stock control.

a A two-way communication link is necessary between the main office and the design staff, who spend a lot of time away from the office with customers.

    i Name a piece of computer hardware that staff need to make this communication possible. State the use of this piece of hardware.

    ii Name a piece of computer software that staff need to make this communication possible. State the use of this piece of software.

b Name **three** other types of software that Complete Bedroom Design needs, apart from your answer to **a ii**. Describe a use for each type of software you have given.

c The senior management of Complete Bedroom Design decide to change to the use of information technology methods to perform the payroll calculations for all their staff. Some staff are part-time and some are full-time.

    i They intend to buy new hardware to record and input automatically the working times of all staff into the computer system. State the name of **one** piece of hardware that would be suitable for this task.

    ii Describe **two** advantages to the firm of making this change.

    iii Describe **two** disadvantages to the firm of making this change.

(EDEXCEL)

6 A pupil database contains two data files. The structure of the two files is shown on the right.

a Why is it better to store the data in two separate files, rather than keeping it all in one file?

b Why is date of birth stored rather than age?

c To find all the pupils in the same form a search can be carried out. In this database package searches take the form

> **<fieldname> <comparison> <value>**

A search for **surname** = "**Robinson**" would find all pupils with the surname Robinson.

Write down the search you would carry out to find all the pupils in the Form called 7B.

d The head teacher wants to be able to send personalised letters to the pupils' parent or guardian.

What extra field would be needed to allow the letters to be produced?

e The pupil record contains four subject code fields. Each of these contains the code of an optional subject studied for GCSE. Subjects can appear in any option group. The system can produce this report.

Pupils

Pupil number
Surname
Forename
Date of birth
Address 1
Address 2
Address 3
Contact phone number
Home phone number
Subject code 1
Subject code 2
Subject code 3
Subject code 4
Form

Subjects

Subject code
Subject name

> **Pupil Options Report**
>
> **Pupil Name:** Paul Freeman
>
> **Form:** 10S
>
> **Optional subjects studied:**
>
>   1   History
>
>   2   Geography
>
>   3   Information Technology
>
>   4   Spanish

i Explain how subject names were included in this report.

ii The system also produces subject lists like the one shown on the right.

The subject code for Spanish is 12. Simple searches can be linked together using the logical operators AND, OR and NOT. Brackets are used to make sure the separate parts are handled in the correct order.

> **Subject:** Spanish
>
> **Form:** 10S
>
>   **Name**
>
>   Rachel Brown
>
>   Graham Ellis
>
>   Paul Freeman
>
>   Sunita Patel
>
>   Mary Williams

Write down the search needed to select the correct records from the pupil file for this report.

(AQA / NEAB)

7 Simulators can be used to gain experience of driving cars at high speed.

a Give **one** example of people who may need to use such a simulator as part of their job.

b Give **two** reasons why a simulator would be used in this situation.

c All simulators rely on rules built into the controlling software. Tick **three** boxes show the rules that could reasonably be built into this driving simulator.

Tick three boxes only

Motorway driving must be fast.	☐
Cars take longer to stop on wet roads than on dry roads.	☐
Cars over three years old must have a valid MOT certificate.	☐
The faster the car is travelling, the greater the distance needed to stop.	☐
Cars should stop at red traffic lights.	☐
Younger drivers pay more for car insurance.	☐

d Name and briefly describe **two** other situations in which computer simulation might reasonably be used.

(AQA/NEAB)

8 Emma and Hannah own a nursery which sells plants to shops, supermarkets and individual customers.

Emma and Hannah have expanded the business so much that they feel they need computer hardware and software to help them run the business.

They want purchasing, stock control and sales information to be produced using a computer.

Kelvin is a friend of Emma and Hannah. He is also a systems analyst. Emma asks him for help.

a The main features of systems analysis are:
- ◆ Investigation
- ◆ Analysis
- ◆ Design
- ◆ Implementation
- ◆ Monitoring

Describe how Kelvin should carry out each of the five stages of systems analysis in helping Emma and Hannah to update their business methods.

b Describe **two** benefits to Emma and Hannah of introducing a new system using information technology (IT) methods.

(EDEXCEL)

9 A supermarket manager is considering how new communication technologies could benefit the supermarket.

a Discuss the advantages and disadvantages to the supermarket of creating a site on the World Wide Web.

b i **Give three** advantages of using electronic mail to communicate with other branches.

ii **Give two** disadvantages of using electronic mail to communicate with other companies.

c A family with children of school age own a computer and are considering connecting this to the Internet. Discuss the advantages and disadvantages of doing this.

(OCR)

10 A microprocessor is used to assist with the automatic control of entry into a car park. When a vehicle is detected at (A) a ticket is issued. When the driver accepts the ticket the barrier is raised to allow the vehicle through. The barrier is then lowered after the vehicle passes detector (B).

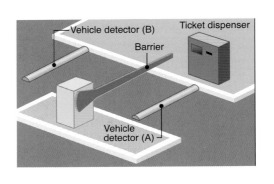

a Complete the table below to show whether each device (as shown on the right) is an **input** or an **output** device.

Devices (as shown above right)	Input or output device?
Vehicle detector (A)	
Barrier	
Vehicle detector (B)	

b Explain why the ticket dispenser is **both** an input and an output device.
c Explain how the principle of feedback might operate in this situation.
d Complete the diagram on the right to show the operation of this system

System diagrams, such as the one on the right, are an ideal means of spotting problems or mistakes in a system.

e Describe **one** problem that could arise from this system as outlined in the diagram on the right.

(NICCEA)

11 Banks allow customers to use automatic teller machines (ATMs), commonly called cashpoints.

a Name **two input** devices found at the cashpoint.
b Name **two output** devices found at the cashpoint.
c Give **two** other **different** services available at the cashpoint.
d Give **two** methods customers can use to ensure the security of their PIN number.
e ATMs are not only found outside bank buildings. Name **two other** types of building where they are likely to be found.
f Describe **two** ways in which the introduction of cashpoints has changed the lifestyles of customers.
g Many banks now offer a telephone enquiry system. Customers can receive accounts details such as bank balance over the telephone.

How can the bank ensure that it is the account holder who is asking for the information?

(WJEC)

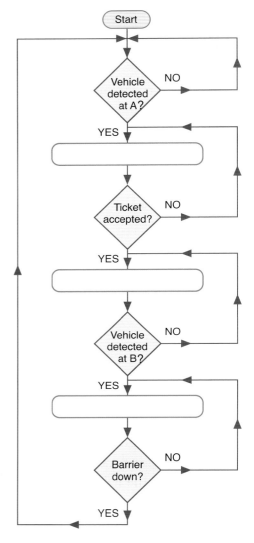

12 A computer-controlled stacker is used in a warehouse. The stacker puts goods on the shelves. Below right is a plan of the warehouse.

a These are examples of instructions used to control the stacker.

Instruction	Action
ENTER	The stacker enters through the warehouse door.
LEAVE	The stacker leaves through the warehouse door.
F6	The stacker moves forward 6 squares.
L90	The stacker turns left 90 degrees.
R90	The stacker turns right 90 degrees.
PUT3	The stacker puts the goods on the third shelf.

This is a program to put goods on the 3rd shelf of shelving unit 2 in aisle 4. The stacker enters through the warehouse door, and leaves through it.

```
ENTER
R90
F6
L90
F2
L90
PUT3
L90
F2
R90
F6
L90
LEAVE
```

	Aisle 1	Aisle 2	Aisle 3	Aisle 4
	Shelving unit 5	Shelving unit 5	Shelving unit 5	
	Shelving unit 4	Shelving unit 4	Shelving unit 4	
Left	Shelving unit 3	Shelving unit 3	Shelving unit 3	Right
	Shelving unit 2	Shelving unit 2	Shelving unit 2	
	Shelving unit 1	Shelving unit 1	Shelving unit 1	

Warehouse door

Write a program that puts goods on the 4th shelf of shelving unit 3 on the right-hand side of aisle 2, and then on the 2nd shelf of shelving unit 4 on the left-hand side of aisle 2.

The stacker should enter through the warehouse door, and leave through it.

b The stacker is sometimes sent to a full shelf. Describe **two** ways that sending the stacker to a full shelf could be avoided.

c The warehouse doors open and close automatically.
  i Name a sensor that could be used.
  ii Name an actuator that could be used.

d Discuss the advantages and disadvantages to the warehouse in using a computer-controlled stacker instead of human workers.

(AQA/SEG 2000)

absolute cell reference   A reference identifies a cell, or a range of cells, in a spreadsheet. It tells the spreadsheet where to look for the values or data you want to use in a formula. Absolute references are cell references that *always* refer to cells in a *specific location*. By putting a dollar sign in front of a column or row reference, the reference becomes absolute and *will not change when copied or moved*.

analogue   The term used to describe a quantity whose value changes continuously. An analogue device is one that uses or measures a continuously varying quantity.

application software   The name given to software that instructs a computer to carry out a specific task. Examples of application software include word processing, databases, drawing/painting and spreadsheets.

attachment   A file that is sent with an e-mail message.

back up   To make a copy of a program, disk or data.

barcode   A set of vertical bars of different widths that is printed on an item for sale, and is used to identify the item and its price. Barcodes are read by a special laser scanner. Libraries also use barcodes to identify books, videos and CDs.

batch processing   A method of processing data where the data is gathered into a series of batches before being processed.

baud rate   The speed at which data can be transmitted by a modem. It is measured in number of bits per second.

bit   A bit (**b**inary dig**it**) is the smallest item of information a computer can work with. It is represented by either the binary 0 or 1.

bitmap graphics   A bitmap program (sometimes called raster graphics or paint program) creates a picture which is made up of thousands of pixels. *See also* **pixel; raster graphics; vector graphics**.

bus network   This is the simplest type of computer network, where the computers (network nodes) are connected in a line.

byte   A byte is a unit of data that is eight bits long. A single byte (**b**inary **te**rm) corresponds to a single letter, number or other symbol on a keyboard. Computer memory and storage sizes are measured in thousands or millions of bytes. The units are kilobyte (kb), megabyte (Mb) and gigabyte (Gb): 1 Gb = 1024 Mb = 1 048 576 kb.

cache   This is a special memory or store where the computer temporarily keeps frequently used data. For example, often-visited web pages are stored in a cache directory on the hard disk. By 'caching' data, computers work faster.

cathode-ray tube (CRT)   A tube in which a controllable beam of electrons is produced and focused on to a screen to produce a visible image. The CRT is the basis of the computer screen and the TV screen.

CD-ROM   A CD-ROM (**C**ompact **D**isk-**R**ead **O**nly **M**emory) is an optical device that uses a laser to store and read data. It can store 650 Mb of data. Being read-only, data cannot be changed or deleted.

cell   The position on a spreadsheet where a row and a column intersect. *See also* **absolute cell reference**.

central processing unit (CPU)   The CPU is the 'brain' of a computer and controls how the rest of the computer works. It processes all of the information and instructions used by the computer.

client   A client computer has access to a network but does not share any of its resources with other computers on the network. It imports shared network resources provided by another computer called a server. *See* **server**.

client/server   The term used to describe the splitting of the workload on a LAN between a client computer and a server computer. *See* **server**.

command-line interface   A way by which a user can interact with a computer. The user has to type commands, using a special language, for the computer's operating system to respond. *See also* **graphical user interface; menu-driven interface**.

data-capture form   A form used to collect data, such as a questionnaire.

data logging   The automatic collection of data over set periods of time, such as the collection of weather information.

data processing   Sorting, searching, or performing calculations on data in order to achieve some form of output.

data validation   The process of checking by the software that what is being entered into a field (in a database) or a cell (in a spreadsheet) is allowed.

data verification   The human checking of data for mistakes.

default   When software is installed on a computer, it is automatically set up to start in a certain way. This is known as being installed with the **default settings**. Default settings can often be changed by a user.

digital   The term used to describe the representation of data as different combinations of the binary digits (bits) 0 and 1. *See* **analogue**.

digit versatile disk (DVD)   Using optical storage technology, a DVD can store up to 17 Gb of data – typically 20 times more data than CD-ROMs. This means that full-length feature films can be put on DVD. As a result, DVDs are often referred to as digital video disks.

e-commerce   The buying and selling of goods and services on the Internet and, in particular, on the World Wide Web.

electronic funds transfer at point of sale (EFTPOS)   A system used in shops to read the magnetic strip on a customer's credit, debit or store card. By swiping such a card through a reader, the customer's account information and the cost of the goods bought are transferred to the banking system.

electronic point of sale (EPOS) Shops and supermarkets with EPOS systems have scanners which read the barcodes on goods to produce customers' bills. The barcodes also tell a store what has been sold. Popular goods are then re-ordered automatically.

encryption The process of putting data into code to prevent unauthorised users from gaining access to the data. Often used during the sending of files on the Internet and the World Wide Web.

export To move data from one system or program to another. *See* **import**.

file The basic unit of storage in a computer. A file is a collection of data, such as a program or a user-created document, e.g. a letter created on a word processor.

file compression The process of reducing the size of a file for storage or for sending via the Internet.

file conversion The process of changing one data file or form to another without changing or damaging the data. An example is saving a Word file (.doc) as text (.txt).

file protection Preventing any changes being made to a file by, for example, allowing read-only access or assigning passwords.

file server This is a high-performance computer that is available to all users on a network, allowing them to share application programs and data. *See also* **server**.

formula This tells a spreadsheet what processes (calculations) you wish to perform on any spreadsheet data.

function This is a ready-made formula built into a spreadsheet, e.g. SUM, IF.

gigabyte *See* **byte**.

graphical user interface (GUI) A visual way by which a user can interact with a computer. What makes up a GUI is summarised by the acronym WIMP, which stands for Windows, Icons, Menus and Pointers.

hardware This is the name given to the physical parts of a computer. Hardware includes the central processing unit, the memory, storage devices, input devices and output devices. *See also* **peripherals**.

hub The device to which each computer in a star network is connected.

hypertext Links between text, or other objects, on web pages. Hypertext links (usually underlined words displayed in a different colour) enable users to jump to another web page or to another website.

HyperText Markup Language (HTML) A computer language used for documents on the World Wide Web.

hypertext transfer protocol (HTTP) This is the set of rules (protocols) used to show web pages on a computer that have been retrieved from web servers. The abbreviation 'http' in an address tells you that it is a website.

import To bring data from one system or program into another. *See* **export**.

information system A term to describe any record-keeping system – manual, mechanical, mechanised or computerised.

integrated software This is a program that joins together, in a single package, all the major types of application – word processing, spreadsheet, database, etc.

Internet A worldwide network linking up millions of computers.

Internet service provider (ISP) This is a company that provides access to the Internet for individuals, businesses and other organisations.

intranet A private network, based on Internet standards, available only within an organisation or business. Nobody else is allowed access to this network.

key field This is the field in a database that always has a unique value, regardless of how many records there are. It is also known as the primary key.

kilobyte *See* **byte**

local area network (LAN) A LAN is a group of computers, printers and large hard disks linked up to form a network, usually on one site.

magnetic-ink character recognition (MICR) A method of input that reads characters printed in magnetic ink. MICR is used by banks to process cheques.

mail merge The joining together (merging) of data – usually names and addresses – into a personalised letter.

megabyte *See* **byte**.

memory A device where data can be stored and from which it can be retrieved. A memory usually consists of a silicon chip (or chips) that temporarily stores data and instructions. *See* **random-access memory; read-only memory**.

menu-driven interface A way by which a user can interact with a computer. The user controls the computer by choosing commands and available options from a menu using a keyboard or a mouse. *See also* **command-line interface; graphical user interface**.

modelling Using a computer to predict the outcomes of ideas. Modelling allows a user to ask 'What if?' questions.

modem An input/output device that enables a computer to send data to, and receive data from, another computer over a telephone line.

musical instrument digital interface (MIDI) This connects computers to musical instruments and music synthesisers.

network The linking up of computers to share files, programs and other resources. The computers can be in the same site or different sites. *See* **bus network; local area network; ring network; star network; wide area network**.

network card This is an interface, known as 'card', that is put inside a computer to allow it to access other computers or printers on a computer network.

operating system (OS) This is the software that controls the hardware and how all the other software works. The operating system is the software on which all applications depend.

optical drive A disk drive that uses lasers to store and read data. Examples are CD-ROM, CD-R and DVD.

optical mark recognition (OMR) OMR is a method of entering data by precisely positioned marks on a form, e.g. a lottery ticket. The marks are read by a special scanner and the data input to a computer.

peripherals Devices which can be added to a computer system, such as a printer, a scanner and a modem.

pixel Short for picture (**pix**) **el**ement. Thousands of pixels make up the image seen on a computer monitor.

random-access memory (RAM) RAM chips hold data *temporarily* in memory whilst programs are using the computer. This is the place where the central processing unit (CPU) receives the instructions and data it needs to do its job. Data held in RAM is lost when the computer is turned off.

raster graphics The name given to images that are made up of pixels. *See* **pixel; vector graphics**.

read-only memory (ROM) Random-access memory in which the basic input/output instructions are fixed when the computer is made. These instructions can be read, *but not changed*, and are available every time the computer is switched on.

real time The term used to describe a computer system which processes data *as it is generated*.

record In a database, a record is a collection of related fields.

relational database A database that has links (relationships) with data held in more than one table or file.

ring network In this type of computer network, the computers (network nodes) are connected in a closed loop or ring.

search engine A software application used on the World Wide Web for finding websites using keyword searches. Search engines have their own websites.

server A computer that is on a network and shares application programs and data with other computers connected to the network. A file server may be dedicated only to the task of managing shared files or may be used as a client as well. (*See* **client**.) Some networks also use a printer server that is dedicated to managing all printers on a network. *See also* **file server**.

simulation Using a computer to imitate (simulate) something real or imaginary. Examples are computer games and flight simulators to train pilots.

smart card A plastic card which has a microchip inside it. The chip can be loaded with data, allowing the card to be used for many purposes, such as paying for goods, making telephone calls and storing music.

software The computer programs that tell (instruct) the hardware what to do. *See* **hardware**.

stand alone A computer that is not networked.

star network Each computer is connected to a central hub, giving the network a star-like appearance.

storage devices Devices which allow a computer to permanently store data. They include floppy disk drives, hard disk drives, CD-ROM drives, DVD drives and magnetic tape drives. *See also* **digital versatile disk; read-only memory**.

system life cycle This refers to the key stages in the development of an information system. They are: analysis, design, implementation, testing, user documentation and evaluation.

template A predesigned file that sets up a structure for a document. For example, a word-processing template contains all the settings for a document, such as fonts, menus, page layout, any special formatting and styles.

uniform resource locator (URL) Every site on the Internet has an address known as a URL. In order to access a site, you enter its URL into the Internet browser e.g. www.bbc.co.uk.

user interface How users interact with and use a computer. *See* **command-line interface; graphical user interface; menu-driven interface**.

vector graphics The name given to images that are made up of objects created by lines not pixels. Close up, no distortion of the image can be seen. *See* **bitmap graphics; pixel; raster graphics**.

video conferencing The transmission of live pictures and sound between two or more computers. It is also the name given to a 'meeting' between people who are based at different locations and have multi-way sound and TV link-ups.

virtual reality A simulated 3-D environment which a person, equipped with a special headset and suit, can experience and explore as if that person were really there.

web browser Software that enables users to view HTML documents and web pages.

website A collection of web files that have been published, using a HTTP server on the World Wide Web. Most websites have a 'home page' that users go to first when entering a site.

wide area network (WAN) A large network, located over a wide geographic area or world-wide, which links up many small and large computers.

WIMP The acronym formed from Windows, Icons, Menus and Pointers. These make up a graphical user interface (GUI).

World Wide Web (www) The World Wide Web is the main way of accessing the information on the Internet. The Web is based on pages of information linked by hypertext. These pages are 'published' on HTTP servers and viewed by a web browser.